Sir John Betjeman said of *English Architecture since the Regency*, 'it is still to me like St. Paul's Epistles: you can find more in it every time you turn back to it'. Kenneth Clark called Goodhart-Rendel 'the father of us all'; that is, of everyone writing on Victorian architecture in the twentieth century. First published in 1953, Goodhart-Rendel's witty and penetrating 'interpretation' of the period 1820 to 1934 broke new ground, and led towards the present appreciation of Victorian and Edwardian architecture.

Originally given as Slade lectures at Oxford, it addresses a non-specialist readership and does not hesitate to condemn familiar but over-rated buildings like the British Museum, nor to praise unpopular ones like Keble College, Oxford. The frequently subversive judgements were not the result of whimsical prejudice, but of Goodhart-Rendel's reasoned philosophy of architecture, supported by his own experience of architectural practice, and his immense first-hand knowledge of the buildings themselves. Illustrated with drawings and prints, *English Architecture since the Regency* provides the most readable and entertaining guide through the dense thickets of Victorian style ever written, and the later sections are a provocative survey of the period Goodhart-Rendel himself lived through as a working architect.

An introduction has been written for this new edition by Alan Powers who has also provided additional notes.

Harry Stuart Goodhart-Rendel was born in 1887 and developed an appreciation of architecture early in life, although he studied music at Cambridge. He became a practising architect and Resident of the RIBA. He inherited Hatchlands, the Georgian house near Guildford, which he presented to the National Trust in 1945.

Alan Powers is an artist and an architectural historian who has specialized in inter-war architecture, writing for a variety of publications. He organized the Goodhart-Rendel centenary exhibition at the Architectural Association in 1987.

A CLASSIC OF ITS AGE

Manchester Town-hall (1869)

ENGLISH ARCHITECTURE SINCE THE REGENCY

An Interpretation

H. S. GOODHART-RENDEL

CENTURY

LONDON SYDNEY AUCKLAND JOHANNESBURG

IN ASSOCIATION WITH THE NATIONAL TRUST

First published in 1953 by Constable

This edition first published in 1989 by Century, an imprint of
Century Hutchinson Ltd, in association with the National Trust
for Places of Historic Interest or Natural Beauty, 36 Queen
Anne's Gate, London SW1H 9AS

Century Hutchinson Ltd, Brookmount House,
62–65 Chandos Place, London WC2N 4NW

Century Hutchinson Australia Pty Ltd, 89–91 Albion Street,
Surry Hills, Sydney, New South Wales 2010, Australia

Century Hutchinson Group New Zealand Limited,
PO Box 40–086, Glenfield, Auckland 10, New Zealand

Century Hutchinson South Africa (Pty) Ltd,
PO Box 337, Bergvlei, 2012 South Africa

Cover painting "St Pancras Hotel and Station" by John O'Connor

British Library Cataloguing in Publication Data

Goodhart-Rendel, H. S. (Harry Stuart)
English architecture since the Regency.—
(National Trust classics).
1. England. Architecture, 1830–1987
I. Title   II. Series
720′.942
ISBN 0–7126–1869–4

Printed in Great Britain by The Anchor Press Ltd.

Published in association with The National Trust, this series
is devoted to reprinting books on the artistic, architectural,
social and cultural heritage of Britain. The imprint
covers buildings and monuments, arts and crafts, gardening and
landscape in a variety of literary forms, including histories,
memoirs, biographies and letters.

The Century Classics also include the Travellers, Seafarers and
Lives and Letters series.

CONTENTS

ILLUSTRATIONS

Illustrations

Illustrations

FOREWORD

Sir John Betjeman said that '*English Architecture since the Regency* is still to me like St. Paul's Epistles: you can find more in it every time you turn back to it'.[1] Lord Clark called Goodhart-Rendel 'the father of us all', because he had begun the serious study of Victorian architecture long before Clark published his pioneering study *The Gothic Revival* in 1928.[2] Who was Goodhart-Rendel? Why should his book, published in 1953 and never previously reprinted, be recognised as a classic?[3]

Harry Stuart Goodhart-Rendel was born in 1887, the son of a brilliant young fellow of Trinity College, Cambridge. His maternal grandfather was Stuart, First Baron Rendel, a Liberal politician connected with the armaments business of Lord Armstrong, so that when Goodhart-Rendel wrote of Cragside (p. 168), he did so from the experience of many childhood visits. His father moved to Edinburgh as Professor of Classics, before a tragic early death, and Goodhart-Rendel recalled being pushed around the Neo-Classical streets in his pram, shouting out 'Doric', 'Ionic' or 'Corinthian' at the various columns as they passed. A solitary childhood spent with his over-protective mother gave him the

1. Sir John Betjeman 'A Preservationist's Progress' in *The Future of the Past* ed. Jane Fawcett, 1976, p. 58.
2. Kenneth Clark 'A letter to Michael Sadler' in *The Gothic Revival* 1950 edn. p.4.
3. See *H. S. Goodhart-Rendel 1887–1959* ed. Alan Powers, catalogue of exhibition at the Architectural Association, 1987, with list of works and bibliography.

opportunity for further self-education in architecture, with a parallel enthusiasm for music. One of the Rendel family was married to Hasley Ricardo, the talented Arts and Crafts architect famous for his interest in colourful tiled buildings. Goodhart-Rendel also had the opportunity of meeting architects employed by his grandfather at Hatchlands, near Guildford, the house of Admiral Boscawen where Goodhart-Rendel lived from 1913 until shortly before his death in 1959, and which he presented to the National Trust in 1945. To the chaste Georgian brick box of the house, Lord Rendel added a 'Wrenaissance' music room in 1902 to the designs of Reginald Blomfield. The young architectural critic asked the self-important architect why his sash windows had 'ears' extending down from the sides of the upper sash-frames, when no genuine eighteenth-century sashes had them. On receiving no satisfactory answer, he began his lifelong animosity towards Blomfield and other English architects who used classical forms without taking account of the rules governing them.

It was not long before Goodhart-Rendel was able to build himself, starting with estate cottages when he was 16, and continuing in 1907 with the facade of a large office building in Calcutta, Gillander House, still standing as a testimony to the skill of an untrained twenty-year old, who was actually studying music at Cambridge at the time. By 1909 he had decided against music as a career, although he continued to compose and improve his knowledge of obscure nineteenth-century operetta and musical comedy, which his friends considered as great as his knowledge of obscure Victorian architects.

Instead, he took up architecture, training briefly with Sir Charles Nicholson before establishing his own practice. As an architect, Goodhart-Rendel therefore partici-

pated in the movements described in the later chapters of
his book. His early buildings reflected his love of the
Regency and the period of Jane Austen (his favourite
novelist), but they were never pastiches. The same
attitude governed his use of architectural themes from the
Gothic Revival. It is clear from *English Architecture since
the Regency* how much Goodhart-Rendel admired the
architectural philosophy initiated by Pugin, and brought
close to perfection by Butterfield and Street. In the 1920s,
such a view was rank heresy, although Goodhart- Rendel's
lectures on the subject were immensely popular. As Sir
John Summerson has recalled, 'It was well-known that
Victorian architecture was bad or screamingly funny or
both. Rendel begged to differ, but what really stunned his
audiences was that he knew, and knew in great detail, what
he was talking about.'[4] This knowledge was manifested in
architectural designs like the extensions to St. Mary's,
Graham Terrace, Pimlico, 1922–36, in which Goodhart-
Rendel developed the 'vigorous' style of the 1860s until it
arrives, at times, at Art Deco. He believed that the giants of
the Gothic Revival had already tackled most of the
challenges posed by the proponents of functionalism and
modernism in the 1920s. His own reaction to the new
movement was Hay's Wharf, London Bridge, 1930 (see
page 267), apparently a break with the past, yet so grounded
in a certain historical tradition that when asked what style it
was in, he replied 'the Early French Gothic style'.

It is appropriate that Goodhart-Rendel leaves the last
word in *English Architecture since the Regency* to a
building of his own, the Church of St. Wilfrid, Brighton,
1932–34. Not only did he prefer to be considered
primarily as an architect rather than as a writer and critic,

4. Sir John Summerson, Speech on receiving the Royal Gold Medal
for Architecture, 1976.

but this church was the result of a severe architectural self-inquisition, bearing fruit in a sequence of highly creative church designs for the remainder of his life. The regrets on page 80 at the Victorians' failure to adopt a version of eclectic Romanesque have a personal meaning, for this was the style which Goodhart-Rendel developed, with the hindsight of the Gothic Revival, in such masterpieces as Holy Trinity, Dockhead, Bermondsey, 1957–60.

The finishing date of his book, 1934, obviously fails to tally with the date of publication, 1953. The reason, explained in the Author's Note, being that it is assembled from Slade Lectures given at Oxford in 1934, published with little alteration, since Goodhart-Rendel had neither the time nor, perhaps, the inclination to write a separate book on the subject. His literary efforts had been concentrated on the perfection of the hour-long lecture, which perfectly suited his sense of irony, wit and well-timed delivery. It was this, he explained to Sir John Summerson, that prevented him from writing a conventional history of nineteenth-century architecture. His book needs no apology, however. Goodhart-Rendel's encyclopaedic knowledge was disciplined by the need to engage a non-specialist audience. Looking at buildings with the eye of an experienced architect, he was able to see beyond the prejudices of art history, its obsession with originality and its concern to categorise and evaluate styles, to the intrinsic merits of the buildings themselves. The subtitle 'An Interpretation' shows how the aim is to understand a sequence of ideas, and the actual names of architects are often omitted from the text in the belief that 'to write a history of architecture as a history of architects is to misplace emphasis and divert attention from the typical to the personal characteristics of their work' (page 35).

Although architecture from all the periods covered in

the book is now appreciated and enthusiastically preserved, Goodhart-Rendel's unconventional assessments still have a subversive edge, for instance in his dim opinion of Sir Robert Smirke and Sir Thomas Graham Jackson. By 1934, the genealogists of the Modern Movement had already started telling English readers that the only worthwhile buildings from around 1900 were those of Mackintosh and Voysey. Having lived through this period and outgrown these influences, Goodhart-Rendel disagreed. Instead, his praise of a building such as Stratton House, Piccadilly, illustrated under the title 'Polished Urbanity' baffled Sir Nikolaus Pevsner when he reviewed the book in the *Architectural Review*, and probably continues to baffle most informed opinion today. Yet he remained sufficiently true to his unprejudiced disregard of styles as an index of quality to be able to praise the work of Connell, Ward and Lucas.

The lively unorthodoxy of Goodhart-Rendel's judgements will always keep his book fresh. His way of looking at buildings is an education in itself, and his verbal wit, while exposing much of the absurdity of architects' aspirations, was also used to elucidate complex thoughts. Readers will discover his mastery of the extended metaphor, while phrases like 'a Gothic game played with neo-Classical counters' have entered the folklore of architectural history. To quote Summerson again, 'He stands alone among architectural writers. Scrutinize any one of his many essays, and you will not find a single commonplace sentence. Of how many writers from Vitruvius onwards can that be said?'[5]

Alan Powers October 1987

5. Sir John Summerson, Speech on receiving the Royal Gold Medal for Architecture, 1976.

THe lectures of which this book consists were delivered at Oxford in the year 1934. They deal with particular sections of a subject to which their author hopes shortly to do better justice in a general history. When first he determined upon that inevitably elaborate work, he imagined it as amplifying the matter of the lectures and incorporating many of their passages. He soon perceived, however, that to this method the matter was inappropriate. In a series of lectures, each lasting an hour, an account of a subject can be made memorable only by concentrating upon significant themes and minimising connecting narrative. To convert this deliberate desultoriness into the continuity required by an exhaustive history would necessitate rewriting so extensive that little of the original would be left.

In the belief, however, that a short and not exhaustive history may have its special uses, these lectures, with all their limitations, are offered to the reading public. Some of them have been rearranged, some abridged, and some slightly amplified. In all of them the author has retreated from the first into the third person, not from cowardice, but from his feeling that in print the many 'I's and 'me's of the lecture-room might seem unmannerly. In the last two lectures what at the time of their delivery was the present has now become the past, and the tenses of verbs have accordingly been altered.

The date added to the mention of any building or

alteration of a building is that of the year in which it is believed that that building or alteration was designed. In the nineteenth century the process of building was often lengthy, and the dates at which the buildings were completed do not properly reflect the sequence of architectural development.

Five of the illustrations in this book are reproduced from drawings specially prepared; that of St. Matthew's, Clubmoor, by Mr. J. P. van de Waal—that of Christ Church, Streatham, by Mr. J. Raymond Binns, and those of Bryanston, Pollards, and St. John's College, Hurstpierpoint, by Mr. E. Whiteley. The drawing reproduced of the British Museum Extension was lent for the purpose by Sir John Burnet, Tait and Partners, that of Scarisbrick Hall is reproduced by permission of Miss H. C. Allen, Principal of St. Katharine's College, Liverpool. The view of Keble College, Oxford, is from a print in the late E. H. New's publication *The New Loggan*. The illustration of St. Chad's Cathedral, Birmingham, is from a print lent by the Rt. Rev. Mgr. Canon L. S. Emery, Prot. Ap., Rector of Oscott College, and that of St. Luke's, Chelsea, from a print in the Chelsea Public Library. Illustrations have been made also from a print of the Edinburgh High School, lent by Mr. W. G. Dey; of St. George's Hall, Liverpool, lent by Mr. C. F. Stell; of Stratton House, Piccadilly, lent by Mr. W. Curtis Green, R.A.; and of the Cathedral Church of Christ, Liverpool, lent by Sir Giles Scott, O.M., R.A.

For all these loans and for the kindness and courtesy with which they have been made the author expresses his gratitude. He also records most gratefully his indebtedness to Miss Elizabeth S. Young for her untiring help in proof-reading, index preparation, and the discovery and verification of dates.

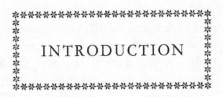

INTRODUCTION

WHEN the lectures upon which this book is founded were delivered, they had been immediately preceded by other lectures upon general aesthetics. A critical standpoint had been defined which may here be summarised in three postulates—that a work of art should contain no otiose ingredients, that the ingredients it does contain should be integrally united, and that the very existence of art is contingent upon its comprehensibility by beholders or by auditors. In other words, that a work of art must be a single organism, every bit of which can work efficiently upon the sensibility of those who hear or see it. Above this general foundation however, each particular art has a theoretic sub-structure proper to itself, and the basal theory of architecture is misconceived so often that a few remarks upon it are here necessary.

The architecture of the nineteenth century, for example, is apt to be dismissed as wholly imitative and unauthentic because these adjectives are justly applicable to many of its formal elements. To critics unaware of essential values these formal elements are everything. Any club-house with pedimented windows is described as an imitation of a Roman *palazzo*, any chapel with four corner-turrets as a derivative of King's College Chapel at Cambridge. The club-house may be absolutely novel in the proportional relations of its parts, the chapel may display familiar forms in the boldest and most unfamiliar combinations, but such real originality more often than not will pass unnoticed. The familiarity of the forms will be commented upon, the use made of them ignored.

The fine art of Architecture rests upon the useful art of Engineering, and without that art underlying it, can seldom exist. Rarely if ever can it claim the complete autonomy enjoyed by Painting or by Sculpture. The painter may choose what forms he will. The sculptor has the laws of gravity to reckon with, but is otherwise hardly less free than the painter. The architect's choice, on the other hand, is strictly limited by the exactions of a difficult stability, of a utilitarian necessity often complex and unyielding. Structure is his chief preoccupation, his chief obligation to provide shelter. With this preoccupation, beneath this obligation, his art has grown from its very beginning; so that few indeed of the traditional forms at his disposal are without some appearance—true or false—of usefulness either in support or in accommodation. Moreover, with the notions suggested by this appearance their aesthetic significance is inseparably compounded. Actually useful they may or may not be, but from a useful origin they have derived a nature that cannot be disregarded. A column laid down on its side, a cornice climbing vertically up a wall, would make not architecture but nonsense. When serving their proper purposes the column suggests support, the cornice protection; notions attached by human experience to vertical and horizontal lines respectively; notions which, by multiplying their characteristic lines, the fluting of the column and the moulding of the cornice will enforce.

Such enforcement of natural appearances is of all architectural processes the most fruitful. Through its operation the resources of architectural expressions are continually enlarged by changes and developement in methods of construction. Once acquired, however, these expressive

17

resources have always, in historical architecture, been extended to include the use, for their emotional value only, of cognate appearances unwarranted by the facts of structure. The Greek builder, having aestheticised wooden eaves to his satisfaction, carved their likeness in marble across pediments where no eaves could be. The Roman veneered his arcuated structures with mimic columns and lintels. The Romanesque church-builder panelled his walls with miniature representations of the pillars and arches that elsewhere he was constructing in reality. His mediaeval successor went further, adorning niches, furniture, and even goldsmith's work, with toy pinnacles, windows, and buttresses; and eventually, in England, carrying over the whole surface of his building mullions, transomes, and tracery, like those he had invented to hold his window-glass. The Renaissance designer revived the Roman decorative application of inactive columns and pilasters. He also attempted, and this he did first of anybody, to put upon grouped buildings a mask that should disguise their diversity beneath a simulated unity, that should give to multiform buildings the appearance of one.

The typical architect of the first half of the nineteenth century too often collected these and all other such devices into an excess so great that there is nothing surprising in the reactionary Puritanism he provoked in the minds of Lethaby, Philip Webb, and their followers. The doctrine of this Puritanism survives strongly to-day, and is, probably, of all the things the nineteenth century gave to architecture that which in its day was most unquestionably new. It is a doctrine essentially protestant, essentially negative; unlikely to gain many adherents except at moments of surfeit and disgust.

To architects untroubled by the sick scruples of utilitarianism—to all architects of the past, that is to say, and to many of the present—the normal process of design is to aestheticise, to dramatise, the physical character of buildings and to adorn them with sculpture. For sculpture is the proper name to give to all the mimic architecture with which real architecture is customarily adorned. The Romanesque wall arcades, the mediaeval gablets and pinnacles, the Renaissance rows of pilasters, stand in exactly the same relation to real arches, roofs, and colonnades as that in which stone saints or statesmen stand to saints or statesmen of flesh and blood. Sculptural, too, in their essence are the mouldings and flutings by means of which the natural appearances of construction are usually emphasised. It is possible, no doubt, to make architecture without any added sculpture whatever, without even any mouldings or flutings, as certain designers of all times have discovered. In contrast with this, architecture that is nothing else but sculpture, architecture in which every constructive element is dissembled or concealed, was produced in the days of Baroque. Of the two processes, therefore, the aestheticisation of physical character and the addition of sculpture, one only will suffice to make architecture of a kind; but it is rare that both should not be employed.

Both were employed profusely at the end of the British Regency, the time at which this architectural survey is to begin. Not that they were employed systematically; periods of systematic art are rare, and the Regency had certainly not been one of them. The artist in any age produces by means of subconscious transmutation of material he has subconsciously absorbed, and it is only when such influences as the exploitation of the ribbed vault or the translation of Vitruvius have brought the building ambitions of an age to unanimity that he can feed simply enough to avoid all mental ferment and indigestion.

The architect of the period immediately succeeding the

19

Regency had browsed in many pastures, he had been led to the banks of the Ilyssus by Smirke, to Salisbury by Wyatt, to an Arabian wonderland by Nash, and to a wholesome purgatory by Soane. It is consequently not surprising that his outlook was sometimes a little confused, his behaviour a little erratic. Like his post-Renaissance predecessors, he believed that what one man built at one time must always be organised into a formal and regular composition, except upon occasions ruled by the painter's fantasy and demanding the picturesque. Like those predecessors, also, he expressed his somewhat tepid interest in construction by means of ready-made architectural symbols at some remove from reality.

These symbols were normally Grecian or Gothic, Italian being tolerated only when it was such as could be described as Roman and truly antique. The ingenious novelties of Soane found imitators, many rather than successful. The Arabian, the Moorish, the Turkish;—it was not agreed which of these was in fact the Prince's style at Brighton, so that it seemed safer to apply to it the epithet *Mahometan*. Mahometan, then, was available for special occasions and made among other appearances a very surprising one in a Unitarian chapel at Devonport. The architects of Crockford's, by having that club furnished in what they believed to be the Louis XIV style, had pointed out to upholsterers a way of escape from the prevalent severities of the French Empire. None of these capricious experiments, however, was on a scale large enough to confuse or compete with the general Grecian and Gothic tendencies in Regency architecture taken as a whole. The architectural paraphernalia of Wren were admired by some, but by none imitated; those of Adam, and of Wyatt's youth, were not yet old enough to be anything but unfashionable and stale.

It has been customary to regard nineteenth-century architects as little more than stylemongers, owing to the far-fetched variety of their material; to ignore the essential qualities in their work, and to poke fun at the non-essential. Stylemongers among them there were, typified by George Wightwick (who in his book *The Palace of Architecture* unconsciously reduces stylism to its ultimate absurdity), by Peter Frederick Robinson, and, later in date, by George Somers Clarke (who, while capable of original design, occupied himself largely with reproductions in inappropriate surroundings of various models of foreign Gothic). In the heyday of Victorian prosperity, moreover, the mass-production of churches, houses, and public buildings tempted many harassed practitioners to trade extensively in stock patterns, but these patterns owed less to the buildings of an earlier age than to former products of the office that issued them. Details might be borrowed from far and wide, but composition usually displayed the Victorian character natural to its place and age.

The architect of the nineteenth and twentieth centuries need only differ essentially from the architect of preceding periods by having more than one string to his lyre. It may be customary to assume that designs whose details are derived from buildings contemporary with them and near at hand must be distinct in kind from, and greatly superior to, those that display the eclecticism of a wide knowledge; but the assumption is hard to justify. Indeed it would seem to be based upon the erroneous but popular conception that architecture must make the architect rather than the architect architecture, that what is called a style must always grow, culminate, and wane of its own agency, irresistibly compelling artists to materialise its various stages. That this has sometimes seemed to occur in the past and never seems likely to occur again cannot be denied; but its occurrence or non-occurrence can hardly be allowed to set up a radical distinction in works of architecture between the original and the unoriginal, between the creative and the mimetic.

It is very improbable that any architectural design, however original it may appear, can be other than a transmutation or an imitation of something in its author's experience, whether his memory of the model be conscious or subconscious. What that model may have been, old or new, from near or from far, is of no essential moment; what matters essentially is whether it has been transmuted or merely imitated. The distinction between transmutation and imitation is all it is wise to allow as the distinction between originality and unoriginality. A mediaeval steeple exactly like the slightly older one in the next village—that is an unoriginal work, however great its beauty; a Gothic cinema, impressing old forms into a new service—that, be it never so deplorable, is an original one.

Architecture that is original may indeed be otherwise unsuccessful, whereas that which is unoriginal may nevertheless be valuable and satisfactory. In the only proper testing to which a work of art can be put—that of whether or not it pleases in the way intended by its maker—considerations of originality and unoriginality are of no importance. They have been discussed here because of the prevalent belief that the architecture of the last century was inevitably spurious, and that of all preceding centuries authentic. A much more reasonable belief is that in every age there have coexisted works of spurious art and works of authentic art, and that the provenience of the raw material for the authentic works is entirely impertinent to their value as finished products. Once we have learned, indeed, to regard architectural style as nothing more than the medium of architectural expression, we shall rid ourselves of the delusion that has caused so many historians to bury

architecture at the near edge of the eighteenth century and
to recount in a hurried and sceptical last chapter its supposed
re-appearances, posthumous and improbable, between then
and now. Recent writers have certainly been apt to place
the tomb a little nearer to us, so that the first twenty years of
the nineteenth century now stand on its farther side: but,
wherever it be made to stand, it can never be anything but
an unmeaning cenotaph.

Architecture is as fully alive now as ever it was, and is
extremely unlikely to be outlived by men. The action of the
artist's will upon the thought and emotion of the spectator
is of exactly the same kind in the Cathedral at Westminster
as in the Abbey, in the Government buildings now rising
in Whitehall as in the Horse Guards on the other side of the
way. Even for the faults to which the work of the last
century and of our own must be particularly liable, for the
faults that spring from confused knowledge, from conflict-
ing possibilities, precedents in all ages can be found. One
such fault is alone peculiar and unprecedented, the fault of
trying to make a new building seem to be an old one. This
curious ambition has sprung up at intervals throughout the
last century and a half, but has always hitherto resulted in a
quick reaction toward healthier habits. The forms of old
buildings, their disintegration and their scars, seem as
models to have been reserved for the apes of latter days. At
the moment we may be in reaction against such foolish
mimicry, but it would be rash to claim that we are immune
against its recurrence. Were it endemic it might give some
justification to those who make it the mark of architecture's
fallen state, but even then the justification would probably
be insufficient. As an epidemic it can have no permanent
consequence, and should it arrive, need cause no anxiety
whatever. Temple Moore and Lutyens produced much
architecture of high quality only yesterday in spite of their

excessive preoccupation with ages not their own. Creative talent will always pierce through the thickest pretences of masquerade. And the masquerade will never be kept up for very long. The future may now seem remote in which anyone will have either the means or inclination to start it again, but it is rash to assume that it is passing into history finally. Follies die hard. Sometimes, too, it may be sad when they die.

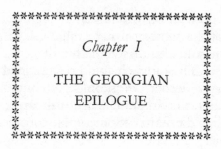

Chapter I

THE GEORGIAN
EPILOGUE

THE Regency ended, and the scope of this history begins, in the year 1820, by which time architects were already trying upon occasion to make new buildings seem to be old ones. This practice—as has been said in the Introduction—is almost without precedent in former times, and is supposed by many to be the peculiar failing of the nineteenth and twentieth centuries. It never has been as prevalent, however, as superficial appearances may seem to indicate, and was only indulged in by Regency architects and their Georgian predecessors upon provocation that might be called fantastic. Picturesque landscape, as it had come to be understood, required a large number of castles, hermitages, and ruins, in appropriate situations, and these objects the architect was called upon to provide. Hermitages and ruins, being intended only to excite a pleasing melancholy in the beholder, were given artifical decrepitude; but castles, which their owners would have to inhabit, were made as modern and convenient as was re-concileable with the provision of romantic silhouettes. At Beckford's Fonthill (1786), certainly, romance had got the

25

upper hand, a fact more than hinted at in Rutter's published description of that extraordinary building. 'If the Abbey,' he says, 'were a fair specimen of the total of the requisites for domestic comfort, which could be obtained with such a display of magnificence, we should certainly have the prejudices of all our countrymen in hostile array, when they know the scanty means it possesses.' He considers, however, that prejudices in favour of 'warm sitting-rooms and airy chambers' should be mitigated by the reflection that 'as we know that more might have been obtained if more had been thought desirable, we are bound to consider the present conveniences of the Abbey well adapted to the particular establishment for which they were provided.'

Requisites for domestic comfort, of course, were not yet expected in residences other than those of the gentry; and the decrepit hermitage or ornamental ruin might often be designed to serve as the peasant's humble dwelling. Less disagreeable abodes for the peasant were produced at the time in model villages, composed of cottages whose style sometimes departed little from the building traditions of the countryside. Ordinarily, however, the 'old English cottages' of such collections, (like the buildings in the delicious toy-village of Marie Antoinette), were deliberate, and often charming, exaggerations of the type; artificial as beseemed the artificiality of the occasion. Such exaggeration, though usually regarded as deplorable, may reasonably be defended as giving real value to what would otherwise be mere inapppropriate imitation. That a noble lord should build as a yeoman might build would have seemed then both eccentric and disgusting; obviously the noble lord's enlightened taste in bargeboards and twisted chimneys should be expressed by a more than ordinary emphasis upon those pretty rusticities. The cottage when built for and not by the cottager should surely be sophisticated in its ornament.

That, at any rate, is what people felt a hundred years ago, and reason does not side against them.

If cottages to be occupied by the cottager proper were thus idealised, much greater was the elaboration of picturesque character in *cottages ornés*, the name then appropriated to cottages intended as retreats for the gentry. Endsleigh (1810) in Devonshire is one of the first in date of such buildings, and is fairly typical of them in general. They are usually low and irregular, and covered with steep roofs heavily overhanging at the eaves and the verges. Their wall surfaces are of rubble stonework, of Roman cement, or of rough-cast plaster; since visible brickwork was for long condemned by all persons of taste as prosaic and mean. Their windows were large, (small lattice casements being allotted only to the labouring classes), and on the lower floor generally opened down to the ground. Ornamental enrichment was concentrated as a rule in the woodwork of porch, verandah, and gable, which all would help to support the creeping plants with which the building was to be covered; rose, wistaria, and magnolia on the garden front; ivy at the back. Considerable elegance was displayed in the internal finishings, the prevailing simplicity of which did not forbid marble chimney-pieces surmounted by glasses, and crystal chandeliers. Growing flowers were brought indoors, not only to that new delight the conservatory, but also into the sitting-rooms, where *jardinières* of wood or metal were provided for their display. Everything, in short, was sentimentally simple and highly appropriate. That the decoration and furniture of a room should accord in character with the dress and manners of its occupants was a truth that had not yet been lost sight of; the cottage aspect outside was a concession to the surrounding landscape, but the blessings of civilisation were preserved indoors.

27

Endsleigh, Devonshire (1810)   A COTTAGE ORNÉ

So well did this type of house accord with the tastes and habits of the nineteenth-century *bourgeoisie* that, in various stages of degradation, it continued to be built occasionally within living memory. In England it acquired as time went on the staider rusticity of the correct parsonage, and was finally purged of all its characteristic extravagance in the routine building of late Victorian suburbs. In Scotland its original romanticism had a longer run, and in the 'seventies was still the normal expression of the Glasgow merchant's rustic whim. The Glasgow architects well known as 'Greek Thomson' (1817-1875) and his brother relaxed very frequently in this direction. Such *cottages anglais* also contributed largely to the formation of a cognate type in France, merging there with the native *chaumières rustiques* that had been popularised by sentimentalists of the Revolution. Even now this type is not entirely obsolete.

Some stress has here been laid upon buildings of this style, which may be called, according to our predilections, the *villegiatura* style or the fretwork-and-earwig style, because its historical importance has generally been greatly underrated. In it more than in anything else was relearnt the lesson, long forgotten, that a building can be an architectural composition without possessing bilateral symmetry on any of its faces. In the eighteenth century such irregularity seemed intolerable, in the nineteenth it became not only tolerated but sought. To appreciate the enlargement of architecture produced by this change of feeling let us try to analyse the prohibition it did away, the permission it secured.

The word *symmetry* is used in many senses, but seldom in other than one when applied to architecture. This one sense can be described, in words selected from the definition given in the *Concise Oxford Dictionary* as the quality that 'allows of an object's being divided by a . . . line . . . into . . .

parts exactly similar in size and shape and in position relatively to the dividing line.' Furthermore, the dividing line is assumed to be vertical; the word 'symmetry' would not be used for the combination of a building with its reflection in water. Commonly, therefore, an architectural object is called symmetrical when its two sides, but not its top and bottom, balance and match each other.

It is often said that such bilateral symmetry is a characteristic of neo-Classical architecture and is absent in the Gothic. In saying this people mean that they expect to find the front door in the middle of a Georgian house, whereas in a Tudor house it may be anywhere. In a simili-Tudor house of the present day it may indeed be anywhere, but in an authentic house of the Tudor period it will be just as regularly placed as in a Georgian one. The Tudor doorway will always be in the middle of something, but in the middle only of the passage into which it opens—the 'screens'—and not necessarily in the middle of the whole façade. Such real antithesis as there is here between Georgian and authentic Tudor lies in the fact that in neo-Classical styles the front of any building whatever will appear as an integrated unit, whereas in Gothic and other styles the front of any complex building will show smaller units in irregular aggregation. The units, however, will almost always be symmetrical in themselves; no Gothic builder ever voluntarily threw a church window out of the middle of its gable or sloped that gable's two sides at different angles.

In the matter of bilateral symmetry, then, the opposition between neo-Classical and Gothic amounts to no more than that in the one a façade is commonly designed as a whole, in the other it is loosely composed of separately designed parts. The requirement that every building, however irregularly sub-divided, should be outwardly regular and self-sufficient seems to have originated at the Renaissance, when the characteristics natural in the simple buildings that form most of the architecture of antiquity were forced upon the complex buildings of the later age.

From this process there often resulted much grandeur, and still more often much inconvenience. In very few sub-divided plans can all that is on the right be equalised with all that is on the left without many of the compartments becoming smaller than they ought, or larger than they need to be. In monumental buildings waste of space may make for nobility, and the general scale may be grand enough for nothing to have to be squeezed. In domestic buildings completely symmetrical planning usually proves impracticable, so that the question arises whether irregularities that are unavoidable should or should not be concealed behind a symmetrical façade that will inevitably be more or less of a misfit. Whether such unnatural symmetry ever has the value in reality that it has on paper is open to doubt, but if it has, that can only be in open situations where it can be viewed without interruption by trees or adjoining buildings.

Houses of our *villegiatura* style were never intended to preside over parterres; they were for the woodland lawn, the shrubbery, the shelter of cedars. Here they enjoyed their new-found freedom, breaking out into gables whenever and wherever they felt inclined, although seldom if ever indulging in irregularity for irregularity's sake. The error of such indulgence, which was to lead even to the conceal-ment of natural symmetry, to the wanton variation of things that logically should have been uniform, did not arise until later in the century.

Free composition, once rediscovered, was not long confined to the 'Old English' style, in which it was at first developed. Architects upon their Italian travels soon became enamoured of those Tuscan villas and farms in which flat-pitched roofs and arcaded windows were combined with an insouciance as great as that of our native tradition. In France the illustrations of such buildings published by Percier et Fontaine, and afterwards by Scheult and by Normand, had already led to their imitation, and Mr. Summerson in his recent study of John Nash has discovered three houses of this character designed in the first decade of the nineteenth century. It was probably the publication at later dates of Hunt's *Architettura Campestre* (1827) and Parker's two volumes entitled *Villa Rustica* (1832 and 1833) that caused these forms to be generally exploited in England, and so eager was the exploitation that the word 'villa' acquired forthwith what is now its commonest significance. Tuscany came to St. John's Wood, to Cheltenham, to St. Leonards; indeed, in the outskirts of almost every growing town what was not a 'cottage' now became a 'villa.' In 1829 Peter Frederick Robinson (1776-1858) attempted a diversion in his Swiss Cottage north of the Regent's Park, and thereafter many crossbred villas displayed the *châlet* strain. Pure *châlets* were and have always remained rare upon English soil.

The 'villa' fashion spread even to the design of large houses of which the remodelled Walton House (1837) in Surrey remains a conspicuous example. Here, as also in the smaller specimens of its type, the belvedere tower is a conspicuous feature. Villas also appeared that really would have been called villas in the land of their origin; symmetrical mansions of Italian character, with visible roofs and without the decoration of columns or pilasters. One of the first of them to be built (in 1829) is now the Xavierian Seminary at Brighton. With this Italian character the Grecianism practised by the older school of architects was to fight an unequal and a losing battle. The pilastered walls, the two-storeyed portico, the terrace-roof surrounded

by a parapet, the noble but inconvenient flight of steps;
all these Grecianised Palladianisms of the Regency were
due to die. Of what was conceived as the pure Grecian
style examples had always been rare; the incongruity with

A VILLA

Design from Papworth's *Rural Residences* (1818)

their surroundings of such houses as Trelissick in Cornwall
(*c.* 1825), or the Grecianisation of the Grange in Hampshire
(begun as early as 1809) was perceived and avoided by most
people. Other neo-Grecian houses whose purity was less
uncompromising, settled down well enough in the stylised

GRECIANISATION

The Grange, Hampshire (1809)

parkland, lake, and landscape garden that formed their customary setting. Satisfying to the eye as they might be however, their formality, their costliness, and their frequent inconvenience gave them small chance of survival in a generation whose tastes wavered between baronial magnificence and the elegant *al fresco*.

'The rich man in his castle,' sang Mrs. Alexander, and *that* in the '40's, when she flourished, is where most people would have looked for him first. East Cowes (1778), Belvoir (1801), Eastnor (*c.* 1808), Kinfauns (*c.* 1820), Gwrych (*c.* 1820), Mitchelstown (*c.* 1820), and very many others, varying in date and size, had all been due to the widespread feeling that if you could not live at Windsor, at Arundel, at Alnwick, you nevertheless did the best you could. Many houses of the eighteenth century, like those at Mulgrave in Yorkshire and Hawarden in Wales, had been recased and castellated at great expense. Of the new castles mentioned above, Eastnor, of pre-Regency date, shews no emancipation from the fetters of neo-Classical symmetry, although in the others those fetters are broken through completely. Belvoir and Mitchelstown are romantically irregular in the noble manner; Kinfauns, East Cowes, and Gwrych are irregular, but perhaps less noble.

To write a history of architecture as a history of architects is to misplace emphasis and divert attention from the typical to the personal characteristics of their work. In every age, however, there will be one or two architects so influential that it would be false to refuse them a spotlight. James Wyatt (1746-1813), the architect of two buildings already mentioned—Fonthill Abbey and Belvoir Castle—only lived to see two years of the Regency, but his influence upon younger men was so powerful that something must be said here of his achievement. At Fonthill, at Belvoir, at Ashridge (1808), and in much work in several cathedrals, his

CASTELLISATION

Hawarden Castle, N. Wales (1804)

use of Gothic forms although avowedly eclectic and arbitrary was based upon a knowledge of detail that for his time appears astonishing. His powers of composition both in Grecian and Gothic mark him as a great architect, however we may regret the justification that there is for the name he won by his dealings with cathedrals—*Wyatt the Destroyer*. Interiors at Belvoir and at Ashridge prove his scenic skill, and shewed his contemporaries that a building Gothic externally might, at least in part, reconcile the same style internally with modern elegance. Before the coming of Wyatt, although neo-Gothic furniture and decoration of one kind or another were at least as old as Horace Walpole's Strawberry Hill, they had seldom moved far out of the toyshop. But the Gothic grandeurs of the Fonthill saloons and galleries, now all laid in the dust, had been such as to take men by storm; and, if the discomfort of Beckford's Abbey was all that Rutter implies, that discomfort could be laid at his own door rather than at that of his architect.

After that architect had first shewn what he could do in the London Pantheon (1770), 'several noblemen, desirous of retaining him in England, and of setting him at once out of the way of seeking emolument in any way but the fair and even pursuit of his profession, agreed to allow him each a stipend, amounting in the aggregate to twelve hundred pounds per annum, for which he was to act as architectural supervisor to their mansions.'[1] Wyatt more than anybody was the chosen and subsidised architect of the nobility, and he served them well. He knew what splendour meant, and when working for sensible men did not undervalue convenience.

Castles and abbeys, however, were mainly for nobles and for rich men well on the way to ennoblement, whereas for old English gentlemen, and for those whose antiquity and

[1] Hunt, *Architettura Campestre*, Introduction.

gentility were being sedulously cultivated, *manors* or *granges* made more appropriate habitations. The manor-house as understood at the beginning of our period was planned after the normal pattern of houses not manorial, but designed outside in a style between that of the *cottage orné* and the plainer parts of the contemporary castles. Gables it had and sash-windows sliding behind mullions, and emphatic chimneys, with a little buttressing and battlementing here and there, and possibly a pinnacle or two. If visible brickwork were used in the walls its colour would be yellow or buff, the Georgian view still prevailing that red bricks were greatly inferior to those whose colour resembled that of stone. What did actually appear to be of stone in dressings and ornament would probably be of Roman cement. Any pointed arches that occurred would have the flattened 'Tudor' form.

Wyatt's Gothic houses when not castellated had never relapsed into the prose of the manor-house, but had followed Strawberry Hill in its romantic combination of details largely ecclesiastical. Priories they would naturally be called, or abbeys; not manors or granges. Toddington Park in Gloucestershire (1819), designed—it is said—by its noble owner, was a true descendant of these, and perhaps the most important Gothic mansion of its age. It is remarkable for the intricacy of its internal decoration, in which everything is as Gothic as the plasterer could make it and all compromises with neo-Classical conventions have been eschewed.

Ordinarily the architects of the time were less thorough, or their employers less patient, and the vaultings and traceries that put such difficulties in the way of the upholsterers were confined to the hall, the staircase, and one or two important rooms. The interiors of the more comfortable manor-houses were often unblushingly neo-Classical from the threshold inwards. As in the *villegiatura* style, the outside of a house would conform with the landscape, the inside with the necessities of elegant life.

From the dissolution of the monasteries until now the architecture most characteristic of our country has been domestic; and in that category is properly included the architecture of universities and public schools, perhaps our most characteristic institutions. In the typical Oxford or Cambridge college the plan of such a house as Haddon Hall survives with hardly any modification, and is repeated in new foundations to-day.

During the years immediately following the Regency many great changes took place in the appearance of Cambridge University, and it was inevitable that the taste for mediaevalism then prevalent in house-building should be strongly displayed where mediaevalism if not surviving had never been forgotten. The Grecian ideal pursued in Downing College (1806) at Cambridge was overwhelmed and discredited by the later activities of Wilkins (1778-1839), its architect, in that University, by his neo-Tudor courts at Trinity and at Corpus Christi, by his remarkable buildings at King's. All these, together with the new and equally neo-Tudor buildings at St. John's and at Peterhouse, were begun in the years 1823 to 1827 inclusive, a period during which the only undertakings of the kind at Oxford were the modest new ranges at Balliol and at Hertford College. Both of those were obstinately neo-Classical; indeed, at Oxford since the completion of Hawksmoor's quadrangle at All Souls, Gothic experiment had been confined to the alteration of buildings already existing. No middle type was thought tolerable, as the drastic Tudorisation of the seventeenth-century buildings at Pembroke College, Oxford (1829), and at Sidney Sussex College, Cambridge (1821), painfully testifies. If a façade was neither neo-Classical nor neo-Tudor it had to be made one thing or the other. Soon the alternative disappeared, and the banishment of neo-Classical became complete. What was true of all universities was also true of public schools, in which battlement and buttress now utterly routed pilaster and pediment. One of their earliest victories had been won at Rugby School in 1809; and Lampeter College (1829) shewed later that even a Cockerell must stoop to Tudor when popular sentiment compelled.

Architecturally there is little in the style of most of these buildings to distinguish it from that of the contemporary 'manor-houses' already described. Even at Cambridge, where three of the more characteristic old colleges are built of red brick, the resumed use of that material was not yet thought admissible. Stone, Roman cement, or white brick was the rule, and the Wyatt tradition of eclectic detail, generalised from examples in many different places, was preferred before any observance of local peculiarities.

A range of college chambers is unlike most buildings demanded of the architect in that its practical requirements have remained almost unchanged throughout more than four hundred years. If, then, the neo-Tudor blocks of the early nineteenth century were comparable in every respect with their archetypes, and in every respect less valuable than they, they could have no possible defence. It is arguable, however, that the better among them have a particular value of their own which the nature of their archetypes had not allowed. The older buildings of the kind were related to their surroundings in the accidental way we may consider natural and proper, and the skill with which the newer often are organised as parts of a large all-pervading design may seem to us skill misplaced. Yet if we judge by its appropriate standard such a composition as the court of Corpus Christi College at Cambridge, if we think of it as one integral design, satisfying a desire for harmony that had increased with each passing century, we can hardly dismiss its claims upon our respect. To say of such a building that its neo-Tudor details are unsuitable for such un-Tudor use is easy, but to give any reason for saying so is harder. Even if they were so, even if they were as wildly irrelevant in their application as the Classical orders piled up against the tower of the seventeenth-century Schools at Oxford, they would remain but details, incapable of stultifying design in the large. The sentiment of the present day enjoys in Tudor forms a naïveté that was as little valued one hundred years ago as it would have been by Tudor builders themselves, had they been conscious of it; and this naïveté, which nowadays we are anxious to recapture, the early designers of neo-Tudor were anxious to avoid. In their manner of designing it would certainly have been incongruous, but, with it eliminated, the Tudor convention suited them well enough. The screen at King's College, Cambridge (1823), is not an old story haltingly retold, but a new story elegantly phrased in an idiom fancifully archaistic.

As we turn from the domestic architecture of this period to that of its public buildings we leave Gothic behind us altogether. When the Regency began, the chief architects in our country had already set a Grecian fashion that for eight years after the Regency's close seemed securely established and unchallengeable. The designs of the General Post Office (1823), the British Museum (1823), the Royal Institution at Manchester (1824), the Edinburgh High School (1825), and London University College (1827) were all as Grecian as could be; and whatever departures from purity there might be in the style of the Board of Trade Offices (1824) or of St. George's Hospital (1827) were certainly not in the direction either of Gothic or of the new rival shortly to appear—Italian. The use of an accepted receipt for the façades of public buildings was one to make little variation possible; all effort was concentrated upon a large Grecian portico, everything else being kept as negative and as much out of the way as possible. Soane's[1] strange and beautiful interiors at the Bank of England, which can now be studied only in photographs and drawings, were entirely eccentric. They stand outside all generalisations; and also, from the date of their designing, largely outside our period.

The year 1829 saw three hard blows delivered at Grecianism in the designs of three new buildings of unusual importance. In that of the State Paper Office (1829) (destroyed long since) the ageing Soane ran neck and neck with young Charles Barry (1795-1860) in introducing Italianism into the west end of London, Barry's mount being his famous Travellers' Club (1829); and Philip Hardwick (1792-1870), whose father had remained an obstinate Roman until his death at the beginning of the year, carried on the family tradition in the antique but eminently un-Grecian ornaments of Goldsmiths' Hall (1829). In the same year also, the most scholarly of our architects, Charles Robert Cockerell,[2] saved the prevailing fashion from decay when in Hanover Chapel (1824) (now gone from Regent Street) he gave to neo-Grecian formulas a meaning and a rationality that in this country they never had had before. A time of change was at hand.

Not before change was needed. What Fergusson,[3] the critic, called the 'Classical Revival'—what nowadays we describe vaguely as the 'Empire style,' first French and then of other countries—was slow in Great Britain to produce anything of much value. Our eighteenth-century

[1] Sir John Soane (1753-1837).   [2] James Fergusson (1808-1886).
[3] Charles Robert Cockerell (1788-1863).

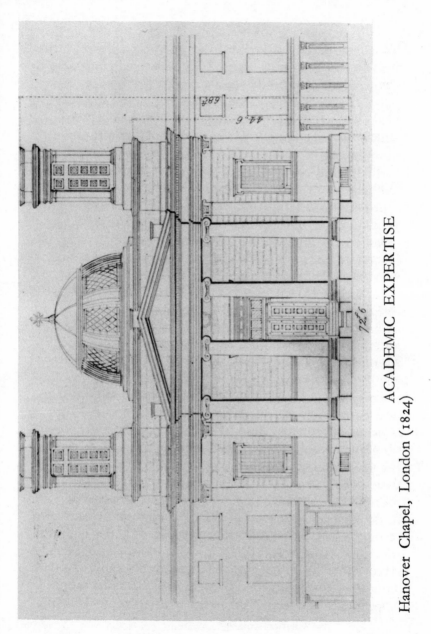

ACADEMIC EXPERTISE

Hanover Chapel, London (1824)

Palladianism, however dear to us now through sentimental association, had been a very provincial affair measured by the grand work of the same century in France, and its peculiar virtue of ingenuous earnestness was exactly what a change of idiom from Italian to Grecian was likely to make ridiculous. The heavy but amiable fancy of our Georgian designers has been most amusingly and endearingly distilled for our generation in decorative caricature by Rex Whistler:[1] similar caricature of the chaste inanity of our Grecian converts if it amused at all would have a bitter taste.

In the year 1809 the opera-house at Covent Garden had been rebuilt in a Grecian Doric style as frigid and as unsuitable to the purpose of the building as any style could be. Its designer was Robert Smirke (1781-1867), the protagonist in the dreary Greek play that took twenty years of British architecture in performance. The British Museum and the General Post Office were Smirke's; and so, too, were the additions to the Mint (1809 and 1815), the Royal College of Physicians with the old Union Club (1824), the remodelling of the Customs House (1825), and many important buildings beside, both in London and in the provinces. Never can so large an acreage of superficial architecture have been made of elements so few and so monotonous. One kind of Ionic order, one kind of window-dressing, one kind of doorway, seemed to Smirke, one must suppose, the kinds that were absolutely best, so he gave us nothing else. The frugality in draughtsman's time in his office must have been extraordinary. His order, his window, his door, are all good things, but good things of which one can easily have too much. Nor did he vary his method of composition any more than absolute necessity demanded. Almost all of his repertoire can be seen in the building partly occupied by the

[1] Obiit, 1945.

Royal College of Physicians that still takes up the west side of Trafalgar Square. (This building in its original form had a skilfully designed attic storey, partly projected, partly recessed, of a kind that occurs also in many other of Smirke's buildings and is the least uninteresting of the effects of his strictly regulated routine.)

It is customary to credit Smirke—not upon very convincing evidence—with considerable skill in planning. If his buildings are staid and ultra-conventional in appearance, some of them are at least reasonably well arranged. Without contesting or supporting this claim, it must be said that skill in planning, never the *forte* of British architects, deteriorated steadily in our country during the nineteenth century, with only the achievements of exceptional men like Barry or Waterhouse to keep the international repute of our architecture from collapse. Both Smirke and his less well-known contemporaries were already too often content that a very perfunctory and unarchitectural disposition of apartments should lie behind a duly porticoed façade. In later days than Smirke's, moreover, when façades had lost their porticoes and become generally less unaccommodating, planning, which should have become better, ordinarily became worse; and the cause of this phenomenon is perhaps not very hard to find.

What is commonly called a good plan is one of which every part is of a size proportionable with its nature and is appropriately placed. Such a plan will serve all physical needs, and in doing so will give some degree of satisfaction to the mind. Yet to give aesthetic pleasure it must go further; means of communication must be thought of as stages in a man's pleasurable progress from one apartment to another, an agreeable relation must be secured between each apartment and the next, the eye of the spectator must be led along every vista to no disappointment at that vista's end. The temple cella must culminate in its statue, the cathedral choir in its altar, the vestibule, staircase, gallery, and ante-chamber of a palace must culminate in the throne. When a plan is complex, the only eligible alternative to this organisation is to let chance play the same part in associating architectural elements as that which it plays in associating those of a natural landscape, to secure actual convenience by the simplest adequate artifice, to let the spectator's surprise or the fulfilment of his expectation come to him by chance. This method of design is not necessarily idle or cowardly; indeed, it is all that was usually attempted in complex buildings before the Renaissance, and is rich in possibilities of what is called the *picturesque*. It can be the indirect cause of aesthetic pleasure, although it cannot give it directly. To walk through a building arranged thus loosely need be no more disconcerting than to walk through a city, where closer organisation, being seldom possible, can seldom be expected. The seventeenth and eighteenth centuries, however, with their mania for making every building a monument capable of being taken from its context and presented, neatly self-sufficient, in a drawing or an engraving, gave no quarter to plans in which irregularity was not either absent or concealed. Difficulties already great were aggravated by the fact that the method of architectural design then normal was still that of dividing and subdividing a building whose external form had already been arbitrarily presumed; a method in which the nature and convenient disposition of apartments was just as frequently lost sight of as not.

For a hundred years before the close of the Regency, the conflict between two forces in architecture had continually sharpened. During all that time the style approved for external architecture had grown steadily simpler and stricter, and the needs of internal convenience had complicated and become harder to satisfy. Something would have to be yielded on one side or the other, although for a time Smirke and his compeers postponed the necessity of any decision by persevering in laborious compromise. Windows were slightly enlarged from the Palladian norm, skylights were contrived for spaces that porticoes darkened, the excessive height of small apartments forced to range with great was reduced by means of false ceilings. Such concession might long have been found sufficient had not the freedom allowed in neo-Gothic practice relaxed the technical skill of architects while it raised the expectations of their employers. Greater convenience was required than Smirke had provided, and, if buildings were to remain as regular as his, such aesthetic qualities as his planning possessed must be sacrificed entirely in a scramble of small attempts to fit accommodation in somehow—to make things do.

British architects of the neo-Classical school have ordinarily been more successful in small things than in great, and much, consequently, of the most valuable civil architecture produced in England during and after the Regency can be found in country towns. It would have been hard to conventionalise small town-halls and assembly rooms into the nullity of architectural expression that a false taste had successfully imposed upon larger undertakings. Markets also were too active to tolerate stiff clothes even in the metropolis, for prisons no complete Grecian disguise was physically possible, and workhouses, before the Act of 1834, were protected by frugality from aesthetic falsification. Most of these utilitarian buildings, even when they were works primarily of engineering, were designed by architects, and designed more often well than ill. The modest little market at Launceston in Cornwall may be instanced from among many other satisfactory examples. Covent Garden

Market (1830), naturally the grandest of them all, seems never to have been sufficiently praised; its workmanlike construction and simple architecture are very skilfully united, and the now destroyed Hungerford Market (1831) at Charing Cross by the same architect could have been praised in the same terms. The old Corn Exchange at Winchester (1838) is a later example of the kind, a little too Tuscan perhaps, but creditable to its designer. Important bridges, too, were still architect's work, although the newly specialised profession of engineers had arisen to collaborate in their execution. Already, indeed, the engineer sometimes enlisted the services of the architect, rather than the architect those of the engineer. Thus, in the obituary notice published in *The Gentleman's Magazine* of John Linnell Bond (1766-1837) we read that 'his design for Waterloo Bridge, justly considered one of the finest ornaments of the metropolis . . . with all the necessary estimates, was made by him for the projector, the late Mr. George Dodd, engineer.' The writer of this notice may be presumed to have known that the fine ornament of the metropolis, an ornament then only twenty years old, was designed by Bond, to whom it is attributed also in Redgrave's *Dictionary of Artists* and in *The Dictionary of National Biography*. On the other hand, Samuel Smiles in his life of John Rennie (1761-1821) assumes that when before the bridge was begun Dodd as engineer was replaced by Rennie, Bond disappeared from the scene. It is recorded that Rennie prepared two designs at this juncture which certainly differed from Bond's first proposal in discarding the form of arch known technically as *corne de vache*.

The architectural subtilty of the bridge as built, however, contrasts so strikingly with Rennie's own maladroit handling of a similar conception at Kelso, twelve years before, that Bond's authorship seems a much more likely cause of it

than Rennie's artistic increase. Bond has left in the front
of the Stamford Hotel (1810) a work of high quality. The
Stamford Fish Market (now the Public Library) (1807) and
the charming little town-hall at Bourne near by, look very
much as though they might have come from the same brain
as the hotel. If Waterloo Bridge (1810) was his also—and
this has been the object in discussing its authorship here,
he might well be taken as the type of many almost forgotten
architects in a small way, whose productions surpass in
merit those of the too successful Smirke.

For example, of Daniel Alexander (1768-1846), the architect of Dartmoor (c. 1809) and Maidstone (1810) prisons, it
was well said by a eulogist that 'in his hands the architecture,
whatever it was, was ever made to grow out of and to form
an inherent necessity of the structure. . . . He ever distinguished between the sense of an original architectural
feature and the nonsense of a false adaptation of it.' Here
again is praise which to Smirke would have been altogether
inapplicable.

Looking at post-Regency Grecianism as a whole, an
English critic of his national architecture cannot feel any
great satisfaction. The smaller monuments may be good,
though even they are invariably surpassed by coeval French
monuments of the same kind. In the larger monuments the
difference in merit between English and French becomes
enormous—the rich Classical tradition of Percier et Fontaine has for its parallel little else than the frigid pedantry of
a Smirke. Yet, if we forgive it the pompous irrelevance of
its peristyle, the British Museum shews in several of its
parts that Smirke could make use of opportunities that
suited his vein.

When criticising buildings by other hands than Smirke's
it is usual to disparage the National Gallery (1832) because it
is not what its architect would have made it, had he not

been interfered with; but the building as it stands is probably a great deal better than what most of its detractors would prefer. Of University College, London, an impressive monument to the eye, the internal arrangement seems to have escaped the architect's attention altogether, and it is difficult to imagine that the equally impressive High School at Edinburgh can ever have been found really convenient. The Edinburgh High School, however, attains with the National Gallery and University College a degree of purely architectural merit never reached by Smirke; indeed, in the design of each of these there can be detected some germ of the freedom that was to develope so remarkably at a later date in the riper neo-Classicism of Cockerell.

Of church architecture produced during the earliest years of our period there is not much to say. Most of what was done was the first-fruits of the Church Building Act of 1818, an Act whose first object was to drown what now might be called Socialism in the preaching of many voices from many new pulpits. It was generally agreed that the buildings containing these pulpits must be neo-Grecian or neo-Gothic, such neo-Romanism as is displayed in the parish church of St. Marylebone (1813-17) having become exceptional. Soane's suggestion of Romanesque as a third possibility bore very little fruit at that time, but at Walworth (1823) on Bethnal Green (1824) and in Trinity Church, Marylebone (1824), Soane turned his own idiosyncratic style to effective ecclesiastical use. In general, these early 'Commissioners' Churches' are mere preaching-houses of little architectural worth, neo-Grecian or neo-Gothic details being incongruously applied to a conventional model with parsimony or profusion as funds would allow. Of the neo-Classical variety, few, if any, can compare with St. James's, Bermondsey (1827), where every peculiar architectural difficulty of the type is solved in a design of

ATHENS IN BRITAIN

The High School, Edinburgh (1825)

great dignity and good sense. Every student of English eighteenth-century architecture knows the troubles that arose from Gibbs' unhappy attempt at St. Martin's in the Fields to combine a spire and a portico into one symmetrical compositon: architects felt thenceforth that the two brought together must not again be separated, and yet too often left the problem no further toward solution than it remains at St. Martin's. At St. James's, Bermondsey, the spire, instead of appearing to be perched astride the portico's roof, stands grandly at the west end, upon a mass which the portico only abuts, the nave overtopping the portico by the height of a clerestory. The solution is complete, but nobody seems to have thought of it before. The designers of St. Pancras' Parish Church (1819) certainly had not, when they piled up one of the least assimilated masses of beautiful second-hand details that have ever been offered to the public as a work of architecture. At St. James's, Hackney (1823), Smirke improved upon Gibbs' practice only by making his portico very heavy—Grecian Doric, in fact—and his spire, or rather his cupola, very light. At St. Anne's, Wandsworth (1820), he curved a peristylar portico round a circular steeple (as Nash has done in Langham Place, in order to close the vista of Regent Street); and at St. Mary's, Bryanston Square, London (1823), with characteristic economy of effort, he repeated exactly what he had done at Wandsworth.

Throughout the whole of the Georgian period churches had occasionally been designed in the Gothic style as understood at the time, and in the increasing number of these that appeared in the quarter of a century before Queen Victoria's accession two types can be distinguished, although not always very clearly. In both of these types a plan and arrangement adapted to Protestant worship is joined with architectural forms derived from Catholic antiquity, but in one kind the principal motive is the arrangement, in the other the principal motive is the architecture. Churches of this second kind, churches in which the aisled and clerestoried nave is the essential and all the lumber of box-pews and galleries but the accident, may be attributed not so much to the revival of Gothic as to its attenuated survival. In such re-appearances the style, however imperfectly recaptured, is always in the phase that it attained before its abandonment in the sixteenth century, whereas in works of arbitrary revival all phases were confounded together by imitators having no tradition as their guide.

It is therefore not inappropriate to include such churches as St. Peter's, Brighton (1823), in the Georgian Epilogue although their details reach a degree of correctness that anticipates Victorian revivalism. In this class St. Luke's, Chelsea (1820), is exceptional, its groined vault being really of stone and provided with flying buttresses, whereas in most other examples the vaults are but make-believe affairs of lath-and-plaster. The interior of St. John's Episcopal chapel in Edinburgh (1816), has merits above the average in this category.

Theale church near Reading, when it was finished in 1828, was the subject in the *Quarterly Review* of an article praising the correctness and singularity of its style. That style is 'Early English' of the Salisbury variety, rather awkwardly assumed, but giving evidence in its details of careful study on the part of its architect. A church with imitation 'Norman' details had been built some years before at Wolverton in Buckinghamshire (1815), and it was not long before revivalism of other mediaeval styles than the latest became epidemic. Such revivalism was at first only detail-deep, the general forms and proportions of the buildings in which it occurred remaining strictly Georgian.

GOTHIC REAWAKENING

St. Luke's Church, Chelsea (1820)

Toward the end of the eighteenth century the experiment was occasionally made of adapting to Protestant worship octagonal and other amphitheatric plans, and in the nineteenth century this experiment was continued with Gothic material. The church of St. Dunstan-in-the-West in Fleet Street (1830) has an octagonal nave and an exceptionally elegant steeple: it is much better than others of its kind, and therefore perhaps is not truly representative of them. There is no need, however, to specify others of less worth in what is but a general review. The conventionality of most churches of the period, whatever their plans, exhibits British Conservatism and unimaginativeness at its worst, and the slender interest they possess is merely that of anticipating better things to come.

A review of beginnings is all that this chapter has purported to be. The beginnings of many things that are tangled together and could not have been traced sequentially without falsification. For the scope of this book a length has been cut, arbitrarily enough, from the skein of history, and the threads have been traced back no further than to the fragment's severed end. All that has been attempted has been to knot them firmly enough to stand the strain of our future disentanglings without coming apart—and this should be enough; seeing that in the examination of art immediate context is far more significant than remote provenience.

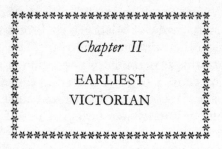

Chapter II

EARLIEST
VICTORIAN

HOWEVER determinedly the student of history may
shun the diversions of biography, he is bound to find
that the tendencies and aspirations of many epochs
are personified in his mental picture by particular men. The
Georgian Epilogue on the architectural stage suggests
vividly a curtain tableau of character and attitude. Its central
figure is Sir Robert Smirke, displaying with a complacent
gesture a group of models representing Ionic porticoes of
identical design but neatly graded sizes, and pretending not
to notice the rival model of a *cottage orné* to which Sir
Jeffry Wyatville (1766-1840), late Jeffry Wyatt, is trying
to attract the attention of the audience. Each of the two
knights is numerously supported by esquires, some of whose
eyes are turned uneasily toward the as yet undubbed John
Soane, standing quizzically aloof. Behind these groups are
ranged younger men, bringing in their arms toy castles and
churches from a landscape in which can distantly be seen the
towers of Fonthill and of Belvoir. In the foreground of that
landscape a huge mass of collegiate buildings is rising, soon
to conceal with its turrets and pinnacles the porticoes of

Downing College behind it. Thomas Telford, the engineer, has adopted no attitude: his whole attention being given to the labours of some bridge-builders. The mountebank Nash postures extravagantly, in oriental costume, but nobody notices him.

John Nash (1752-1835) has hardly yet been mentioned in these chapters for just this reason—that nobody else in our tableau would be paying any heed to him, and that he would hardly seem to belong there at all. Being the Regent's man he naturally had his sycophants, but the eyes of his contemporaries, having focussed but imperfectly upon the grandeur and picturesqueness of his conceptions, were disgustedly averted from the cynical shoddiness of their architectural realisation. He had cut Westminster in two and was joining Marylebone to London, and as Farington had noticed, 'put himself very much forward' on that account. But when he 'put himself forward' in their direction, more respectable architects drew back. Smirke and Wyatville may have been amused by the fellow's Gothic and Mahometan antics, but can hardly be expected to have taken seriously his attempts at classical quotation. He was obviously a good man with roads, trees, and water; and Soane, never squeamish, had not refused to design a façade in his new street.

When the collegiate buildings are complete they will dominate the scene, which will then be filled by a crowd of ordinary Englishmen who have come expressly to admire them. The taste for English Gothic was a national taste and a popular one, although neither architects nor public yet wished for a return of the style in its integrity. Had the first repudiation of neo-Classicism been—as it is so often represented to have been—a literary or a religious gesture, a yearning for the world of Mrs. Radcliffe's fancy, or a spiritual revolt against the evils of Erastianism, it would have been a gesture more violent, but one only of a few.

The architecture it then would have produced might well have had a strong foreign flavour, since romanticism and catholicism acknowledge no frontiers. It would have been enthusiastic in the sense that made that word dreaded, and almost certainly as inconvenient as sentimentality could make it.

The repudiation actually made was quite different from this. Neo-Classicism was suddenly seen as something alien, never really acclimatised here, Gothic as something indigenous to which patriotism required our return. Nevertheless no radical change was contemplated except in the shapes of ornamental forms; the internal arrangement and the structural workmanship of the buildings the age required were generally agreed and not thought of as subject to revision. The polish of neo-Classicism seemed then to be characteristic not of one kind of architecture but of all civilisation, and the combination of this polish with the romantic forms of more savage times was the task especially confronting builders in an age of Progress.

It may be that the tamed and sophisticated neo-Gothic that was thus evolved did not in the end justify its existence. It may be that if from Gothic forms all irregularity and quaintness are eliminated not enough remains to make an expressive style for conventional use. In the Cambridge buildings mentioned in the last chapter, in St. Katherine's Hospital in the Regent's Park (1827), in the now destroyed hall of the old Christ's Hospital (1825), all good examples of their kind, nothing perhaps suggests that their designers would not have done better to say it with pediments and pilasters. All this may very well be true, but what about the Houses of Parliament?

In the Houses of Parliament (1835) we see a complex building, elaborately and artificially organised in the post-Renaissance manner, wearing clothes made of Tudor

'TUDOR DETAILS ON A CLASSIC BODY'

The Houses of Parliament, London (1835)

material although of modern cut. Every relation between one part and another is carefully adjusted where by the Tudor builders it would have been ignored. The towers excepted, nothing breaks the general regularity of the composition, a regularity that in some parts of the design has even imposed the necessity of sham windows. On the other hand, the general patterning of the façades is as Tudor as its designers could make it, which is almost to say that it actually is Tudor in everything except date. Yet it would be difficult to find any building in which there were fewer elements of aesthetic discord than in this, any building in which theoretic inconsistency is architecturally so innocuous. There has been, as is well known, much bitter and foolish controversy over the question asked in the title of a pamphlet, *Who was the Art Architect of the Houses of Parliament?* 'Foolish' controversy because that question itself was foolish; what can be the meaning of the preposterous term *Art Architect?* If it were to mean designer of surfaces most of the honour would go to Augustus Welby Pugin, to whom all the internal, and much of the external ornament is due. If it were to mean composer of plan, disposer of masses, the answer to the question would be its appointed architect, Sir Charles Barry. Sir Kenneth Clark's book on the Gothic Revival and Mr. Trappes-Lomax's recent biography of Pugin well recount the dispute in its interesting, although unedifying, progress, but our concern here is with the building rather than with its authorship.

A compromise between two strong and convinced opponents is likely to be more definite, more taut, than a compromise made between two opposing influences in the mind of one man. The Pugin-Barry compact certainly proved firmer than the compact in the design of Corpus Christi College between Wilkins the Romantic and Wilkins the symmetrician. At Westminster the equilibrium is so just and delicate that criticism must pause before it. The application, in Pugin's regretful words, of 'Tudor details' to 'a Classic body' may seem a roundabout way of making good architecture, but here it seems to have succeeded extremely well. The circumstances of its success have never recurred, and recent attempts to reproduce them have led to no success as marked even as that of Wilkins. In years less recent, when the Houses of Parliament were still newish or new, nobody tried to repeat the essential peculiarities of their style. Victorian architects were barking up another tree.

In the advertisements of the competition held in 1835 for their design, it was absolutely required that the style of the new Houses of Parliament should be 'Gothic or Elizabethan.' This requirement raised two synchronous storms, one of applause, the other of protest, but can hardly have been surprising to those most in touch with the feeling of the nation. What the promoters who framed it expected to get cannot be clearly imagined; they could not have foreseen Pugin, and their conception of an Elizabethan palace of legislature was probably inchoate and unrealisable. Sir John Soane, however, had already been compelled to Gothic design some years before, in the external additions he had made to the old palace: and in the new palace popular sentiment would be likely to favour some degree of stylistic harmony with what remained of St. Stephen's Chapel, with Westminster Hall, and with the Abbey. Westminster, moreover, was an exceptional place; the new building proposed there was one that would inherit exceptional associations. Elsewhere in 1835 the most enthusiastic Gothicist would not have dared to dream of an ordinary legislative or official building's being clothed otherwise than classically.

If any proof were needed that neo-Classicism was first

assailed not by the romanticism of the literary but by an awakening of national self-consciousness, this permission of 'Elizabethan' as an alternative to Gothic would supply it. Few people in 1835 were quite sure what 'Elizabethan' architecture was, John Britton (1771-1857), the antiquary, complaining that it might mean anything from Tudor to Renaissance. Nevertheless, it could not but be English and that was enough. The crude, coarse, ornament that is its distinguishing mark had been regarded in the eighteenth century as of antiquarian interest (which, if the truth be told, is the only interest serious criticism is likely to allow to it), and in the first decade of the nineteenth century had been dutifully continued in new works at old houses such as Longleat (1801) and Wollaton (1804). Anything 'Old English,' however, even if by origin bastard German, was sure of popular favour, especially if it could be associated with the legendary 'Good Queen Bess.' Confused strapwork and paunchy grotesques came to be not only admired in old buildings but copied in new.

J. Hakewill's (1778-1843) study of the style was published in 1835, C. J. Richardson's (1806-1871) in 1837, and John Shaw's (1803-1870) in 1839; the last book being by far the most valuable of the three. Amid the execrations both of classicists and mediaevalists Elizabethanism won its way in the domestic architecture of the '30's, bringing with it a revived use of red brick and a homeliness of character that were welcome enough to a generation accustomed to pallid Grecianism and unfriendly castellation. Babraham Hall near Cambridge (1832) is a remarkably early example of this type. Nor was the style entirely confined to the country. Fortnum and Mason's old house in Piccadilly, obviously the work of a very accomplished architect, displayed Elizabethan forms in the shop-front, cunningly supported by little sympathetic oddities in the other

'ELIZABETHAN'

Harlaxton Manor, Lincolnshire (1834)

details of a severe and beautifully proportioned façade. Of its date it can only be said with certainty that it was pre-Victorian; the more pronouncedly Elizabethan offices of the Law Life Assurance Coy. in Fleet Street were begun in 1832, and the designs of the two buildings look very much of an age. This urban Elizabethan, although seldom as satisfactory as it was at Fortnum and Mason's, had usually involved enough modification of ancient models to acquire new value at first hand.

Except for the coming of neo-Elizabethanism no considerable novelty can be observed in house architecture during the first fourteen years of Queen Victoria's reign. Castle-building abated; there was a lull, even, in the magnificent reconstruction of Windsor, and what little continued was done more reasonably than before. Peckforton Castle in Cheshire (1847) is an exception to this, being a miracle of mediaeval reproduction, achieved at the expense of the modern allowance of light and air that Wyatt and Nash had never refused to their employers. Scotney Castle in Kent (1837), an early work by the architect of Peckforton, is a castle only in name and can be taken as representative rather of the very numerous neo-Tudor houses built by Early Victorians, of which it was a typical specimen. The design of these was developed from that of the manor house as understood by the previous generation, with the buttresses, pinnacles, and other ecclesiastical elements of that curious conception eliminated. In them bilateral symmetry was more and more discarded, and a tower, irregularly placed, soon came to be thought indispensable. White brick having been succeeded in popular favour by red, cement now was no longer accepted as a substitute for stone, and roofs grew steeper and sprouted into rich crestings of iron-work or tile. Windows, although mullioned and transomed, were very skimpily so divided and were extremely large in proportion to the area of the walls in which they were set. The large new house added to the old one at Aldermaston in Berkshire (1848) from designs by the son of the architect of Babraham epitomises the modifications made in the manorial style during sixteen years.

Not that this style was the only one in domestic use. What in the last chapter was named the *villegiatura* style retained its popularity, and Italianism continued to rule town and suburb. Sir Charles Barry, whose conversion in 1837 of the Georgian Highclere House into a towered Elizabethan palace had caused great wonder and delight, was employed upon several other transformations no less surprising. In these his usual style was Italian and sumptuous, towers and colonnades being added to old buildings that were themselves dressed up with new cornices, balustrades, window-dressings, urns, and what not, so that they might not disgrace the splendid patches put upon them. Trentham Hall in Staffordshire (1838) is the classic example of these doings and was surrounded, as was also the more gently handled Harewood House (1842), with an Italian garden of great magnificence.

Nevertheless, with the exception of such palaces, nine out of ten early Victorian houses of any size were professedly 'old English,' which was the aristocratic style of its time, such neo-Italian houses as still appeared being built chiefly for the prosperous middle-class. In smaller houses also the use of the neo-Italian style came to be restricted in the main to those whose owners would boast that they had stood no nonsense from their wives or their architects. Their prudent architecture seldom possesses novelty or merit.

In street-houses the neat brickwork of Georgian days gave way everywhere to cement, some London estates actually making the cementing of the front an obligation when granting a renewal of lease. Neo-Italian was here sup-

reme, rarely rising to the excellence displayed in that
block of Prince's Gate, Knightsbridge (1840) which was
designed by the architect of St. George's Hall in Liverpool.
Attempts at Gothic or Elizabethan town-houses were rare.

When in the last chapter neo-Grecianism was shown to be
threatened by the Italianism from which it was soon to
suffer defeat, no detailed explanation was attempted of what
that Italianism was, or of how it was new to England. The
first little villas were described as Tuscan, which in in-
spiration they certainly were, and the larger works of Barry
as Italian more generally; examples of those being the
Xavierian Seminary at Brighton and the Travellers' Club.
The Travellers' Club together with the Reform Club,
which came in 1837 to occupy the site adjacent to it, might
perhaps be best called 'palatial Italian' in style; indeed, the
façade in Pall Mall of the Travellers' has been supposed to
have been suggested by that of the Pandolfini Palace at
Florence, that of the Reform by that of the Farnese Palace
in Rome, in both cases foolishly but understandably. Whatever their derivation, the club façades are anything but
Palladian, and upon Palladianism was founded the only
Italian architecture that untravelled Englishmen then could
know.

What is called in schools 'the application of an order'—
that is to say the more or less flat representation upon a
façade of the elements of an antique colonnade—was no
Palladian monopoly; but the particular formula by which
the 'order' was made to embrace two storeys, another
storey underlying it as a basement, and yet another sur-
mounting it and being conventionally called an *attic*,—this
formula was especially Palladian and was the foundation
of most neo-Classical European building outside Italy.
The pilaster running through more than one storey and the
extra storey called the attic were its peculiar characteristics,

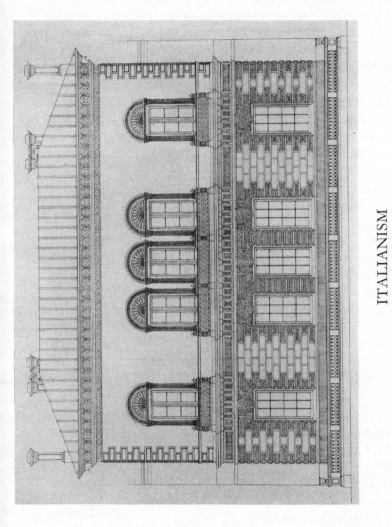

ITALIANISM

Travellers' Club, London, Garden Front (1829)

characteristics whose convenience obtained their continuance in the neo-Grecian style by all architects but the most hidebound. But the neo-Grecian conscience was never quite easy about them. Purity was the order of the day, and pilasters and attics would hardly seem probable in the temple of Vesta. Yet virtue was difficult; antique patterns of purity seldom had more than one storey, whereas modern buildings needed several. Basements and attics must go, and those buildings that could not be veiled, as the British Museum and Fitzwilliam Museum could, with Classicism unsullied must stand forth naked and, as far as possible, unashamed.

At this difficult juncture Sir Robert Smirke retired from practice, leaving the unusual choice between nakedness and impurity to his younger brother Sydney (1798-1877). In the first Carlton Club (1835) Sir Robert, probably influenced by the two club-houses newly built in Waterloo Place, had done without any order of columns: Sydney now confused the issue by rebuilding it (1846) with two, in a reduced copy of St. Mark's Library at Venice. To others less hesitating, Barry's Italian pointed an easy way out of their dilemma. Pilasters must go, but not cornices; the necessary order could be present bodily at the top, but elsewhere present only in spirit. Furthermore, the cornice could be of any size, being proportional no longer to the largest columns that could be used with convenience, but to an imaginary order that might embrace the whole building. Provided such a cornice were large enough, it never need be put below the top, and no attic storey need ever appear above it. Palladio never did thus, but careful consultation of Letarouilly's *Edifices de Rome* and Cicognara's book on Venice revealed that other Italian architects had done thus most of the time.

If you walk down Eaton Place in London, going south-west, you pass architecturally through the years this chapter purports to cover. At the north-eastern end of the street the houses are designed on a neo-Grecian variation of the Palladian formula; the dining-room storey forms a basement for an order running through the drawing-room storey and the storey above it—and the cornice proper to that order is surmounted by a storey treated as a classical *attic*. As you go on, the street gets gloomier and even produces an illusion of narrowing; the cornices have gone up to the top, and their projection is proportionally increased. The houses look higher, although they are not really so; they also look what the house-agent calls 'handsomer.' Within them you no longer find neat classical plasterwork and woodwork, but bolder things in a style certainly not neo-Grecian. The Doric columns of the porches have changed from Greek to Roman, and support far richer balustrades. Victorianism has arrived.

In the days of true neo-Grecianism the highest praise a work of architecture could receive was conveyed by the epithet *chaste*. To say that chastity went out of fashion with the last Georgians would probably, in any general application, be unhistorical. Nevertheless, the last Georgian style has an unmistakeable air of knowing more than it used to. Let us say that in due time the neo-Grecian style became matronly, and that what in the succeeding style might be mistaken for voluptuousness was in reality nothing but the chubbiness of a new-born innocence. For *chubby* seems to be the exact adjective that will describe the character of neo-Classical architecture in its Early Victorian phase. Possibly this chubbiness was not necessarily infantile, but was the desired antipole of the aristocratic, the academic, the esoteric. It may thus be explained as a cherished characteristic in a style that was deliberately, proudly, middle-class.

It was certainly not unrecognised, choice specimens of it having been described by their producers as in the 'Fancy Style.' Every man might have his fancy—he need no longer be ashamed of taking simple pleasure in the ornate. The tawdry of the fair ground was no sin, why should only gin-palaces exuberate?

Probably the Fancy Style was largely a confluence of the upholsterer's 'Louis XIV,' attempted at Crockford's and elsewhere, and the upspringings of Elizabethan already noticed in the last chapter. Neo-Grecian characteristics it retained, particularly in those vegetable motifs of ornament that suggest honeysuckle and celery, but the essential rectangularity of neo-Grecian was deliberately avoided. The two well-known books of designs by George Smith for domestic furniture, published, one in 1808 and the other in 1826, shew very well the change in taste that took place between those years. In the first book the designs follow the Grecian, Gothic, and Chinese routine of the Regency—in the second the Fancy Style has made a most significant appearance.

The new ornament, although initially used only in internal decoration, was not slow in creeping out of doors, first curling round shop-fronts and in course of time spreading over whole buildings. Theatres gave it readiest support, one of its most successful cultivators being the romantic Samuel Beazley (1786-1851), playwright, actor, and architect. Of his theatre façades that of St. James's Theatre, finished in 1837, is the only one in London that remains intact; it combines dignity with an appropriate theatrical flavour in a happy way that now, alas! appears to be forgotten.

Sir Charles Barry, according to the *Dictionary of National Biography*, was son of a 'well-to-do stationer,' and it is said that the business of Sir Charles's father was conducted in the

THE FANCY STYLE

Design from Collis's *London Street Architecture* (1837)

71

shop that used to exist by the entrance to the old Egyptian Hall in Piccadilly. This suggests an explanation of the son's constant preference for the Fancy Style in decoration, if the tradition be true that 'Barry's' was the great place for the expensive wedding presents in which ormolu and incrustations were to be expected. Certainly, once he had lost the white robe of his Grecian youth, Barry rarely refused himself anything that was going in the way of rich ornament, and the contrast between the elegant simplicity of the Treasury in Whitehall when it left Sir John Soane's hands in 1828 and the juicy elaboration of Barry's remodelling of it in 1846 is great enough to be disconcerting. The Fancy Style attracted in some degree nearly all the mass of the architectural profession, and came naturally enough to the theatrical Beazley and to coarse-fibred men like Sir William Tite (1798-1873), (who so unaccountably won in competition the designing of the Royal Exchange). The greater architects, however, with the exception of Sir Charles Barry, seldom would have anything to do with it.

Barry's share in the Houses of Parliament, his extremely clever planning both there and elsewhere, his leadership in introducing the neo-Italian style, his two club-houses in Pall Mall, and the large patronage he received from the nobility, have all combined to give him a very prominent place in English architectural history. This place it would be ungracious to grudge him, yet the critical student must wish honour to be shared more equitably than it is between him and several architects that were at least his equals in everything except opportunity. The surface beauty of architecture such as that of the Ashmolean and Taylorian Building (1841) at Oxford was far beyond Barry's power to achieve; and that the name of a Cockerell should rank in popular estimation below that of a Barry gives to power an unfair pre-eminence over sensitiveness. Barry stands first perhaps in reflecting his time: his boldness, his professional competence, his not too discriminating veneration for Italian art, mark him the true Victorian. Cockerell, on the other hand, with his acute intellectual curiosity and his aristocratic disdain of the insensitive and the conventional, fits oddly enough into an age of plebeian complacency. Barry led and represented the general body of well-meaning architects in his day and what he did first others could soon learn to do nearly as well as he did. Cockerell was lonely and inimitable.

Had Cockerell been a Frenchman he would not have been thus aloof, since the particular tendency of his genius accorded with the aims and practice of the best Parisian architects of his time. While the Smirke machine had been turning out innumerable Ionic columns as easily as though they had been sausages, the French had been occupied, as always, with delicate problems of architectural developement. The classical researches of the late eighteenth century had deposited all over the rest of Europe a collection of forms, hitherto forgotten, from Greece and Rome. For some time the architects of most nations were content merely to play with these as though they were new toys, but the French had set to work at once to see what valuable thing could be made of them. All the experience acquired by a Mansart, by a Gabriel, in the aesthetic interplay of rustication and plain surface, of column and pilaster, of arch and lintel, could not be discarded in favour of a process of antique veneer. New methods and materials, too; the cast-iron girder, the large sheet of glass, the metallic or composite roof-truss, must all be allowed their expression. In such developement Cockerell early took an active share, while most of his compatriot architects were content to let approved formulas save them the trouble of any real self-adaptation to an age of change.

Cockerell was not strongly influential (it would have been better for our architecture had he been so), since few among his contemporaries had the wit to appreciate, let alone to emulate, his exquisite skill, his egregious habit of mind. Emphasis upon his personal art, however, is unavoidable for another reason, that of its intrinsic excellence. Never has there been a more accomplished English architect than he, nor one more originally creative. Many of his buildings by now have been destroyed or mutilated, but among those that remain the houses of the Bank of England at Liverpool (*c.* 1844), Manchester (1845), and Bristol (*c.* 1847), with the Taylorian and Ashmolean Building at Oxford, are the most important. The Westminster Assurance Office (1829), Hanover Chapel, and the Westminster Bank in Lothbury (1837) have been allowed to disappear without a protest by a generation ever anxious to hold up a public improvement to save the meanest Tudor cottage. The Sun Assurance Office (1843) has had an extra storey thrust into its middle— as tenderly as possible, but with great damage to its proportions. Other work of his was lost only recently in the savage pogrom of architecture at the Bank of England.

Beside the works of Cockerell, there are not many neo-Classical designs of the post-Regency period in England that can be of any great interest to others than Englishmen, and even for Englishmen the value of most of them must be historical rather than aesthetic. The Offices of the Duchy of Cornwall in Buckingham Gate (1854), though small, have elegance and dignity in an unusual degree,[1] and high praise was deserved by two other works of their architect (Sir James Pennethorne (1801-1871)) that have since been

---

[1] These, having escaped death in a war injury, have now met a worse fate at the hands of reconstructors. Their unviolated form is well recorded by a measured drawing published in Professor Richardson's book on Monumental Architecture.

pulled down. These were the Museum of Economic Geo-
logy in Piccadilly (1848) and Holy Trinity Church in the
Gray's Inn Road (1848).

Neither Cockerell, nor Barry, nor Pennethorne, however,
was the architect of the two important neo-Classical
buildings whose designs were obtained by competition
about the time of Queen Victoria's accession; the Fitzwilliam Museum at Cambridge (1835) and St. George's Hall
at Liverpool (1839). Of the design of the Fitzwilliam
Museum hard things have sometimes been said, and its
enormous portico certainly cannot be regarded as suitable
either to the building behind it or to its place opposite
nothing and terminating no vista. It is a very handsome
portico, all the same, and the hall and staircase to which it
gives access are noble enough. Cockerell was to have
decorated them after their architect's death, but in the end
the decoration was done by another hand; in a style very
different from Cockerell's but possibly in better accord than
his would have been with the hyper-Corinthian luxury of
the exterior. Cockerell did complete and decorate (1848)
St. George's Hall at Liverpool when its brilliant young
architect, Harvey Lonsdale Elmes (1813-1847), had been
cut off by consumption; and the result of the two men's
labours is rightly famous as the grandest neo-Classical
building in England. To adapt the forms of the baths and
temples of Roman antiquity to the public halls of a modern
British seaport may be—indeed is—a highly irrational pro-
ceeding, but art can operate within many illogical hypotheses
provided those hypotheses be consistently upheld. St.
George's Hall, both in the proportions and organisation of
its plan and in the aesthetic disposition of its masses, is the
work of a master; and to say that Cockerell's designs for the
interior are worthy of this building by another man is no less
than it would be to say that they are worthy of himself.

75

ROMAN GRANDEUR

St. George's Hall, Liverpool (1839)

The civil engineering of early railways had aesthetic merit so considerable that the architecture of the first railway stations seems somewhat tame and inappropriate in comparison with it. The terminal stations at Blackwall (1840) and London Bridge (1843) were predominantly domestic in character, and those at Brighton (1840), Nine Elms (1838), and Southampton (1839) also differed little in appearance from private houses except by their extended porches for the shelter of carriages and cabs. The two last were among the very many designed by Tite, the architect of the Royal Exchange. At Cambridge (1845) such a porch became an enormous arcaded loggia itself forming the whole façade of the building. Both at Euston Square (1838) and at Birmingham (1838), the railroad connecting those two places was entered by passengers through a tremendous portico, whose purpose was entirely spectacular. About ten years younger than these two striking works by Hardwick are the large stations at Carlisle (1847) and Perth (1848) in which Tite saw fit to go extremely Gothic. The Newcastle station (1848), which has been much praised, is a grand exaggeration of the type displayed at Cambridge; the carriage portico, huge and long, being as high as the station wall behind it, and most richly Roman in style. The front of King's Cross station (1852) has been hailed with relief by three generations of critics because of its freedom from irrelevant motifs of applied architecture. Its simplicity and size win for it a grandeur that, although deserving our gratitude, might have been greatly increased by more skilful emphasis and adjustment in its designing.

All of these buildings were entirely devoted to the purposes of the railway, and what parts of their design may appear to be domestic were in reality only waiting-rooms or offices of the Company. The magnificent hall at Euston, one of the noblest rooms in London, has, in spite of its palatial appearance, no function but that of losing the footsteps of hurrying travellers. Railway hotels had not yet been thought of, and little was demanded of stations by the traveller beyond shelter from rain.

In the architecture of churches, between the passing of Grecian and the great Gothic inundation there had been little time for the Italian episode that might perhaps have been expected. When France had again taken to church-building after her revolutionary troubles, she evolved a style in which details of Renaissance character were combined with the general form and pattern of the Romanesque basilica. Designs of this kind were published in the books of Normand and others, and had a small but recognisable influence upon one or two English churches built at the time. In the elegant and fashionable-looking chapel of St. Andrew at Hove next Brighton (1827), an early work of Barry's, the Italianism looks as though it had reached England via France, and a few unimportant churches are scattered about the country whose designs had we encountered them in Normand's book would not have surprised us. Such are All Saints' (R.C.) Church, Hassop in Derbyshire (1818), the parish church of Woore in Stafford-shire (1830), St. Mary's (R.C.) Church at Grantham (1832), and, of a later date, the church of the Holy Trinity at Plymouth (1845). In the beautiful and original twin churches of St. Raphael (R.C.) at Kingston-on-Thames (1846) and Christ Church, St. Alban's (1847)—designed by Charles Parker (1800-1881), the author of *Villa Rustica*, an ecclesiastical counterpart of the neo-Tuscan villa is perfectly supplied. The church, now superseded, of the old Spanish Embassy in London (1792) had anticipated such an Italian-ate style, and in its day was much admired.

Among Catholics of the time the tendency to revert to the architecture of the Church's youth is understandable. The

rebuilding of St. Paul's at Rome and the building of the
King of Bavaria's great basilica at Munich may have
pointed the way, but the impulse was rather one of sentiment than of artistic imitation. Anything associated with
the eighteenth century was ecclesiastically out of favour,
and the alternative of mediaevalism, bound up as it was with
legitimism in France and with neo-Catholic claims in
England, was regarded by many as dangerous and contro-
versial. Basilican churches, on the other hand, were
universal, ancestral, and safe.

Occasionally, throughout the nineteenth century a like
fear of mediaevalism and a like desire to assert primitive
simplicity induced church-builders of the Establishment to
attempt a like revival of basilican forms. The sumptuous
church at Wilton (1843) may owe its Italian Romanesque
style to nothing more than the preference of its founder;
but it must be noted here as the earliest example of a type
that reappears intermittently with the full support of Protestant sentiment.

Not altogether unlike such Italian was an eclectic
Romanesque that appeared fairly constantly between 1835
and 1845; most of it was miserable enough, but Christ
Church, Watney Street (1841), and St. Jude's, Bethnal Green
(1842) in the east end of London were admirable buildings
in the style. Christ Church, Streatham, built in 1841-2, was,
and is, unrivalled in its excellence as a specimen of a modern
basilica designed with spirit and grace. If the early enthusiasts for Gothic had had more buildings of this class to
contend with, their victory might have proved harder to
win than it did. As things happened, they seldom had
opponents less easy to overthrow than the ambitious but
unsuccessful church in Duncan Terrace, Islington (1839),
so unkindly satirised by Pugin in one of his books. The
English style called Norman might occasionally be allowed,

Pugin had used it himself, but eclectic Romanesque—no!
Upon this all good 'Ecclesiologists' were agreed, and it was

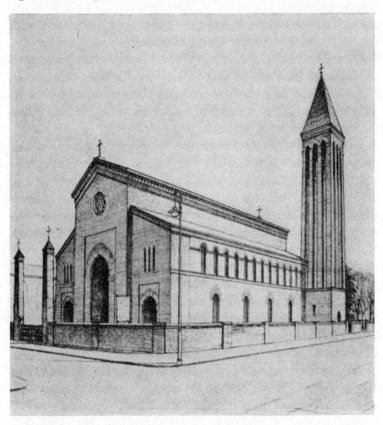

NEO-ROMANESQUE

Christ Church, Streatham, London (1841)

the Ecclesiological Society that decided in the long run
what kind of churches Englishmen should build. What the
Ecclesiological Society was will be told in the next chapter.

GOTHIC as understood by Georgians had been a fashion, a style, a mark of nationality, occasionally even a symbol of religion, but never a method of construction. Probably the notion that to build cleverly and well could in itself make a style had not occurred even to those antiquaries who had some real learning about mediaeval remains. John Carter (1746-1817), the best known of these antiquaries to-day, designed for Bishop Milner as flimsy and unreal a church at Winchester (1792) as any of its time; and the church at Theale, already cited for the singularity of its style, appears artificial and lifeless enough to us, although it was the work of an architectural theorist of much ability. Indeed, despite innumerable researches and theorisings, some aspects of the nature of Gothic were hardly guessed at before Pugin appeared to explain them.

Augustus Welby Pugin (1812-1852), as everybody knows, was not only an architect but a theorist, whose passionately held opinions accorded ill with the way in which he was compelled to work at the Houses of Parliament. These opinions were to be far more influential than his practice, which, hampered elsewhere in other ways than at Westminster, resulted nowhere in perfect realisations of his ideals. On the other hand, his *True Principles of Christian Architecture* was a book that initiated a way of regarding the art before which all principles then current were to fall. The Gothic style, regarded then as one among several flavourings eligible for stylish Architecture, was to Pugin the only style allowable to Christian men. This exclusive justification it owed to its exclusive possession of Truth.

Now Truth, as Ruskin was later to point out so frequently, is really very nice indeed. Yet there is a limit to its power of excusing things otherwise regrettable, and Pugin certainly did not care for it greatly when displayed in tall chimneys and cast-iron bridges. His insistence upon its necessity, an insistence always less shrill than that of his successors, was a natural consequence from his two great rules of design, but it was with those rules themselves that he was primarily occupied. The first of these was 'that there should be no features about a building which are not necessary for convenience, construction, or propriety,' and the second 'that all ornament should consist of enrichment of the essential construction of the building.' Notwithstanding all his acuteness and power of expression, Pugin's absorbing love for mediaeval art and his detestation of neo-Classical art often led him along doubtful paths of reason. He hated porticoes, therefore they were 'features' not justified by convenience, construction, or propriety. He loved spires;—perhaps they were not 'features,' or was propriety their justification? Festoons and frets were heathenish; they therefore could not be enrichment of essential construction. Crockets and niches apparently could.

Earnest Early Victorians seldom stopped to analyse the meanings of words; to them features were features, enrichment was enrichment, and any further definition mere vexatious hair-splitting. The new doctrine promised to clear confused issues in a delightfully simple and moral way. The Gothic style, so dear to all generous hearts, need not be reconciled, after all, with improved science in design, but could safely remain untutored as of old. You just had to construct what was convenient and proper and then to enrich your construction. Nothing could be easier. Hearts less generous, to whom the Gothic style was permissible for churches if—as seemed probable—it generally came cheaper than the Grecian, but to whom the notion of Gothic for other buildings seemed altogether uncivilised, were attracted nevertheless by the suggestion of an architectural return to Nature. The disingenuous façades and make-believe materials of Palladianism began to lose their defenders; forced symmetry was disowned and visible brickwork approved as 'honest' even by confirmed Grecian men and neo-Italian. It seemed as though all the mysteries of architecture had been suddenly revealed to the eyes that were innocent. Young Gilbert Scott, upon reading articles by Pugin, felt 'awakened from a feverish dream.'

The story of Early Victorian architecture in England is largely the story of a battle, with Pugin as chieftain leading an ever-increasing army of the faithful against an unbelieving world. The age was easily stirred by projects of social reform, such reform being obviously much needed; and in Pugin's mind the return to a Christian State, for which he spent his life fighting, was symbolised by the return to a Christian architecture. Give to the people the visible forms of mediaeval piety, and that piety will pour back through those forms into the realities of brotherhood and service. To say that his theories are but imperfect rationalisations of his noble and generous impulses, his talents those of the brilliant improvisatore of rich backgrounds for religion, may seem to be underrating a great teacher and architect. Nevertheless, to take his *True Principles* as the compendium of his creed, his realised designs as the consummation of his potency, would be to underrate him much more seriously.

The brilliance, the nobility—perhaps we may even say the greatness—of Pugin, the man, penetrates all the prejudice and unreason of his theories. Inconsistent in things of the mind, never was a man more consistent in things of the heart. His burning love of truth dazzled his readers into accepting his definition of it; few could share his vision but many could, and did, adopt his thoughts. Inappropriate as we may find his and their practice of bringing ethical standards to bear upon matters naturally aesthetic, we can nevertheless understand how great the boon seemed that he offered to a generation wearied by doubts and frivolity, the boon that many grasped with such desperate eagerness. Here was a faith that was simple, a rule of art and a rule of life in one. Decorate your construction, avoid shams, fit the several parts of your buildings to their proper uses, letting each tell its own story without thought of the others. Live arduously and frugally, devote your superfluity of time and money to the works of mercy, suffuse your work and your leisure with prayer. So doing you will be active as architect of a world that forsakes error and recaptures truth, of a world that discards pilasters and entablatures and becomes more and more Gothic every day.

Pugin died, worn out, in 1852, having lived only forty years. Of the realised designs that he left behind him the external and internal decoration of the Houses of Parliament is by far the most important. In domestic building his monastic and conventual buildings have significance that is now chiefly historical, and of houses for laymen he built few. Scarisbrick Hall in Lancashire (1837) is the best speci-

THE CATHOLIC SEIGNEURY

Scarisbrick Hall, Lancashire (1837)

men of his powers in this kind, and the contrast between its architecture, so passionately sincere, and the sentimentally unreal architecture of the Wyatt school, still current while Pugin was building, is strong and significant.

Stronger and more significant still is the contrast between his churches, the works of his heart, and those built by the architects of his day that refused to become his disciples. When young Pugin joined the ranks of active churchbuilders a change was taking place that tended to increase the difficulty of his crusade of reform. The Commisisoners' churches for the Establishment, the Catholic chapels, mean or frivolous, or both, had improved superficially while remaining radically unchanged in their imperfect form and arrangements. Thomas Rickman (1776-1841), the Quaker, who had classified English mediaeval architecture into three phases that he named Early English, Decorated, and Perpendicular, and illustrated that classification in a book still valuable to-day, had himself turned architect. He was now teaching by example as well as by precept how plausibly a building of the kind detestable to Pugin in its essentials could be given an air of Gothicism more genuine than had hitherto been secured by anybody else. His church at Ombersley in Worcestershire, designed as early as 1825, shews him at his best, and the aesthetic attractions of even his inferior work, such as the Catholic church of Our Lady of Mount Carmel at Redditch, Worcestershire (1834), must have seemed sufficient to many whose discontent Pugin longed to arouse. Others beside Rickman had acquired like, if less, skill; as can be seen in buildings all over the country by many different designers. St. Mark's, Leeds (1823), St. Peter's, Great Yarmouth (1833), St. Ignatius' (R.C.), Preston (1835), and St. Michael's, Bath (1835), are representative of these. Three churches in or about Islington—Holy Trinity,

Cloudesley Square (1826), St. John's, Holloway Road (1826), St. Paul's, Essex Road (1826) (together with the church of St. Peter, Saffron Hill, Holborn (1830)), are commonly instanced as among the best of their time, for no other discoverable reason than that they were designed by Sir Charles Barry. Far more successful, and possessing some real novelty of invention, was the church of Holy Trinity, built upon Blackheath Hill near Greenwich in 1839 by the versatile architect of Christ Church, Streatham. In all these buildings, however, the mediaevalism of the details was unsupported by any return to mediaevalism in the provisions made for the conduct of worship.

To this theft and misuse of his fire Pugin responded with churches having chancels stalled and screened, having the space for the congregation divided into many compartments, having all the supposed improvements of Georgian comfort carefully discarded. Yet so convincing was the beauty of architecture and decoration in such churches of his as St. Chad's (R.C.) Cathedral, Birmingham (1839) and St. Mary's (R.C.), Derby (1839), that all but the most stubborn doubters among his co-religionists determined that they must in future suffer in order to be Gothic. Before Pugin's death in 1852, Catholic churches at Sheffield (St. Marie, 1846), Burnley (St. Mary, 1846), Hackney (St. John the Baptist, 1847), Clapham (Our Lady of Victories, 1850), Greenwich (Our Lady, Star of the Sea, 1851), and many other places had arisen to testify to the loyalty and competence of his architect disciples. But more important historically than these was the enormous output of his followers within the Tractarian party of the Establishment.

If, standing in the Mediaeval Court of the Great Exhibition, (the arrangement of which court was poor Pugin's almost last activity), we had been able to see, as in a *camera obscura*, a panoramic view over two decades of English

PUGIN

St. Chad's Cathedral, Birmingham (1839)

architecture, we should at first sight have observed little
else but a forest of towers and steeples. In this forest all
would be Gothic, and most would be far more correctly
mediaeval in outline and detail than they could ever have
been without Pugin's precept and example. Yet their architects had been many:—Wardell, Hadfield, Derick, Harrison,
Stevens, Clarke, Carpenter, Ferrey, Scott, Chantrell, Dawkes,
—the list could be continued almost without end. The
buildings attached to the steeples would mostly be of the
type the master had promoted as truly and exclusively
'Catholic,' yet with the exception of those by Wardell and
Hadfield and some few dissenting meeting-houses, all had
been built to serve the Establishment. None of them could
any longer be found to resemble Mr. Newman's chapel at
Littlemore, which, ten years before, had been hailed as the
ideal type for Tractarian reproduction. Indeed, that chapel
within those ten years had itself been brought up to date,
its wanting chancel supplied, its architectural details added
to and modified. Its original form was little more than that
of a college chapel, an unbroken parallelogram, the east end
of which was arranged and furnished in the then strange
fashion of Tractarianism, in common parlance of Puseyism.
Its masonry, although not its proportions, could be called
'Early English Gothic,' its wooden roof modified 'Perpendicular.' Having Newman's authority it had been the
model for many copies in various parts of the country, and
some of these copies remain unchanged. Nevertheless, only
a few years after it was built, an improved version of its type
was inaugurated at Roehampton and thenceforth took its
place as the pattern for Tractarian chapel-builders. But
before Pugin died, it had come to be held unanimously by
Tractarians that any church pretending to correctness must
be much more elaborately organised and stylistically correct
than this. A structural chancel there must be, separated

from the nave by a high screen, and long enough to be stalled for priests and choir. Eastward of this the altar must stand in a place curiously misnamed by Tractarians the *sacrarium*. Lateral chapels, whose proper use was not then tolerated by the Anglican episcopate, were provided to seat school-children or to hold an organ. The reading of prayers in the nave was passionately discouraged, so that reading-desks, the successors of the middle decks of three-deckers, were either dispensed with or made as little of as possible. An absolute taboo was laid upon galleries, and, instead of pews with doors, open benches were commanded. The Commissioners' churches, whose form had been conditioned by the requirement that as many of the congregation as possible should see the pulpit, were referred to contemptuously as 'preaching-houses,' although the altar had not yet in most churches of the Establishment taken the pulpit's place as the focus of attention.

Actually, so little convenience was required of architecture at this time that a supposed correctness could dictate almost unhindered both the general lines and the minutiae of ecclesiastical design. Congregations unprepared to worship in a Catholic way were willing to worship in buildings of Catholic form if it were understood that they did so without prejudice. Even Dean Close, who in his first alarm at Puginism had preached a Guy Fawkes' Day sermon entitled 'The Restoration of Churches is the Restoration of Popery,' shortly afterwards himself built a cruciform 'Norman' church with an apsidal chancel. Except among the stricter sects of Dissenters, the mediaeval revival soon was unresisted and complete.

The organisation of the revival was the work of the Cambridge Camden Society (named after 1846 the Ecclesiological Society), a body at first formed largely of graduate and undergraduate members of that University, but afterwards containing members of many stations, callings, and abodes. The Society's main occupation was with ritual and with architecture in its ritual aspect, for the science of which the name *ecclesiology* was coined and adopted. A journal duly called the *Ecclesiologist* was founded in 1841 and continued for twenty-seven years, and in the volumes of that journal are recorded all the significant facts concerning one of the most surprising chapters in English architectural history. Almost every page offers judgement, pronouncement, or instructions, whether upon general practice in style and arrangement, or upon the merits and defects of some particular new building. In the index to the third volume there is printed after each name in the list of new churches one of three capital letters, P for *praised*, C for *condemned*, M for *mediocre*; and the same index contains names of architects classed under the headings 'Architects condemned' and 'Architects approved.'

Not that all architects of Tractarian churches were Tractarians themselves, nor that all who were Tractarians had always been so. The great Ecclesiological army, with its battle-cry *Donec templa refeceris*, enlisted its regulars from strange recruiting grounds and employed many mercenaries. Even the architect of the Protestant Martyrs' Memorial at Oxford (1841), and of the great Lutheran church of St. Nicolas at Hamburg (1845), enjoyed their frequent sanction, perhaps unwillingly given. Latitudinarian he might be in matters of faith, but in matters of architecture his orthodoxy was often found to be sufficient. Indeed, although it was far from being due to the Ecclesiologists that this compromising young man, Scott (1811-1878), should eventually become the eminent Sir Gilbert, leader of his profession, his early conversion to Puginist architecture saved him from any severity of persecution at their hands.

A few churches, on the other hand, had been built by

men less skilful, but in a faith that was as correct as their
architecture was faulty; and these harbingers of approved
ecclesiology were, by the new critics, very tenderly handled.
Dr. Pusey's church of St. Saviour, at Leeds (1842), was an
early profiter by this condonation, and the ungainly parish
church in the same town (1838), by virtue of its arrangement,
but not its unstomachable architecture, was an earlier one
still. In the style of this parish church, together with that
of a few others like it, we come back to something not
unlike the eclectic late Gothic of the Georgian Epilogue:
there is no great dissimilarity between the details of Leeds
parish church and those of Wilkins's college buildings.
Even in its strange characteristic of displaying bilateral
symmetry in its flank elevations (a characteristic that could
only be proper in a church if it contained two altars of equal
importance, one at either end), the Leeds church corre-
sponds with the artificial neo-Classical composition of many
a secular building contemporary with it.

A characteristic in Early Victorian Gothic architecture
for which the Ecclesiologists have to answer is the very
great predominance therein of forms derived from what
Rickman had christened the 'Decorated' phase of English
Gothic, a phase that Ecclesiologists preferred to call the
'Middle Pointed' and upon whose exclusive claim to re-use
they never tired of insisting. The theory upon which this
claim was based may perhaps be most appropriately stated
in the words of Sir Gilbert Scott, who, if no Ecclesiologist,
was too prudent to undervalue or misrepresent any opinion
supported by the influential among his contemporaries.
'It was argued,' he says in retrospect, 'that it was the duty
of those who guided the Mediaeval Revival to see that its
course should not be wildly eclectic, but that we should
select, once and for all, the very best and most complete
phase in the old style, and, taking that as our agreed *point*

de départ, should make it so thoroughly our own that we should develope upon it as a natural and legitimate nucleus, shaping it freely from time to time to suit our altered and ever altering wants. . . .' Assuming this theory to be sound, it was further argued that the '"Middle Pointed" is the true point of perfection which we should take as our nucleus of developement; that however admirable may be the vigour of the earlier phases, and whatever beauties we may find in the later, this middle style has the undoubted merit of completeness.'

In consequence of this theory the lofty and relatively convenient churches of the fifteenth century that had been chosen as models particularly capable of Protestant adaptation by the generality of the pre-Puginists were by the Ecclesiologists indignantly discarded as debasements of a nobler pattern. Their regularity of form also was condemned, the haphazard grouping of older English churches being at that time wrongly attributed to design rather than to accident. Steeples, the normal position of which had in English churches always been central and usually at the west end, were now most commonly placed on one side, the fancied picturesqueness of this position bringing the collateral advantage of a practicable reduction in their size and cost. A steeple tall enough to lift its bell-chamber above the ridge of the nave roof cannot but be an expensive thing, whereas one that has only the eaves to overtop may be both 'correct' and economical.

Pre-Puginist churches had been well lighted, Ecclesiological churches were dark; pre-Puginist churches were high in the wall and low in the roof, Ecclesiological churches had exceedingly steep roofs rising from walls relatively low; the towers of pre-Puginist churches seldom carried spires, whereas without a spire the tower of any Ecclesiological church was thought to be faultily incomplete. These are among the more obvious results that had been already reached through the action of Puginism, the reaction from Rickmanism, in the year of the Great Exhibition. In the building materials chosen, too, a great change had taken place. Pre-Puginist churches were smooth, their walls being of dressed stones, of cement, or of evenly coloured brick. Ecclesiological churches were rough, Kentish ragstone being carried all over the country for use where the equally approved walling material, flint, could not be obtained. Freestone, from Bath if not imported from Caen, was used for the dressings and ornamental details necessary to develope a proper intensity of 'Middle Pointed' character in the architecture.

Now, all the buildings we can discern amidst our forest of towers and steeples (and to every tower or steeple a building of some sort must presumably be attached)—all these buildings are very much alike, although they have been built by people most various for most various forms of worship. Their common form has been imposed by an authority the religious tenets of which most of their builders strongly repudiated. The Oxford Movement inspired the Ecclesiologists, and the Ecclesiologists succeeded even in bouncing the Manchester Unitarians into building an extremely Catholic-looking chapel. If anyone believed in what used to be called the 'spirit of the Age,' he would conclude that Ecclesiology preached to the converted, that what it prescribed men were already minded to perform. On the more rational hypothesis that in all mass movements the detector of origins must seek the instigator, the success of neo-Puginism would appear to be due, not to Pugin directly, but to the man in the street, and, indirectly, to the man who builds the street. Mr. Gilbert Scott of Messrs. Scott and Moffat, the successful firm of workhouse architects, found satisfaction of his tastes, and the materials for constructing an enormous popular reputation, in what might maliciously be called, in modern phrase, 'service to clergy of discernment.' Gothic architecture had always been his hobby, and now his hobby could become his trade. Moffat and workhouses discarded, he rose by rapid stages to the head of his profession.

Among church-builders outside Puseyite influence, Sir Gilbert Scott considered himself to be the best, and certainly in this he did no injustice to many. Yet all over England there can be found churches dating from the 1840's that now seem as good to us, at the very least, as those Scott was then building, although they were not designed by him. To take an example at random, Osmaston church near Derby, dating from the year 1845, is one of many by a local architect now little remembered that reaches a general excellence of design that, in that year, Scott could but doubtfully have equalled and certainly not have surpassed. St. John's Church on Notting Hill, London (1844), also suggests that a world with Scott left out of it need not have been as unfortunate as he supposed.

Scott's professional position became rapidly so pre-eminent that it has been needful to point out that his success in occupying and maintaining it was due chiefly to talents other than artistic. Nevertheless, the proper business of this history is with the comparison of buildings rather than with that of men. Of Scott's own early work the example it is kindest to choose is the very elegant church of St. John, Holbeck, Leeds (1847), in which the design of the choir of the Temple Church in London is faithfully and unstintingly reproduced.

That the architect who, during a working career of forty years, built or interfered with nearly five hundred churches, thirty-nine cathedrals and minsters, twenty-five universities and colleges, and many other buildings beside, was a remarkable man it would be foolish to deny. That the designs he issued, the making of which must, considering their number, have been in more or less degree deputed to others, should mostly possess a strong flavour of their issuer's idiosyncrasy is as remarkable as it might be unexpected. That that idiosyncrasy, however, was compounded of any qualities more valuable aesthetically than prudence, industry, and a strong sympathy with the popular taste of the moment, cannot be easily maintained. Throughout the first forty years of Queen Victoria's reign, large buildings of Scott's constantly check the historian's progress, some of them deserving more admiration, some less. None, however, is likely to justify in our eyes the judgement of an age that throned him upon an eminence relatively loftier than that occupied by any other British architect since the day of Sir Christopher Wren.

In a brief survey of an enormous body of not greatly varied material Osmaston church may be supplemented only by mention of St. James's, Weybridge, Surrey (1846), and SS. Thomas and Clement's, Winchester (1845), to typify the better class of 'Middle Pointed' design in which forms approved by Ecclesiology were adopted without any consent to their Catholic significance. A writer of the year 1851 remarks that the only visible distinction between the Catholic and Protestant churches then being built was that in the former the niches would be filled, in the latter empty; a distinction hardly commensurate with the difference between the uses of the two. So general became the understanding of this accepted method of design that any early Victorian architect of average ability soon could do it on his head, without any particular application to mediaeval study.

The Ecclesiological disapproval of styles earlier than 'Middle Pointed' was generally deferred to, but not always.

Little buildings like the 'First Pointed' church at Nutley, Sussex (1844), never were rare, although in their nature exceptional. Experiments even in the Anglo-Norman manner, however much discouraged by the Ecclesiologists, were not altogether discontinued, a large church of the kind being put up at Morpeth (1844), and Scott obliging with something very richly Norman indeed at Sewerby in the East Riding of Yorkshire (1847).

In the inner circle of Puseyism, churches were, of course, put to the uses their architecture implied, and that architecture could therefore be both mediaeval and sincere. Richard Cromwell Carpenter (1812-1855), whose short lifetime almost synchronised with that of Pugin, was not only the Tractarian's especial protégé, but also a designer whose superiority over most of his rivals present-day criticism can endorse. He built as solidly as Pugin would have liked to have done but seldom could, and in the works of the disciple can often be found the fullest practice of the precepts of the master. St. John's, at Bovey Tracey (1852) in Devonshire, Christ Church at Milton by Gravesend (1854), and the larger church of St. Peter the Great at Chichester (1848) are three convincing proofs of his delicate skill and sensibility.

Even before Carpenter's death in 1855, William Butterfield (1814-1900), his rival in Tractarian favour, had already built a dozen churches or so, and had been at work for five years upon the model church the Ecclesiologists were raising in Margaret Street, St. Marylebone (1849). The church at Sessay in Yorkshire (1847), with its lych-gate and other approved appurtenances, belongs to this, the earliest, period of his career, and is a particularly representative specimen of the ideal village church of its time. At Leeds, Dr. Pusey's not very talented architect had done his best in the pioneer church of St. Saviour already mentioned; and among the

THE TRACTARIAN PARAGON

St. Alban's Church, Kemerton, Gloucestershire (1845)

churches praised upon ritual grounds in the *Ecclesiologist* many more have architectural merit than among those condemned.

By the year 1850 George Edmond Street (1824-1881), second only to Butterfield in Ecclesiological favour and afterwards to be perhaps the most powerful architectural leader of the century, had built at Biscovey (Par) in Cornwall (1848) his first church, the interior of which perhaps recaptures as much of ancient charm as can be found in any equally imitative church built since.

The Gothic spirit waking from sleep, the modern spirit stirring the dry bones of neo-Grecianism; those are the images that should remain in our minds when, stationed in imagination at the year 1851, we turn our eyes from back to forward. Of the Italianism of Barry, of the Romanesque of the experimentalists, of the chubbiness of the fancy warehouses, more remains to be told; lost for ever only is the chastity of Sir Robert Smirke and his followers. But no Italianism, no Romanesque, no fancy chubbiness, can have any place in the foreground of a picture where Smirke and Wyatville have been replaced by Cockerell and Pugin, the first deep in study, the second rapt in prayer. Mr. Scott (who seems to have lost Mr. Moffat) is not yet in the foreground, but can be seen in the middle distance pushing hotly forward. A pressing engagement with the Duke of Sutherland has caused Sir Charles Barry to withdraw, but several rolls of drawings importantly labelled Stafford House, Cliefden, Trentham, and Dunrobin, have been dropped by him in his hasty departure from the scene. Alas! closely behind the kneeling figure of Pugin stand shadowy figures of Madness and Death, while from time to time Cockerell sadly turns his eyes from the plans of St. George's Hall to the newly made grave of their young author. In the background a motley crowd is surging forward, led by a prince the device upon whose banner appears to be a drawing of an enormous conservatory. When next we look upon the scene, the crowd will have invaded it, and Sir Joseph Paxton will explain to us the benefits the world may expect from his vision of glass and iron.

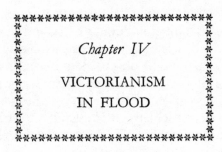

I F we now leave the *camera obscura* in which we may
imagine our forest of towers and steeples to have been
projected, and emerge into the Mediaeval Court of the
Great Exhibition itself, we shall find ourselves surrounded
by prototypes of almost everything that may, since our
earliest recollections, have embittered our experience of
church-going. Dazzling tiles, bristling brass, archaistic
glass-painting, gingerbread-coloured pulpits, sanitary looking altars; all the exhibits can be truly described in as un-
flattering a way as this, and to many people nowadays the
pejorative implication of such epithets would seem to do the
exhibits no wrong. No time need be spent here in contending
that tiles may legitimately dazzle, brass be worked in spikes
and spirals, glass-painting be stylised, oakwork be brown
with oil, marble and alabaster be obviously washable, since,
whatever the justice of these contentions, they affect the
surface of things only, and the surface of things cannot
greatly affect their underlying design. Nor need time be
spent here in considering the design of the particular
exhibits before us, because the Court contains but furniture,

and it is with architecture that our business lies. Much of the decoration exhibited is Pugin's own, and in decoration, if not in architecture, all work of his has great value. Furthermore, it should be observed, in passing, how greatly superior this English decoration and furniture is to that sent from foreign countries. The merits of the Mediaeval revival were displayed chiefly in England, and this, which is even more true in architecture than in furniture, may have something to do with the small esteem we now accord to the movement. A habit of national self-disparagement has succeeded our former happy confidence.

Very far from self-disparagement was the mood of our grandfathers who thronged Sir Joseph Paxton's (1801-1865) great conservatory in Hyde Park. Here, in England, an eighth wonder of the world had been invented and achieved. Here, in one enormous building, English enterprise had collected together samples of almost everything that civilised man hoped to sell to his fellows, and sales promised to be extremely good. Great pride could also be felt in the state of world-civilisation to which those samples testified. Almost everything, even the cheapest and the most utilitarian, was highly ornamental; the Prince would be delighted. Mr. Pugin said dreadful things about everything outside his own strange department, but Mr. Pugin was a Catholic, and so satirical.

Now, the objects exhibited in this astonishing collection cannot be said to have had any considerable influence upon the course of architectural developement. They were symptoms rather than causes, and the diagnosis Pugin made of their significance was accordingly directed, as it must have been, toward cure rather than toward prevention. But the building in which the exhibits were enclosed, the engineering marvel that afterwards became the nucleus of the Crystal Palace at Sydenham, was received with a rapture that found expression in many later and less fortunate experiments with iron and glass. 'A man,' says Fergusson, the architectural historian, 'must have had much more criticism than poetry in his composition who could stand under its arch and among its trees by the side of its crystal fountain and dare to suggest that it was not the most fairy-like production of Architectural Art that had yet been produced.' Victorians believed in fairies, and found them in the engineers If only some of its glass walls could have been bricked up, Fergusson thought that the Crystal Palace would exemplify a new style, 'for certain purposes more beautiful than anything that has gone before.' Indeed, as Eastlake[1] remarked twenty years after, 'sanguine converts to the new faith began to talk as if glass and iron would form an admirable substitute for bricks and mortar, and wondrous changes were predicted as to the future aspect of our streets and squares. . . . Architects were warned that if they still fondly clung to the traditions of the past they had better abandon their vocation altogether. It did not take many years to dissipate the dreams of universal philanthropy to which the Exhibition had given rise' (the quotation is still from Eastlake), 'and with these dreams the charming visions of a glass-and-iron architecture may also be said to have vanished.' Not, however, before the architects of the Oxford University Museum (1854) had tried to glaze in their quadrangle 'without limiting the design to the merely structural features of the Crystal Palace or condescending to the vulgar details of a railway terminus.' Unfortunately their first attempt did not achieve stability, and, to what already must have seemed a remarkably large number of columns to support so light a roof, more supports very soon had to be added. The result appears difficult rather than

[1] Charles Locke Eastlake (1836-1906), author of *A History of the Gothic Revival in England.*

103

graceful. The almost contemporary roof of Paddington station (1854) is, on the other hand, a charming vision that materialised, with its trim rivet-sprinkled columns and the fairy Gothic flames that lick up from the bases of its ribs. Sanguine Paxtonians could exult also in the bubble-like dome that Sydney Smirke blew across the reading-room with which in 1856-7 he blocked up the courtyard of his brother's British Museum. Paxton himself, however, had now turned to something solider than visions, having for some years been sedulously reproducing Wollaton Hall (with improvements) on a site in Buckinghamshire.[1]

In the last chapter but one a short account has been given of the architecture that resulted immediately from the railway mania of the 1840's, the architecture, that is to say, of passenger stations and railway offices. Into such works were poured very large sums of money by speculators and investors of all classes. Shortly after the arrival, in 1855, of the principle of limited liability, (and instantly, in greater force, after the passing of the Limited Liability Act of 1862), speculators and investors rushed, as wildly as they had before into railway construction, into the building of large hotels; and a close connexion soon was established between the two undertakings. As early as 1852 the Great Western Hotel at Paddington had been completed in a style of great stuccoed magnificence, and had been recognised as a railway advertisement more remunerative, probably, than the nobler but less useful efforts of the same architect at Euston. The Alexandra Hotel (1857) and the Westminster Palace Hotel (1858) had also astonished Londoners by their ambition and what then appeared to be their splendour. Both were cement-faced, like the building at Paddington: and neither they nor it departed noticeably from the Franco-Italianate style in vogue when they were built.

[1] Mentmore, Leighton Buzzard (1851).

In the Grosvenor Hotel (1860), however, a new and peculiar character crept into the façades, a character that quickly became general in buildings of the class, for which it is difficult to find a descriptive name. Its most obvious characteristics are an extreme heaviness of ornamental detail, and a horizontal stripiness caused by a multiplication of cornices, impost-mouldings, and bands. Heathcote Statham in his book *Modern Architecture* chose a specimen of it (actually from a club-house, not an hotel) to illustrate what he called a design *destitute* of style, comparing it in this respect with the poetry of Alfred Austin. The leading practitioner of this style, if style it be, was James Knowles (1831-1908), well known afterwards as the founder of the *Nineteenth Century* review; it was he that designed the Grosvenor Hotel; the Cedars Estate at Clapham is covered with his work; and there must be about a quarter of a mile of him along the sea-front at Hove. The Thatched House Club in St. James's Street, of which he was the architect in 1865, is the work Heathcote Statham (1839-1924) chose for pillory.

Knowles's work has an exaggerated appearance of solidity which he deliberately sought by the coarse (he would have called it *bold*) scale of his details, and by sinking the glass of his windows as deeply as possible into his walls. His use of architectural forms was so eclectic that, if his style had to be named, it might be called Romano-Lombardo-Naturalistic —the adjective naturalistic being used sylleptically to cover his insistence upon non-imitative materials and his fondness for carved ivy-leaves and oak-leaves. The two railway hotels designed by another architect as parts of the stations at Charing Cross (1863) and Cannon Street (1864) have been described by that architect's brother as being in the style of the French Renaissance. Perhaps this was a family tradition. If it were credible, it might account for the lack of violence in these designs, in comparison with Knowles's work, and the relatively formal convention in their ornament.

Other specimens of the style are plentiful, but there is no need that they should be enumerated. Perhaps there may be need, however, to point out an important value that these not very appetising buildings possess. Finding the number of their storeys unwontedly large, their designers have set to work to invent a new treatment to suit a new thing. They have tried to invent a style that will suit an indefinite number of storeys, and in a measure they have succeeded; there is no architectural reason why these stripy, pile-of-sandwiches façades should not go up and up for ever. That this was in their designer's minds seems proved by the fact that contemporary hotels of limited height, like the first English hydropathic, at Ilkley (1854), display no exaggerated striation.

The French word *hôtel* is commonly used in England for what in France is one only of its secondary meanings, that of a house for the accommodation of strangers, particularly travellers—the *hôtel des voyageurs*. For its primary French meaning, that of a great town-house occupied by one family only—the *hôtel particulier*—we have no especial name. Perhaps that is because we have never had very many of such *hôtels*, such *palazzi*: most of our nobles and Midases have indulged their taste for architectural splendour in the country, and in London have been content with good roomy mansions in fashionable streets and squares. Family houses in our country towns have seldom belonged to persons 'of family,' and have never affected the architectural graces that make delightful the residential streets of Bordeaux or of Aix-en-Provence.

During the reign of Queen Victoria not many grand houses were added to the existing company in the west end of London, a company then including Northumberland,

Devonshire, Norfolk, Lansdowne, Harewood, and Grosvenor Houses, all now destroyed, and a smaller number that
survive. Among the newcomers three could claim to magnificence, Bridgewater House (1847), Dorchester House
(1849), and Kensington House (1873). The last, being
scarcely finished before Baron Grant, the company pro-
moter for whom it was built, was nearing his spectacular
downfall, was seized and demolished by his creditors after
standing empty for ten years. It was designed by Knowles,
not very well.

Dorchester House was in some measure the personal
creation of its owner, a man of great wealth, great knowledge, and great judgement. Almost monopolising the
services of an able and experienced architect who was not
otherwise very busy, he insisted that a full-size model of
every ornamental detail in the building should be set up
and discussed before the eventual form of it was decided.
In the interior the more important sculpture was entrusted
to Alfred Stevens (1818-1875), and the decorative painting,
which was spread over most of the surfaces not covered
with marble or silk, was put under the control of the most
esteemed art connoisseur of the day. The result of all these
labours, lasting over many years, was a *palazzo*, as Italian as
that word, a monument of taste and scholarship unequalled
in this country. Compared with the older private palaces
of London it appeared an exotic, but an exotic so beautiful
that its destruction between the two last wars was a barbar-
ous act never to be remembered without shame.

Bridgewater House remains with us. It is nobly planned,
and the designing of its façades has been done with great
competence. Like all those works of its architect (Sir
Charles Barry) in which there has been departure from strict
Italian precedent, it has little distinction beyond that given
it by experience and good technique. It represents very

107

Dorchester House, London (1849)

completely the enlightened conservatism of its time; it is Italianate enough, and yet one would not be surprised by a comfortable smell of English cooking in its passages. It is a specimen of thoroughly sound Victorian architecture, and, in a country that has had no accepted academic standards, architectural soundness is no small mercy.

Of urban and suburban mansions not quite grand houses, but corresponding with the smaller *hôtels* and *palazzi* of France and Italy, there is a remarkable collection in the private road called Kensington Palace Gardens, which borders that palace on the west. There is one Gothic house here, pre-Victorian Gothic in character although designed in 1852 by a backward architect; there are two neo-Moresque houses designed by 'Alhambra' (otherwise Owen) Jones (1809-1874), but all the others are either Italianate or more Italian than anything else. None reaches excellence, but many are agreeable enough. All date from the first half of Queen Victoria's reign.

Three houses in the same category as these, but more definitely neo-Roman in style, had been built, some years before, across the corners of the newly formed Belgrave Square. That square itself, the most magnificent and solidly constructed of any in England, shews what exemplary results the famous speculative builder, Thomas Cubitt (1788-1855), could achieve when he was obliged to work under a first-rate architect. Unfortunately the greater part of his later speculations, like those of his less-distinguished rivals, was conducted under guidance no more authoritative than that of a designer connected with the firm, in Cubitt's case of his brother Lewis (1799-1883). In consequence, the output of countless ready-made houses which for many years after the Regency was the main activity in English building, exercised but little art or ingenuity that was in any true sense architectural. What structural art and ingenuity

they displayed was mostly not of a sort to be highly appreciated by their tenants, although profitable enough to those
who practised it. Captain Marryat's scathing article upon
'Modern Town Houses,' reprinted in his *Olla Podrida* (1840),
expresses a dissatisfaction that was widely felt. There is,
indeed, little in these myriads of mass-built streets and
houses to call for attention in a history of architecture
except the fact of their numerousness.

In country houses architectural fashions were unaffected
by the Great Exhibition, castle-building continuing to
abate, and neo-Tudor continuing to gain what ground was
still occupied by any rival style. The designer of Scotney
and of Peckforton Castles, mentioned in a former chapter,
now became the leading expert in the style there named
'manorial,' a style he had long used with skill, and sometimes happy audacity, upon occasions inappropriate for
castellation. His name was Antony Salvin (1799-1881), and
his fame is supported by Harlaxton Hall, Lincolnshire
(1834), and Thoresby Park, Nottinghamshire (1864), striking examples as they are of the use he could make of great
opportunities in both early and late middle age. He took
Wyatt's place as the aristocratic architect *par excellence*.

What Salvin was in England William Burn (1789-1870)
was in Scotland, conventionalising the neo-Baronial inaugurated by Sir Walter Scott at Abbotsford (1816) into a
northern equivalent of neo-Elizabethan. Burn's reputation
with the great rested chiefly, as did that of too few among
his architect contemporaries, upon the convenient arrangement of his plans; and he consequently was encouraged to
poach Salvin's English preserves by those who wished to be
particularly comfortable. His skill in contrivance, however,
was purely utilitarian, and his plans marry none too happily
with his conventional and rather perfunctorily designed
elevations.

Nine out of ten Early Victorian houses of any pretension assume this irregular character, neo-Tudor or neo-Elizabethan. It was the character sanctified by the choice of the governing class; neo-Italian, when less than palatial, being associated with a form of prosperity that might be not untainted by trade. If Osborne House (1845), that remarkable joint production of the Prince Consort and Cubitt, his builder, makes an exception from this generalisation, it may be suggested that the notion of a Royal marine villa was itself exceptional and might lead naturally to forms that had been somewhat unnaturally appropriated by St. John's Wood. Be this as it may, what might still be thought suitable in the Isle of Wight would certainly no longer be thought suitable in more ordinary situations, when Sir Charles Barry himself, who first had popularised such neo-Italian simplicities, was every day becoming more enamoured of rich pseudo-Jacobean complication. Upon one thing opinion was united: nothing could be more spiritless, more unworthy to be the seat of a man of consequence than the heavy unornamental Queen Anne or Georgian house in which too often he had been born. Something had to be done about that, and a great deal generally was.

In an extended treatment of the subject which this short book attempts to cover much could be said of minor changes of fashion preceding the revolution in the design of small houses brought about by George Edmund Street and young men from his office. Nothing of this can be said now except that the parsonage-Gothic of Puginist church architects, when valuable, as it frequently was, had a powerful influence upon the design of similar houses in general, bringing into the originally frivolous type of the *cottage orné* a new seriousness often very demure and becoming. In Scotland, however, houses too small to be effectively baronial were either *cottages ornés* entirely unpurified by religion or else combined the idea of the Tuscan villa with more or less of the Grecian scholarship that then was the architectural pride of the two great Scottish cities. Some villas designed by Alexander Thomson known as 'Greek Thomson,' are as interesting houses as any that of the nineteenth century produced; they are, unhappily, few, and so peculiar to Thomson's idiosyncrasy that none of the attempts of others to follow him have resulted in anything but failure.

'Those of ourselves . . . who still feel the influence of happy architectural associations connected with the scenes of our education, should be the last to withhold from our poorer brethren, so much more impressionable than ourselves, an advantage which not only influences the childhood, but carries its abiding associations to the end of life.' These words from the report for the year 1851 of the Northampton Architectural Society express perfectly the spirit that sharpened the gables and adorned with tracery the windows of the numberless village schools that then were building, and that still remain the chief ornament of many a village after the church. The Ecclesiologists had a 'correct' model for such schools, as they had for every other building that was ecclesiastical even remotely, and with this model most architects conformed their designs fairly closely. An ideal example, of absolute authority, can be seen in the schoolroom and master's house built by Butterfield for Dr. Pusey himself at Langley in Kent (*c.* 1856). Changed opinions have found the Ecclesiological model defective, both where it is and where it is not so, and Victorian schoolbuildings have in consequence been, for the most part, cruelly havocked or deformed. Where their original charm has been allowed to linger they would certainly seem better for the soul and not necessarily worse for the body than the glary draughty education mills that modern theory prescribes in their place. Granting that many of them are unduly Gothic, it can nevertheless be said that in no other class of building was the Victorian compound of sense and sensibility more happily exerted. Two of the earliest to follow Ecclesiological prescriptions are still two of the most delightful that were built. They date from 1846 and stand a few miles apart at Bisley and at Ripley in Surrey. They are very small, and have not escaped disfigurement and addition, but still can enable us to respect and admire the pains their architect took to give children a picture they could remember with pleasure. If any of our once poorer brethren 'still feel the influence of happy architectural associations connected with the scenes of their education,' they have much for which they should thank the Ecclesiological Society.

In urban architecture other than domestic or scholastic or ecclesiastical, neo-Italian of one sort or another met no serious challenge while the Victorian flood was at the full. The output of it was enormous, torrents of corn exchanges, of town-halls, of commercial buildings, of warehouses, drenching through architects' offices from the reservoir of municipal and commercial ambition into ubiquitous realisation. The nobly designed town-hall at Leeds (1853) set an example to be followed rather closely later by the architect of the town-halls at Bolton (1866) and at Portsmouth (1886), but such excellence, whether original or borrowed, remained rare. Generally the pace proved too quick for artistry to keep up with, and the architectural value to be found in such productions as a whole is not sufficient to entitle them to more than cursory mention. The designs of the markets at Wolverhampton and Bolton (1851) have merit, but not so great as the older Covent Garden and Hungerford markets had entitled the public to demand. The Bank of Scotland's house in Glasgow (1865) exemplifies Scottish superiority in a moment when in England the

MUNICIPAL MAGNIFICENCE

Leeds Town-hall (1853)

genius of Cockerell seemed to flame against a dark background indeed. The warehouses at Manchester designed
by Edward Walters (1808-1872) were greatly admired at a
time when the proper aim of a warehouse designer was conceived to be that of making his buildings look as little as
possible like what they actually were, and it is only in his
Free Trade Hall (1853) that we can see this architect's
powers exerted effectively in their proper field. The façade
of Burlington House in Piccadilly (1872) displays the last
stale remains of the neo-Italianism that had been normal
twenty years before; it has radical faults and superficial
virtues, and need offend nobody who does not examine it
closely.

The famous Battle of the Styles arose suddenly in the year
1857 when Gilbert Scott, in his own words, thought himself
'at liberty to stir' to prevent Pennethorne's being appointed
architect for the new Government Offices. There had been
two competitions, one for the designing of the War Office,
the other for that of the Foreign Office, in the first of which
the determinedly Gothic Scott had come nowhere, whereas
in the second, which was won by a pupil of his, he himself
had been placed third. Lord Palmerston, thinking little of
the winning designs, although they were both in the Italian
manner upon which, as appeared afterwards, he was determined to insist, proposed that with the award of premiums
the competitions should end, and that Pennethorne, the
Board of Works man, should design and carry out the
buildings. This arrangement might have been fortunate
for England, but undoubtedly would have been unfair to
the successful competitors. Scott's 'stirring' resulted
mysteriously in his appointment as sole architect for both
buildings, a change of Government having put his Gothic-
minded friends in power. Alterations were made in the
programme, a new India Office being added to the scheme,

THE LOSER IN THE BATTLE

First design for Foreign Office, London (1856)

and the War Office removed from it. Violent parliamentary opposition broke out against the style in which Scott was known to be working. Of this style we can judge the character from that of the St. Pancras Hotel (1865), which Scott speaks of himself as being 'the same, but divested of the Italian element.' To meet this opposition, perhaps not unnatural, Scott prepared alternative designs in what he describes as a 'Byzantinesque' style, which he tells us that Cockerell, to whom among others they were referred for criticism, 'had the greatest difficulty in swallowing.' Meanwhile another change of Government brought power again to Palmerston, who, describing the Byzantinesque as 'a regular mongrel affair,' gave Scott the choice of going Italian or going altogether. Alas! for Pennethorne's chances, Scott refused to die for his cause. 'To resign,' he says, 'would have been to give up a sort of property which Providence had placed in the hands of my family, and would be simply rewarding my professional opponents for their unprecedented attempt to wrest a work from the hands of a brother architect.' Aided by Sir Matthew Digby Wyatt (1820-1877), in the India Office, who, being the official architect to that office, had been allowed by Scott some measure of collaboration; aided also it is said by the artistic assistance of a young draughtsman of great ability, who died untimely, the successful Gothic practitioner designed a neo-Classical building that to many may seem by far the least unpleasing of his works. As was usual with Scott, everything in it is of the best except the architecture; and since there are here much sculpture, certainly as good as any of its age in England, many elegant details, a great deal of excellent material very finely wrought, and a well-proportioned disposition of masses, the story of the Battle of the Styles may be said to have had a tolerably happy ending.

Indeed, the critical historian's only reasonable grievance

against the building is that it stands where there could have stood one designed by Cockerell, who was never suggested for it, or, in his default, by Pennethorne, who was. Pennethorne has been named in a former chapter as the designer of the beautiful building for the Duchy of Cornwall that has lately been so idiotically mutilated. Not much less recently his Geological Museum met a fate less tragic by being completely destroyed. It had two façades, one in Piccadilly and the other in Jermyn Street, the style of which recalled, but surpassed in delicacy that of Barry's club-houses. The University of London building in Burlington Gardens (1866) is a more ambitious design of his, whose equally rare and sensitive quality is marred only by the inadequate quality and perhaps not very fortunate placing of some of its sculpture. Pennethorne was employed during most of his working life by the Office of Works, and wasted a great deal of time earning his pay in various subordinate and unimportant services. So greatly were his talents respected by his confrères that in the very year in which the Battle of the Styles was begun he had received the Gold Medal of the Royal Institute of British Architects. The west front of Somerset House (1852) is his work, a loyal and exact continuation of the style of Chambers, and so also is the severe but distinguished Stationery Office in Westminster (1847). His largest building is the Record Office between Chancery and Fetter Lanes (1847), in which he has carried for once his peculiar powers of organised design into the Gothic convention. It was originally proposed that he should make a similar experiment in the University of London building, but there, as at the Foreign Office, a change of Government produced a change from buttresses to pilasters. That the idea of strength appropriate in a repository of records should be embodied in semi-castellated forms may seem symbolism that is literary rather than aesthetic. The Record Office has been greatly added to, and now might be described as variations on a theme by Pennethorne. Nevertheless, regarded as a whole, it is a noble building very suitable in a country whose Parliament meets in a neo-Gothic palace, in a city whose Guildhall still preserves its mediaeval aspect.

If English Victorian architects had had any systematic education in their art, Pennethorne's accomplishment in design ought not to have been as exceptional as it was. In England, among the architects who practised neo-Classicism during the last century, he stands, perhaps, third or fourth in order of merit, whereas it must be admitted that in contemporary France there were very many architects no less scholarly and much more imaginative than he. This English inferiority may be partly explained by the lower level here than in France of mental cultivation in the class from which architects are chiefly drawn. Its main cause, however, was more probably the diversion of our best architectural talent into the channel of neo-Gothicism, and when the day comes for our neo-Gothic achievement to be fairly estimated, it may be predicted that the total reputation of our nineteenth-century architecture will be greatly enhanced.

In the Universities, after the completion of the Fitzwilliam Museum and the Taylor and Ashmolean building, neo-Classicism sank into a long sleep. The pre-Victorian Gothic, of which there is so much at Cambridge, had had its Oxford echo in rather brutal mishandlings of older work at Merton, Exeter, and Pembroke Colleges, the last of which, however, received some compensation in the building from 1844 onwards of a hall and range of chambers excellent and thoroughly Puginist in their design. Pugin himself, in 1843, had made elaborate designs for rebuildings at Balliol but was denied employment by the College on account of his Catholic religion. In the following year he built a beautiful gateway at Magdalen, which has unfortunately since been destroyed. The architect of the works at Pembroke was a church designer approved by the Ecclesiologists, and when we turn from the Universities to other colleges and schools we shall find that to such ecclesiological architects is due almost all that is of any value. Neo-Tudor, little tolerated then by purists even at Oxford or Cambridge, on newer foundations would have been regarded as out of the question; the style was inherently debased and even doubtfully Christian. It had been used, and with a success that will be as readily acknowledged to-day as at the time of its employment, for the Hall of Lincoln's Inn (1843), a building the merits of which in its class are exceptional. Even with this example before them, however, early Victorians could not consider neo-Tudorism pure enough to be good for the young. In designing Hurstpierpoint (1851) and Lancing (1854) colleges, therefore, Richard Cromwell Carpenter followed Pugin in concocting a conventional 'domestic Middle Pointed' style, partly by reproduction, partly by invention. In Carpenter's hands this method of design, afterwards travestied by others, was extremely successful, and these colleges of his are buildings that of their kind it would be hard to better. St. Michael's College at Tenbury (1855) is a highly original and picturesque work of later date by another architect who did a great deal of the kind. Being an ecclesiastical foundation, clustering on to a large church, it is properly more clerical in architectural character than the public schools of Hurstpierpoint and Lancing.

The title of this chapter is *Victorianism in Flood*, and of all the streams feeding that flood none flowed more strongly, nor gathered more tributaries, than that springing from the brain and determination of William Butterfield. The next chapter is to be entitled *The Reformers*. In that

SCHOLASTIC GOTHIC

St. John's College, Hurstpierpoint, Sussex (1851)

chapter will appear William Morris, and greatly as Morris probably disliked his work, Butterfield's place is by his side. Both were evangelists whose zeal and whose discontent make them seem brothers in everything except their aims and their personalities. Morris was genial, Butterfield ascetic; Morris was humane, Butterfield bigoted; Morris was sentimental, Butterfield dry. Morris dreamt of universal happiness in this life, Butterfield preferred that all physical comfort should be postponed until the next. Different then as were their ambitions and their achievements, different as were the directions of their special abilities, different as were the tastes and situation of their admirers, the two cannot be separated without injustice. The casual mention of Butterfield that has already been made is no longer sufficient: as the flood abates the depth of his influence becomes apparent and shews him as a force requiring our undistracted attention.

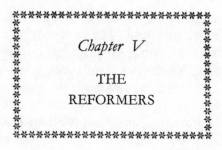

Chapter V

THE
REFORMERS

THE late Lord Baldwin, when opening the centenary exhibition of the works of William Morris (1834-1896), emphasised, as Morris would have wished it to be emphasised, the missionary spirit in which they had been made. 'He passionately desired beauty to be within the reach of all people,' Lord Baldwin said, 'and that they should have, as he had, a discontent in the presence of everything that was either ugly or vulgar, or, as they so often were, both together.' The same could be said of the Prince Consort, though it is to be feared that his notions of beauty, ugliness, and vulgarity would have commended themselves in no particular to William Morris. Morris was a typical Victorian Reformer and therefore, as would be expected, what Lord Baldwin called him, a 'great, glorious, jolly, human being': nearly all of them were. Reformers were like that in those days, and their having been so is an important characteristic of the period to an historian. Morris, however, was also what so many versatile men are not, what few 'great, glorious, jolly, human beings' can ever hope to be, an exquisite technician, and an abnormally resourceful and sensitive artist, yes, a great artist in at least one of his many activities. The power of designing patterns, whether for weaving, for printing, or for painting, as supremely well as Morris designed them, is enough in itself to make an artist great, even without the extraordinary skill and ingenuity in processes with which in Morris it was combined. As a master among art-workers (a disagreeable term for which it is to be feared that he was responsible), Morris's position is beyond all question.

Pugin was a great designer of patterns, too; but except with his pen he was no very skilful craftsman, and was handicapped by not being so. The mediaeval ornament he loved to adapt had, on its first appearance, been largely designed while it was being made and made while it was being designed. The hand, meeting difficulties and opportunities unforeseen, had modified and enriched the preconception of the brain. In contrast with this, all that Pugin attempted to do, in his feverish production, was to record in delicate drawings the work of his brain for another man's hand to follow. Morris may not always have done more than this, but he fought all his life against the conditions that make such a method invariable and inevitable. Art *and* Craft; the conjunction 'and' meant to him not apposition but fusion. The craftsman foreseeing his labour as he made his pattern, the artist adapting his pattern as he did his work; these were to be *one*.

Morris's dream grew vivid ere it faded. At one time it may almost have seemed as though he and his fellow dreamers might carry industrial England back into an imagined past that had never been. Nowadays it is generally realised that, if design and manufacture be at variance, the cure must be to suit design to modern manufacture rather than to antiquate manufacture to suit design. We cannot break the machine to bring back the man, we must use the man to conquer the machine. Nor must this be sad wisdom, bringing with it despair; it must be a counsel of hope. Nevertheless, the doctrines of Morris nourished the artists of his time with food for which they long had unconsciously hungered, and, by him refreshed, they found their way less weary, and rode forth, if not as giants, as men considerably more confident and adventurous than they had been before.

The paper architecture of the eighteenth century (for, after all, that is what it chiefly was) had undergone great changes in the nineteenth; but paper architecture it remained even when Pugin and his imitators had changed all its forms and reversed its principles. So long as the materials and design appeared to be what they were, and that the sacred obligation of truth was nowhere flouted, nobody in Pugin's day cared much how the materials were wrought, provided the shape they assumed corresponded exactly with the architect's drawings. To this indifference was due three-quarters of what we now deplore in the church restoration that formed the Ecclesiologists' major activity. Whatever differences there were between the leading church-restorers were differences concerning the rival duties of conservatism and innovation in design, and it must be admitted that professed innovators were few. To all, however, it seemed only common sense that a new and durable stone should be better than an old and a crumbling one, and the duty of conservatism, being a duty towards ancient and beautiful forms, seemed to enjoin an even greater remaking and rescue of forms in decay than was the obligation of those who held the problem of repair to be one chiefly utilitarian. 'Beware lest one worn feature ye efface,' urged an admonitory poem much quoted by restorers in proof of their conservatism. It was wrong for man to *efface* it, it should be *renewed* to prevent Time's effacing it either. In sharp opposition to this, Morris contended (and the Society for Protection of Ancient Buildings has ever since maintained and tried to enforce) that effacement by Time should be nowhere resisted; that all historical architecture should be patched up just sufficiently to preserve it until it exists no more; and that nothing whatever new should be added to an old building that could possibly appear to have been part of that building originally.

When dealing with buildings whose power of pleasing depends upon picturesque accidents as much as, or more than, upon organic design, such a method of procedure is obviously the only proper one. But to let a valuable and consistent design disappear bit by bit beneath an overlay of formless patches would not seem very sensible. The question of how restoration should be conducted is still a burning one, since even if it be agreed that buildings primarily picturesque should only be patched, whereas integrated works of architecture should have their forms carefully preserved, no general agreement is likely as to the class in which many border-line buildings should be placed. On the whole, it is probable that the labours of Victorian church restorers have preserved as much for us in evidences of the forms of ancient art as they have stolen from us in evidences of history.

At the end of the last chapter the names of William Morris and William Butterfield were coupled together in their common capacity of reformers, although they were reformers in very different ways. In the last chapter but one were quoted some words of Sir Gilbert Scott, in which he stated that the reproduction of English Middle Pointed Gothic, to which all the early Puginists were rallied, was enjoined by the Ecclesiologists merely as a *point de départ* for new developements that were hoped for. Everybody had to be got together before the campaign could be begun.

Butterfield's church at Sessay, already mentioned, was designed at this time of rallying. Like everything of his designing, it borrows from old forms without any exact imitation, and reveals, though here in no pronounced degree, its designer's idiosyncrasy. The church he built for Charles Laprimaudaye, Cardinal Manning's former curate and fellow convert, at West Lavington in Sussex, dates from 1849, but displays the same characteristics; and at a later date still the church he built for Dr. Pusey at Langley in Kent shews that on occasion he could be content to refrain from the daring experimentalism with which by then his name had become associated. His abhorrence of paper architecture was as great as Morris's although very different in its results. Morris would have blank wall-surfaces beautified only by the accidental variegation of hand-made material, by the accidental texture left by the craftsman's tool, whereas Butterfield would fill them everywhere with deliberate patterning, obtained, wherever possible, by the display of constructional materials arranged in contrasting colours. This constructional polychromy, as he called it, reached its climax in the buildings of Keble College at Oxford (1868), and the chapel of Rugby School (1872). It is the most salient and often the least successful element in Butterfield's architecture, his great strength lying rather in the masterly arrangement of masses and harmony of form that pervade every one of his buildings from the vane of the steeple to the hinges on the vestry door. A study of Keble chapel, possibly one of the three or four buildings in Oxford of most architectural importance, will reveal to the spectator, though perhaps not all at once, how all-pervading, how over-riding such harmony can be. It certainly cannot be gainsaid that Butterfield's polychromy has given it a good deal to over-ride. The church of All Saints, Margaret Street in London, preserves the same consistency in spite of

'CONSTRUCTIONAL POLYCHROMY'

Keble College, Oxford (1868)

recent additions to its furniture, whose particular merits may not seem altogether appropriate to their situation. This consistency was achieved in spite of interference from the church's godfather, Alexander Beresford Hope (1820-1887), who has left recorded in a letter that 'Butterfield . . . is honestly fanatical in his colour doctrines, and completely believes that I have marred the world's greatest work.' What Beresford Hope in the same letter refers to as the 'clown's dress' with which Butterfield had 'parricidally spoilt his own creation' must certainly have seemed a heavy price to pay for consistency when the church was new. London smoke has since been kind to it and has softened its appearance in a way one hopes (without being sure) that Butterfield himself would have approved.

There is no denying that Butterfield's constructional polychromy was often not completely successful, but this is not to say that his designs would have been better without it. People perhaps cannot be blamed, if, wincing under some blow between the eyes delivered to them by the master's violence, they feel tempted to protect themselves by counter-attacks with pails of whitewash. Yet any later work of Butterfield reduced to monochrome loses much of its distinctive merit. His zig-zags and stripes are too many, too congested, and often too large in scale; there can be no doubt of that. On the other hand, for the particular effects he had in view it was necessary to string together the shadow-casting features in his closely organised elevations by means of coloured patterns that would conduct the eye across the intervening surfaces. All admirers of his work will lament that he did not do this more delicately, but will regard with dismay the havoc that has been wrought upon some of his buildings by self-confident improvers who, thinking they knew so much more than he, have unconsciously revealed to the world that they knew so much less.

If any historical architecture should be absolutely protected from interference, that architecture should be the best of Butterfield's, which is entirely incapable of being made to behave prettily by modern standards, but will always be esteemed by those strong enough to take the rough with the smooth.

The churches of Sessay and West Lavington are productions of Butterfield in his least defiant mood, but *defiant* is the word that fits the usual temper of this coarse-grained genius; defiance of all the weaker tendencies of his age, of its thought, when evasive, its Erastianism when sanctimonious, its sentiment when insincere. An Anglo-Catholic Puritan; a lifelong celibate; a thorn in the side of his dazed but obedient employers; a man scornful of his detractors, and suspicious of his adulators; was there ever anybody less like Mr. Gilbert Scott? That a church should be warm seemed to him an invitation to drowsiness in devotion. For some years, therefore, he refused to tolerate any form of artificial heating, except by means of braziers of charcoal unpleasant enough to be no more used than necessary. The benches in his churches seem expressly designed to make sitting considerably more of a strain to the worshippers than kneeling. When he built a house, it was he that was to say what was necessary to comfort, and no one else. To a lady complaining of inconvenience in a house he had built for her, he replied only by the question, 'Madam, do your chimneys smoke?' The lady admitted that they did not. 'And you have not thanked me for the boon,' replied Butterfield, ringing the bell. Yet to this man, humble before his God, however arrogant toward his neighbour, many of the most intelligent and discriminating patrons of church architecture gladly submitted. However little he spared them, they knew that he would spare himself less.

Butterfield was twenty years older than Morris although

THE GOSPEL FOR THE SLUMS

St. Alban's Church, Holborn, London (1859)

he outlived him by four years. To discuss the two reformers together is therefore anachronistic, but it is justified by Butterfield's Bourbon-like obstinacy. Indeed, the character of his work and teaching, already mature in the late 'fifties, hardly altered at all during his remaining forty years of activity. That the Ecclesiologists should have put his work above that of all his other contemporaries is understandable enough, even though he flouted their dicta by refusing to obstruct his churches with chancel screens, by paying little heed to their theory of symbolism, and often by shewing a tendency to archaise and make ungainly the smooth perfections of their chosen Middle Pointed style. These trifling insubordinations, however, could weigh little against his Anglo-Catholic orthodoxy and his blameless life. His only known lapse from virtue was that he had once designed a dissenting chapel, a peccadillo, never repeated, that all agreed to forgive and forget. The admirers of Butterfield, however, have been many since and beside the Ecclesiologists, and have included even Norman Shaw, than whom no one could have been expected to be more unsympathetic. Keble Chapel is one of the principal things in Oxford that the well-informed foreign architect wishes to see, and one with which he least often expresses disappointment.

Of Butterfield's work other than churches a great deal might be said, were it not that the same consistency that can be observed throughout his ecclesiastical architecture binds that architecture to his production in other directions. All his buildings, whatever their destinations, are aesthetically of one kind. Of schools and parsonages he built many, the Hampshire County Hospital at Winchester (1863) is his, there is a Convent by him at Plymouth (1850), and anybody who wants to see how he designed a racket-court can do so by examining that treasury of various Butterfieldianisms,

Rugby School. In his buildings at St. Augustine's Abbey, Canterbury (1845), the long unbroken ridge line of the roof shews that even at the beginning of his career one of his most characteristic preferences had fully developed. Where there could be no long roof to have a long ridge line he resorted to a method of pyramidal composition that is no less personal. Examples of this can be seen in many-storied schools and parsonages built upon confined urban sites, such as those at All Saints', Margaret Street.

Butterfield's practice in internal decoration, his tailoring of the 'clown's coat' was ruled less by his choice than by the conclusions to which his theories led him. Everything must be as enduring as possible, mere painting being eschewed by him as transitory. To say that he disapproved of plaster would not be true, since alone among the Puginists he used occasionally on external walls rough plaster very much like what most of them were so busily stripping from churches of earlier centuries. As a general rule, however, he set such store upon permanence in internal decoration that wherever possible he lined his buildings with materials to which time would bring no shabbiness. Decorative painting he therefore held to be less desirable than mosaic, or than paintings burnt into the surface of earthenware tiles. For such mosaics and paintings, as for his stained glass, he did not make the cartoons himself, although he sometimes insisted upon modifying and angularising the work of the artists he employed, probably to their dismay. In wrought ironwork and in marble inlay he especially delighted, taking a great deal of pains in devising their details. Surfaces not intended as fields for pictorial subjects he almost invariably patterned with alabaster, marble, and tiles; with stonework inlaid with coloured mastics; or with bricks. Everything small that he designed is apt to seem oddly imperfect and awkward in itself, but perfect and proper in relation with its surroundings. Had he been an even greater architect than he was, he might, no doubt, have combined particular grace with general harmony and grandeur, but, with that grace lacking, he nevertheless has left to us monuments with which no spectator capable of large appreciation can be seriously dissatisfied.

Morris and Butterfield were undoubtedly strong forces in the history of their time, but were they forces of reform? If reform means the removal of abuses, they were so most certainly; although the abuses they removed may not have been those against which they directed their main attack. Morris hoped to bring our country out of the pains of industrial readjustment into a perpetual May-day in which happy labourers would rollick round the Maypole with old English song and dance. Butterfield hoped to impose upon his backsliding co-religionists a salutary Gothic mortification by means of which all traces of Erastianism would be expelled from a purified national church. Both hopes were disappointed. Nobody danced round Morris's Maypole except Mr. Clifford Bax and Mr. Walter Crane. As soon as Butterfield was out of the way, sinners altered his churches instead of being altered by them. But Morris taught his age that craft can be an equal partner with art, and Butterfield shewed that Gothic was a living language, having words for racket-court, operating theatre, and latrine. Since craft had hitherto been generally kept below stairs, since Gothic had been thought of as a mediaeval style only competent for such modern tasks as had also been mediaeval, the actual reforms promoted by Morris and Butterfield were great. Both developed what Pugin had begun. Morris took Puginism off paper into the workshop: Butterfield reversed Pugin's aim of forcing his age to conform with the necessities of Gothic, and succeeded in forcing Gothic to conform with the necessities of his age.

The antecedents of all the elements of Butterfield's architectural forms are English, and in that respect differ greatly from those drawn upon by the Ruskinians among his fellow architects. Ruskin's direct influence upon the architecture contemporary with him has been greatly exaggerated; it is remarkable considering the numerousness and enthusiasm of his readers how few of his Stones of Venice he induced English builders of churches and houses to incorporate in their work. The Museum of Oxford University is of the Anglo-Venetian style at once the monument and the tomb, and among the innumerable projects of Anglo-Venetian buildings that Eastlake atributes to architectural students of the time, very few seem to have been carried into execution. Ruskin's Venice, pictured in word and drawing, was, however, a quarry that yielded many small treasures to eclectics, and eclecticism was the order of the day. The Middle Pointed régime had collected architects at the *point de départ*; and the thing now was to depart, but whither?

Man's first disobedience to Middle Pointed had resulted in a disastrous fall into the hateful Perpendicular, so that the process of Gothic developement to which architects were now being urged was not without its dangers. Those inclined to play for safety attempted new combinations of the sacred Middle Pointed forms without any re-stocking of their store of material. Bolder spirits ran into all sorts of rootless eccentricities, among which were the experimental designs published by Thomas Harris (1830-1900), in a collection he entitled *Victorian Architecture*, a collection that failed in its presumable object of securing for him a large practice, but niched him in history as the first traceable user of the adjective 'Victorian.' The fiercest, ablest, and most temerarious of these Gothic adventurers built three large country houses—Bestwood Lodge, Nottinghamshire (1862), Tortworth Court, Gloucestershire (1849), and Elvetham Park, Hampshire (1860), which carry modernism tumultuously across the border of caricature. His name was Samuel Sanders Teulon (1812-1873), and as a church architect he had also a large and exciting practice.

Architects predisposed to adventure, as Teulon was, were at this time encouraged to experiment in the building of auditorium churches by those clergy of the Church of England who refused to submit even in externals to Ecclesiological rule. The architecture of the dissenting bodies was at this time at the nadir of its ignoble course, affording us hardly any examples of Protestant developement; but in such churches built for the Establishment as those designed by Edward Buckton Lamb (1806-1869) at Addiscombe (1878) in Surrey, at West Hartlepool in Durham (1854), and at Haverstock Hill (1865), something was achieved towards roofing a large preaching space with ingenious carpentry and adapting pseudo-mediaeval forms to structures of a kind unknown in the Middle Ages. George Truefitt (1824-1902) several times attempted the same thing in a different and highly individual way, and his octagonal church at Tufnell Park (1866), a northern suburb of London, won unwilling praise even from the critic of the *Ecclesiologist*. In Catholic church-building, it was now generally accepted that Pugin's battle was lost, and that the remote high altar, the screened chancel, and the emphasis given to furniture used only at the offices, for all of which he fought so doughtily, were to be regarded as definitely discountenanced by the hierarchy. Catholic churches therefore, although conforming to the Gothic fashion of the time in detail, tended more and more towards the arrangement known as basilican, that is to say towards collecting altar, priests, and people into one uninterrupted area and

'VIGOUR' AND 'GO'

Bestwood Lodge, Nottinghamshire (1862)

137

limiting the use of the aisles to that of processional ways
and approaches to chapels.

Of these enforced developements neither the Protestant
approach to the auditorium nor the Catholic approach to the
basilica seems to have been embraced at all willingly by
architects at large. Lamb and Truefitt have been mentioned
here not because they had any considerable following, but
because their unusual enterprise in trying to give employers
what they wanted might in happier times have inaugurated
a general and a profitable departure from precedent among
church designers. If the Ecclesiologists had objected, as
they certainly would have done, they could have been
reminded that they had asked for developement, and had
got it.

What actually happened was quite different from this. A
compromise had been arrived at by which the Puseyite
church in its structure and in most of its arrangements was
agreed to by everybody, with the mental reservation on the
part of non-Puseyites that once their building was finished
they would behave inside it exactly as they chose. This
Puseyite or, as non-Puseyites would prefer to call it, 'correct'
form of structure consisted of a nave, two aisles or one aisle
or no aisles, according to the number of sittings (Ecclesiologists called them 'kneelings') to be provided, transepts
usually, and most usually opening into the chancel so that
the organ might be put into one of them, a diminutive
vestry, and a steeple (when shortage of funds did not limit
the builder's ambitions to a bell gable or turret). This was
the programme that a very large number of architects of
varying capacities was called upon to work by, over and
over and over again. For the church-building wave was at
its height, and he was an unsuccessful ecclesiastical architect
who was not required to build at least half a dozen every
year. What was more, these churches were all expected to

be novel and striking in character. Architects had had their
Gothic schooling and were expected to get a move on.
Accordingly in the years 1855 to 1870, speaking approxim-
ately, developements followed each other thick and fast—
developements both timely and untimely of the neo-mediaeval idiom that all architects had learnt while at school and
had lately enriched with foreign material of every kind
gathered on their sketching holidays. In an unhappy
moment the brilliant leader of the younger generation had
characterised the style towards which his ambition pointed
as *vigorous*, and thereafter vigour became the avowed aim
of all young Gothicists, being spoken of among themselves
as 'go.' Anybody who has read the writings upon architecture of the first Lord Grimthorpe (1818-1905), (often not
nearly so inept as critic as he was as architect), will remember
that the vigorous style provoked him to very vigorous
criticism indeed. This particular criticism has not much
justice, but certain passages in it are valuable for the
description they give of what he is condemning.

'One of the styles now in fashion,' he says, 'is that
modification of French or Italian Gothic (for it is sometimes called one and sometimes the other), to which its
patrons have dexterously affixed the epithet "vigorous,"
when it would have been just as appropriate to call it
"feeble." But, in fact, any such epithet is nonsense as it
expresses nothing really belonging to architecture. I should
call it the *shadowless* style, for that does express its character
and it is as miserable as the man who lost his shadow. The
great characteristic of genuine Gothic is the abundance of
shadows produced by sometimes quite small cuttings and
projections like eyebrows, requiring no such heavy masses
and large stones as the classical projections do. This vigorous style displays only the vigour of shaving off all such
projections and making the slopes of buttresses without

nosings and twice as steep as they ever were in real Gothic, at least in England. Window tracery is made as though it were cut out of stone flags, and buildings rise out of the ground without plinths or projecting bases as if they were mushrooms.' 'It delights,' he further complains, 'in wood-work of most harsh and ugly outline, totally unlike any old examples, and in all forms of lopsidedness. For some reason or other, this style is peculiarly affected by gentlemen of the ritualistic persuasion, but whether for any other reason than its novelty, which it has already lost, I do not know.'

Most of this description fits the style of that well-known temple of 'gentlemen of the ritualistic persuasion,' the church of SS. Philip and James in North Oxford (1862), and the characteristics of that building make Lord Grimthorpe's allusion to the 'modification of French or Italian Gothic' easy to understand. Cruciform, with clerestoreyed nave and central steeple, it is actually not at all Italian, very little French, and very much English in its general conception, but its details certainly shew that its architect has not wasted his time when abroad. Its style can be hardly called shadow-less, since the bold relief of its pinnacled spire-lights, the deep louvres of its belfry windows, and the projection of its transepts, give it a quality of plastic solidity quite unusual; but it is certainly true that the 'abundance of shadows produced by quite small cuttings and projections like eyebrows,' seems to have been avoided as carefully by the architect here as it was customarily sought by Lord Grimthorpe's god, Sir Gilbert Scott. 'Tracery looking as though it were cut out of stone flags' may or may not be less pleasing than that looking as if it were made out of sticks and pastry-cutters; it is easy to bandy epithets in matters of taste. Here the walls have projecting plinths, so that Lord Grimthorpe could not have called this church a

A TEST FOR TASTE

SS. Philip and James' Church, Oxford (1862)

mushroom. Moreover, plinths are not really any more necessary to the beauty of buildings than crinolines to the beauty of women; both were worn in Lord Grimthorpe's day, but it is possible to be perfectly decent without either. At the time of its building, in the year 1862, this church was a test for taste—it was admired extremely by the sensitive and roundly condemned by the obtuse. Some may think that it remains a test for taste to-day.

Street, its architect, at the time of its building had for eight years been the leader of all young enthusiasts discontented with the correct architecture of their elders, having leapt into that position when, in 1854, the dust of Gilbert Scott's office not long shaken from his feet, he had begun to build the remarkable group of church and secular buildings at All Saints', Maidenhead (1854). If to mingle some Italian details with English Gothic was to be a disciple of Ruskin, then this Maidenhead work proves Street to have put Ruskinism into practice before the master himself got Benjamin Woodward (1815-1861) to work at the Oxford Museum, and it was under the very eye of the master that Street was, in 1858, to build a church with a few un-English marble columns in it at Herne Hill. Nevertheless, Street's own subsequent publication of his book upon buildings in North Italy, and his own inveterate habit of architectural globe-trotting, make it probable that not only did Ruskin influence him little, but that what was derived from Italy in the architecture of his more susceptible contemporaries was due to him and not to the prophet. Very similar to the interior of his Oxford church is the interior of the church he built in the following year at Clifton, near Bristol (1863). In this can be seen the ingenious device, which he had already employed at Oxford, by means of which the arcades separating the nave from the aisles are not allowed to continue eastward far enough for their most eastern arches to come down upon half pillars, but are, as it were, caught up in mid-air on the east wall containing the chancel arch, thus getting rid of a great deal of the masonry that otherwise would have obstructed the view of the altar. In another of its peculiarities, this church anticipates the practice usual nowadays of reducing aisles to the size and function of mere passages.

Both at Oxford and at Clifton, Street's material was stone, and the external colour that the taste of the time demanded has been supplied by means of variations in texture and in tint. Whether, if circumstances had caused these churches to be built of brick, Street would have indulged in colour-contrasts more violent cannot of course be inferred, seeing that Street's appetite for pitiless polychromy may well have abated since his designing of the churches at Maidenhead and in Garden Street (now renamed Thorndike Street), Westminster, S.W.1 (1859). This last church, with its bell-tower completely detached from the buildings (as was that at Maidenhead before the church was lengthened to meet it by his son), is as strongly parti-coloured as any work of Butterfield's, although the patterns are arranged with un-Butterfieldian discretion. Its interior is as rich as coloured materials can make it, and in its general effect is remarkably harmonious.

In a hunt for origins, the details of all these three churches would probably be traced to Italy more often than to France, but the manner of their application, in which their excellence lies, has originated nowhere but in the brain of George Edmund Street. In the later period of his work, foreign influences were to weaken; and, alas!, his astonishing power of architectural improvisation was to tempt him to undertake more work than he could study thoroughly in the time he could spend upon it. In some churches of his his admirers meet him at the top of his form, in too many others he shews signs of lassitude. It is said that he could, and did, make the design and complete the working drawings of a church in a couple of days, and although his days might be other men's weeks, much of what he did needed second thought, and did not get it.

The faults, real and supposed, in the planning of the Law Courts (1871) cannot altogether be laid at his door, for never did the architect of a public building suffer more vexations and interference from authorities than he in this. The architectural treatment of the plan is masterly, though uncongenial to those who require monumental unification in the design of every public building, even when the building is so placed that it never can be seen as a whole. That the external façades of the Law Courts are irregular and loosely integrated is the proper and logical result of their confined situation: any formal or symmetrical façade of the length required along the Strand would have been ludicrous and misplaced in so narrow and crooked a thoroughfare. The great hall internally is magnificent, and, throughout the whole work, inside and out, the originality shewn in the modernisation and other modification of mediaeval form must strike all those with sufficient knowledge of the old Gothic to know a new thing when they see it. Street's candid acceptance of plate-glass sash-windows is a standing reproof to the neo-Tudor specialists of our time with their mullions and transomes and little panes set in lead, transported from the country into the streets of cities. Here again, however, we have to lament the shortness of Street's time. In this case, not of time to which he himself put any limit, but of the time allotted to his life on earth. His seated statue in the great hall looks out with unseeing eyes upon that which he himself never saw in its perfection.

To convey any adequate realisation of all that Street meant, an enormous album would be needed, containing picture after picture of his infinitely varied and numerous

THE GOTHIC SWAN-SONG

The New Law Courts, London (1871)

works. Far *too* numerous, that was the trouble! During
the later years of his life, his architectural output must have
been the largest of any man in England except Gilbert
Scott. Moreover, he deputed to others very little in his
practice. 'Mr. Street works by drawings,' Gilbert Scott
once said, 'I by influence.' This Scott said of stone carving
in particular, but the contrast was of general application.
Street's works, in consequence of his over-production, can
only be judged in the mass; none save the buildings of his
youth being free from the failings of the too facile draughtsman and the too ready inventor. In hardly any of them,
however, is there not some evidence of the originality and
unconventionality of his thought.

Between Oxford and Wantage, in the village of East
Hanney (1856), there is a little early-Victorian church of his
(for anything built before 1860 should still presumably be
called early-Victorian), which must have been an astonish-
ment to his contemporaries. The Puginist chapel at that
time was usually a little manikin church, with a neat little
nave, a neat little chancel, a neat little porch, all with different gables; a pert little bell turret stuck in somewhere, and
an alternation of pretty little buttresses and windows all
round the walls. To the whole thing there would seem to
stick some of the sawdust and shavings in which its architect
had carefully packed it before he sent it down from London.

Street, on the other hand, has built at East Hanney little
more than a barn. The roofs of nave and of chancel are
one, in fact there is only one roof over the whole building,
its slope prolonged downwards over the lateral porch, and
a bit of it prolonged westward at the top to shelter a bell
hung against the wall. There are a few square-headed
windows, spaced irregularly just where light is needed.
Nothing except some details, probably unavoidable at the
time, could possibly be less early-Victorian than this honest,

almost aggressively simple little building, and nobody else, except Street, could possibly have designed it when he did. His parsonage houses are particularly delightful, the later examples sometimes in a style that makes it hard to remember that William Morris's Red House (1859) at Bexley was not one of them. Many are no more than large comfortable cottages entirely free from intimidating Gothicism, others may be a little more formal, but all are pleasant and domestic and as different as possible from the agglomerations of apparent vestries and cells in which the strict Ecclesiologists had hitherto considered that the clergy and their families should be confined.

In 1855, there was an international competition for the design of the Cathedral at Lille. The style imposed by the conditions was primitive French Gothic. Street won the second premium, the first being awarded to Messrs. Clutton and Burges, whose design, in the end, was never carried out. That design, however, together with the publication then in progress of Viollet-de-Duc's dictionary of architecture, turned the attention of English church-builders to the pure original Gothic of Northern France and confirmed young William Burges (1827-1881) in the manner of design from which he was seldom afterwards to depart. It is a tempting antithesis to suggest that Street was greater than his works, but that Burges's works were greater than Burges, although the suggestion would need qualifying before it became true. The contrast between the two men, however, is great; as great as that between the amount of influence they exerted upon others, since whereas Street made every impressionable young architect his imitator, Burges, most of whose few executed designs reach a degree of absolute merit superior to that in any works of Street, received little popular applause, and, by his fellow-architects, was much more admired than followed. Almost all his works, as has been said, were based upon the early Gothic of Northern France, all his ambition was toward a close union of architecture with painting and sculpture. His designs for furniture, for plate, for jewellery, were all those of a master in the particular craft that each employed, and the house he built for himself in Kensington remained a museum of many of these things until their regrettable dispersion by sale between the last two wars. A remarkable piece of furniture of his designing, enriched with paintings shewing pre-Raphaelite influence, was then acquired by the Ashmolean Museum at Oxford, but the fate of the remaining treasures is unknown.

Burges's most complete achievements are the cathedral at Cork in Ireland (1863) and two amazingly rich and elaborate churches in Yorkshire, one at Skelton (1871) and the other at Studley Royal (1871). He also reconstructed an enchanted castle—it can be called nothing less—at Castell Coch in Glamorganshire (*c.* 1875), and gave to Cardiff Castle, near by (1865), its romantic towered silhouette and many interior decorations of the greatest sumptuousness. At Oxford he decorated the chapel of Worcester College (*c.* 1864) in a Renaissance manner that is extremely ingenious and original.

His work is pervaded with the most peculiar and amusing fancy. In his own library in London, all the letters of the alphabet are personified in the carved frieze of the chimney-piece, except the letter H, which someone has dropped in bronze upon the corner of the fender. In another room of his, in another house, an indignant-looking monkey must be robbed of his ivory nut if you would ring the bell. In his own bedroom wardrobe the panels contained paintings portraying the troubles of philosophers. Above these panels ran a cornice, strictly architectural except for an interruption above the figure of Socrates, where Xantippe was leaning out of it to pour some water upon her husband's head.

FROM THE GOTHIC SOURCE

St. Finbar's Cathedral, Cork, Ireland (1863)

149

Henry Clutton (1819-1895), Burges's associate in the Lille competition (but never his partner), was an architect of more various production, although in the magnificent church he built for the Duke of Bedford at Woburn, and in another scarcely less striking for the same patron at Tavistock, the primitive French style of the Lille design is preserved. His place in this narrative, less concerned as it is with men than with deeds, must be only that of the designer of two houses, Minley Manor in Hampshire (1858) and Quantock Lodge in Somerset (1857), in which the manorial Gothic convention is infused by an artistry it had never displayed before. The remainder of his work, and a large remainder it is, contains no landmarks of architectural history, but is delightful to study as that of a little master who never fell below his own high standard.

Our chief concern here is with the work of leaders, with the work of leaders who have been followed. Followers, however, who were later to become leaders can claim our momentary attention. George Frederick Bodley (1827-1907) cannot claim it yet since anything of his that was much more than an echo of Street would, if mentioned here, be mentioned prematurely. Even Philip Webb, the architect most closely associated with William Morris, the earnest, awkward, highly gifted man who laid the fuse that exploded Victorian Gothic, was but a loyal echo of Street in his youth; it is said that he was allowed by the master to contribute much of the design of those parts of the Law Courts that face Carey Street.

In Stratton Street, Piccadilly, there is a brick house (No. 8) the design of which looks as though Street, in a moment when afflatus was withheld, methodically collected therein all that the world regarded as his characteristic peculiarities. Actually he had nothing to do with this house; its architect was Sir Ernest George, whose very different later work will

emerge in a later chapter. Street, Street, Street! In the
period we are considering he is everywhere inescapable.
All the Lord Grimthorpes, all the patrons of Gilbert Scott,
all the five-per-cent. architects-and-surveyors detested him;
but all the young folk that were worth anything adored him.

It is well known that William Morris, although Street's
pupil, did not approve of Street's methods of church restoration, nor of his hurried, swollen practice, nor, probably,
of his too impressionable mood when on his travels. But
the people who approved of Street approved also of Morris.
This is important to realise and is the reason why Morris
has been put into this chapter rather than into the next one.
When we come to the period that is to be described under
the name of *Bric-à-brac*, we shall find Queen Anne revivals,
and flirtations with Japan, and the breeding of strange
Gothico-Renaissance monsters, all being conducted in rooms
papered and chintzed and carpeted by Morris, and we may
be tempted to think that these vagaries were planned at
Kelmscott. Nothing could be more untrue. Morris and
Philip Webb were, and always remained, what Pugin called
'good Gothic men'; their wide sympathies may have kept
them upon excellent terms with their heterodox fellow art-
workers, their unconventional outlook may have established a common factor of modernity between their work
and that of those who innovated upon a Renaissance background, but never did they themselves lower their mediaeval banner. Indeed, Morris's textiles always look essentially inappropriate when combined with eighteenth-century
furniture, in spite of the fact that he sometimes consented
so to combine them himself. Put them, however, into a
room designed by Street, or by Burges, and they will seem
as though they had been expressly designed for the place
they have taken.

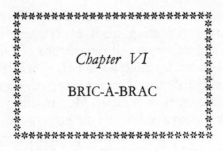

Chapter VI

BRIC-À-BRAC

THE title of this chapter ought perhaps to have been put in inverted commas, because the term *bric-à-brac* is now almost as much out of date as is what it was once so commonly used to describe. In late Victorian days *bric-à-brac* was the accepted name for all that overfilled the drawing-rooms of people pretending to taste—for blue-and-white china, Martin or Doulton stoneware, majolica, dinanderie, ivories, Japanese bronzes, and almost everything else that with them could be dangerously balanced on brackets and above doors, or massed on cabinets and overmantels. The comic opera *Patience* (1881) gives us the classical portrait of the period whose ideals these accumulations expressed. Drawing-rooms that housed them were decorated at first in the manner popularised by Charles Eastlake or Bruce Talbert (1838-1881) and later on in a style become vaguer, ambitiously nicknamed 'aesthetic.' Bric-à-brac instigated the variety in the patterns, all highly conventional and in what were then known as 'quiet shades' of colour, with which every surface, whether of walls, ceiling, floor or furniture, was covered. Furniture itself is not within the scope of this book, but the term *bric-à-brac* can well be borrowed therefrom to name architectural tendencies that resembled and synchronised with the fashion it was primarily used to denote.

The reformers, Pugin, Butterfield, Street, Morris, and most of Morris's immediate disciples, were lifelong Gothicists, hopeful of developement, suspicious of eclecticism. They disapproved of pastiche but shuddered at the moral dangers of stylistic promiscuity. One of their henchmen, writing in 1874, well expressed the longing they all felt for the eventual steadying of mid-Victorian Gothic into a straightforward course of rational inventive building. This course he believed could be steered better by Englishmen than by others, because they had always, 'by a few well-timed reforms, succeeded in correcting the natural tendency which all fully developed styles have to "run to seed." . . . Our most critical period'—he went on to explain—'was the latest form of lancet, but the "geometrical" reform corrected that. Then the geometrical style, in which the Germans stuck . . . had in England no time to decay before it was replaced by the "flowing." This, in turn, was saved from the debasement that awaited it in France, by the wholesome restraint of the "perpendicular" reform. It must, I think, be admitted that in France and Germany the "renaissance" style was at first an improvement on those which it displaced. But in England, when we look at the latest forms of the pure Gothic, and then note what grand works were done in even such a wretched bastard style as our Elizabethan, we are tempted to think that, but for this unfortunate foreign influence, we should shortly have developed a style which would have eclipsed everything preceding it.'

And so we might still: that was the hope underlying these wistful words, words written—as it happened—on the fateful eve of an interruption in the flow of the Gothic

Revival even more violent and far less easily explicable than that which had dammed and diverted the original style three centuries before. George Edmund Street awoke one morning to find his flock all scattered—scattered, as it has proved, beyond recall. All the talented young men who had followed so dutifully in the path of his Gothicism, who had submitted with such docility to his training as future evangelists in a naughty world, decided suddenly that they were not going to be Gothic any more, at least not any more Gothic than they could help. Richard Norman Shaw (1831-1912), who, at Bingley near Leeds (1866) and at Lyons in France (1868), had built two of the best Street-like churches not by Street that exist; Basil Champneys (1842-1935), who, at Kentish Town in north London, had built a church and parsonage of the same kind, with only such minor compromises in the design of the parsonage as Street could easily have tolerated; Thomas Graham Jackson (1835-1924), who had begun his never very enterprising career by mimicking very closely the mannerisms of Street's head draughtsman, Philip Webb (1831-1915); Ernest George (1839-1922), whose enormous house for Sir Henry Peek in Devonshire[1] was one that Street himself must have entirely approved; even Edward Godwin (1833-1886), once straitest of the strait in Gothic orthodoxy; all of these were now to be seen grazing distant and possibly poisonous pastures, far beyond the reach of their master's voice.

Such dispersion was obviously destructive of all hopes of orderly architectural progress. Yet it ought not to have been unexpected. Architecture was still ruled by the aristocracy, of which the Established Church was yet, in the main, a cadet branch. Civic, mercantile, and commercial building might satisfy its material needs, and satisfy them sumptuously, but the manner in which it satisfied

---

[1] Rousdon, 1872.

them was still determined by fashions imposed upon it, whether the imposition were recognised or not, from above. Gothic guildhalls and assize courts were Gothic because the educated patronage of the day had determined that the Houses of Parliament should be Gothic. Banking houses were Italian because bankers had seen and admired the palaces Barry had built either as residences or as club-houses for their more important depositors.

Now, among the architects who served the aristocrats and the plutocrats shortly to become aristocrats, the younger sons in bishoprics and deaneries, and the unclassified sons who were pushing forward to these dignities,—among, that is to say, the leading architects of the age, a doubt had been growing as to whether the rigid Victorian Gothic they had developed would not have to be replaced by some method of building more flexible and convenient. Universal Gothic was the goal, and yet whereas Victorian Tudor and Victorian Elizabethan were usually invited to country mansions and to parsonages, and Gothic town-halls were not uncommon, in new buildings of other kinds the style was still rare. Plainly the thunder of the Italians must be stolen by some new and tempting version of mediaeval principles that would offer greater convenience and amenity, and, if possible, less expenditure of money, than could be obtained by building in any other way.

Gilbert Scott in his *Remarks on Secular and Domestic Architecture* had laid down certain principles by which this new style must be governed. In one or two houses, such as Kelham Hall near Newark (1858) and Walton Hall near Warwick (1858), he had put his theories into effect. There is much in these buildings that at their date must have seemed commendably modern, and for that reason superior to the opportunist compromise with archaeological Tudor offered by the school of Salvin; but their pitiful artistic

inferiority to contemporary works by Scott's juniors, such
as the additions to Betteshanger House, Kent (1856), by
George Devey (1820-1886), and Quantock Lodge, Somerset,
by Henry Clutton, makes Scott's pretensions to leadership
seem comical indeed. The Meadow buildings at Christ
Church, Oxford (1863), date from about the same time, and
were designed with the same intention, but their architect
failed in them, as Scott himself failed afterwards in the St.
Pancras Hotel, through being much too self-consciously
stylistic. Scott's town-hall at Preston in Lancashire (1862)
is a building of which he himself was very proud, and is
certainly more reasonable than the hotel at St. Pancras, but,
criticised by modern standards, can hardly be thought
reasonable enough.

Alfred Waterhouse (1830-1905) is an architect whose
stock at the moment is down at bottom, and Oxford is probably not yet ready to reconsider the adverse judgement
passed upon the new buildings at Balliol (1867) in the days
when Sir Thomas Jackson led the taste of the University.
Nevertheless, five years after these buildings were finished
Charles Eastlake wrote enthusiastically of the 'breadth and
vigour' of their design, and continued with some remarks
that it will not be unprofitable for us to read. Admitting
that the new buildings contrast strangely with the old ones
by which they are surrounded, he suggested that 'as a matter
of sentiment it may be questioned whether such a contrast
is not an advantage when it is explained by a difference of
style as well as of date, while, as a matter of taste, posterity
alone will fairly judge between the Oxford of the fifteenth
and the Oxford of the nineteenth century. Is a high-
pitched roof more picturesque than one raised at an obtuse
angle? Is an equilateral arch better than a four-centred
flat one? Is such a lintel as Mr. Waterhouse used for his
windows—we need not say the comeliest which might have

been devised—but more comely than the ordinary type of Tudor window-head? Does the building altogether present a richer variety of features, a greater refinement of mouldings, and on the whole more indication of artistic study than if it had been a mere imitation of Brasenose or All Souls? If these questions can be answered in the affirmative, and he must be a bold critic who would answer them otherwise, we must plainly leave the rest to the hand of Time, whose artistic touch has exercised, perhaps, a more potent influence than we suppose on the opinion of modern amateurs.' Posterity has not yet fulfilled Eastlake's obvious expectation. In 'matters of taste' it still is coy when Waterhouse's work comes before it for judgement. Yet it cannot be denied that these buildings at Balliol have far greater architectural value than most of the imitative Tudor or imitative Renaissance work that has appeared in Oxford since their completion. They are the work of an age that, like the original Tudor age, was not frightened to be itself; and in their conception common sense has been combined with a great deal of skill in making virtues out of inevitable irregularities. In them there is *rien d'indécis*, they are definite, logical, and brave. Perhaps the reason why they are still disliked is that the 'artistic touch of time' has not yet had long enough to work its magic.

Among the practitioners of this logical domestic Gothic, Waterhouse surpassed all others in ability, and was largely employed in producing it for some years after the defeat of his less competent fellow-workers by opposing fashions. His largest opportunity was the rebuilding of Eaton Hall in Cheshire (1870) in a manner then considered appropriate enough but now made by subsequent associations to seem more municipal or commercial than domestic. Afterwards he, too, was to relax Gothic rigour, taking with him into what—in his hands at any rate—proved an inferior style, his large grasp of planning, his mastery of architectural organisation; and his fondness for angular outlines and unsympathetic materials. In the disposition of plan he was without a rival among his contemporaries. Indeed, in the general shaping of a complex building he has had few superiors in his own country before or since. The Manchester Town-hall (1869) is perhaps his most perfect achievement and continually surprises those who dislike its style into unwilling admiration. Here, as at Eaton Hall, the walls are faced with excellent masonry. St. Paul's School at Hammersmith (1881) is built of his favourite scarlet brick and terra-cotta, and is still too much like a piece of raw meat to be pleasant to most people. Its grouping and silhouette, however, are magnificent, as can be seen in the kindly monochrome of photographs. If architecture were studied, as often it should be, by means of small models and outline drawings, the defence of Waterhouse would not be hard to make. In colour and in texture, however, his buildings are usually so forbidding as to lead naturally to their being undervalued.

Comparison of Waterhouse's Natural History Museum at South Kensington (1868) with the museum of Oxford University will shew how greatly rationality in architecture had advanced in the years between the building of the one and that of the other. In the Oxford Museum the planning is puerile, everything being sacrificed to an unnecessary, though not unbeautiful, cloister; and, as has been already told, the engineering of the glass roof was so ineptly designed that it only stood a few years before it became necessary to prop it up underneath and tie it together, by extra metallic members. The architectural design of the façade depends for its effect upon the relative smallness of the windows, through which in consequence much less light finds its way than is needed internally. All the ornament in the building has the air of being itself an exhibit, unrelated to the essential facts of the structure. At South Kensington, on the other hand, plan and structure are everything, all the decorative details being appropriately subordinated to their situation. The style of the exterior is a developement of the Romanesque that, whether we approve it or not, must be acknowledged to be extremely well-adapted to the material in which it is carried out. That material is terra-cotta and of it a few words must now be said.

In the late years of the eighteenth century, a Mrs. Coade with her partner, Seely, founded what soon became an extraordinarily flourishing manufacture of terra-cotta at Lambeth. The excellent material they produced was not quite like anything that had been seen before in England and has not been equalled since. It was sold as 'artificial stone' and was used not only for a variety of isolated ornamental objects but also for the decorative parts of architecture in conjunction with fine stonework, from which it now cannot often be easily distinguished. Much of what appears to be delicate carving in the St. Pancras parish church (1819) is of this material, and few ornamental buildings contemporary with that church are without some specimen of Mrs. Coade's manufacture. When her factory disappeared, her particular kind of product disappeared also, and, with the exception of some sporadic and not very successful attempts to reproduce it in Staffordshire and Lancashire, very little was to be heard of terra-cotta in England for many years. Its first important reappearances were in the Albert Hall (1867) and the Royal College of Science (1869); and in these buildings it took the fancy of the public. It attained enormous popularity in the '70's, by which time some of the more successful architects had come to regard it as a material superior in every way to stone.

When it is properly burnt, its superiority in resisting the acid-laden atmosphere of cities is undeniable, and this advantage may still recommend it to us to-day. Its other peculiar quality, that of lending itself to the cheap multiplication of ornamental forms, may seem less of an advantage to us than it did to our fathers. The consideration on the other side,—that its appearance is excessively mechanical, no doubt seemed less of a disadvantage to them than it does to us. Even by them it was little used in rural situations, except by Waterhouse, who was not only the material's chief populariser but seems to have been so convinced of its universal appropriateness as to use it on almost every possible occasion. In the first days of its popularity its use was not frequently extended to church-building, but in time even that came about, though never very generally. Neither Philip Webb nor Norman Shaw would have anything whatever to do with it, but few other eminent architects of the period resisted its attraction.

Waterhouse was no disciple of Street, and was therefore not concerned with the rebellion against that master's doctrine. The leader of that rebellion it is difficult to name. Suspicion must rest upon William Eden Nesfield (1835-1888), whose design for Cloverley Hall in Shropshire (1862), orthodox though it was in the main, had some queer and ominous things about it. At first sight it might have seemed merely what was to be expected by a nephew of Antony Salvin (which Nesfield was) who had studied Street's peculiarities and moved with the times. But on close inspection many significant peculiarities appeared. Little bits of diaper pattern cropping up here and there in metalwork and plasterwork were positively Japanese, and inside the house there were paintings by Albert Moore (1841-1893) that were certainly not at all Gothic. These omens might seem of little import, were it not that before

Cloverley was finished, its architect had started upon a much larger house, Kinmel Park in North Wales, of which the style—could it be believed?—was half-way between that of a French Renaissance château and that of an English house of the period of Sir Christopher Wren. Furthermore, Nesfield's past record was not reassuring, seeing that he had already started building in Kew Gardens (1866) a dangerously charming cottage in the style he was now exploiting at Kinmel. Plainly, however Gothic he still might be on occasion, he was not a man for true Gothicists to trust.

It has been customary with historians of what, in the '70's and '80's of the last century was called the 'Queen Anne' style, to represent it as a rootless anti-Gothic reaction suddenly inaugurated by Norman Shaw. If its first appearance had been in Nesfield's cottage at Kew, (for the style of that and of Kinmel Park is the style for which the epithet 'Queen Anne' came to be generally misused), no correction of the popular view would be necessary beyond that of putting Nesfield's name instead of Shaw's at the beginning of the story. This, however, would be to forget, as all writers on the subject seem to have forgotten, that the domestic style of Wren had already been tentatively used earlier in the century by architects outside the main Gothic movement. The old Royal Naval School built at New Cross in 1843 was an early work of the kind by another Shaw—*John* Shaw, and less than twenty years later the same John Shaw designed Wellington College, near Sandhurst (1856), in very much the same style that Nesfield was afterwards to resume. John Shaw was not the sort of architect those of the Street entourage would be likely to know much about, so that it is almost certain that the affinity between the two buildings was accidental. It exists, nevertheless, and serves to shew that public taste was not altogether unprepared for what was to be submitted to it. In Kensing-

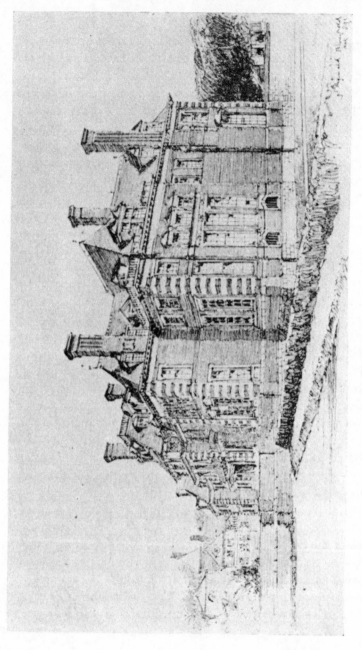

'QUEEN ANNE'

Kinmel Park, Denbighshire (1866)

ton Palace Gardens, Thackeray the novelist had built in
1861 a red-brick house intended to be in the style of the
early eighteenth century; and many house-builders beside,
who objected to turrets and gables, were looking about for
another alternative to Gothic than stucco Italian. A red-
brick Italian had indeed been evolved, and used for houses
which, when symmetrically treated and unadorned by any
tower or loggia, were not altogether unlike our native
Georgian. Plate-glass windows they would have, no doubt,
and distinctly un-Georgian roofs and eaves; but notwithstanding these differences, the distance between their style
and that of Kinmel Park would not be very great. Whatever Georgianism they displayed, however, was accidental,
and contradicted by the Victorian Italian flavour of their
details, whereas the flavour of the English eighteenth century
in John Shaw's work is plainly intentional.

In the 'Queen Anne' style for which the younger, unrelated, Shaw—Richard Norman Shaw—became famous,
there is much more variety than there is in that attempted
by his namesake, John, but much less likelihood that it
would have been recognised by the monarch after whom it
was so unaccountably named. Historically, it could better be
called the 'Board School' style, seeing that its earliest appearance upon any considerable scale was in the many buildings
for the School Board called into being by the Education
Act of 1870. The architects of most of these buildings (J. J.
Stevenson (1831-1908) and E. R. Robson (1836-1917)) were
the first to develope it fully, bringing together into a consistent convention many peculiarities that had occurred
unrelatedly in the works of the first seceders from Street's
Gothicism. Chief among these was the sash window with
sturdy bars dividing the glass into small panes, and with its
woodwork conspicuously painted white. The revival of
such windows changed the whole character of the domestic

'QUEEN ANNE'

Lowther Gardens, S. Kensington (1878)

164

architecture in this country, at once becoming extremely popular with those wearied of peering between the mullions of the Gothic revival. The large use of white-painted wood-work in cornices, doorcases, and balconies was also a marked innovation and an extremely important element in the general effect.

Other peculiarities may here be catalogued: mostly small things, but small things upon which the effect of this delicate style depends. Windows, taller in proportion to their breadth than is customary in other styles, are surmounted by segmental arches having brick keyblocks, their arches being frequently surmounted by a brick moulding following their curvature. Gables, when there are any, are curved and shaped. The panels of glazed doors, and sometimes the upper parts of windows, are often filled with leaded glass, sometimes plain and sometimes lightly painted in grisaille. Chimneys are extremely tall and are commonly ornamented by vertical projecting ribs in their brickwork, and elaborately capped with oversailing courses. Where there is any-thing like a door-hood or a balcony to be supported, large thin stone brackets of ogee outline do the work. Rubbed and gauged brickwork (which means the very fine-jointed smooth brickwork familiar in the works of Wren) is extensively used, not only in its traditional place in window arches, but also in mouldings and ornamental features generally. As a decorative motif, the sunflower is all-pervading. Sometimes it will be of metal or terra-cotta, crowning the hip of a roof, sometimes scratched in outline upon plaster panels in the gables, sometimes it will be carved in this gauged and rubbed brickwork, sometimes represented in the glass panels of the front door. Internally, it will be worked in crewels upon art-serge portières, will appear in copper lustre upon the tiles of the fireplace, will be beaten in brass or silver in the sconces for candles, and will very likely be painted upon the door panels. In its most complete form this favourite flower will grow from a squat two-handled pot. Below the sunflower in popularity, but still extremely characteristic of the style, are the pomegranate and the orange. The tops of roofs and of projecting porches will be fenced with turned wooden balustrades, of course painted white. If any such balustrades are not of wood but of iron, they will display alternating arrangements of straight and wavy bars interrupted by little cast panels. Almost all these peculiarities luxuriate very prettily at Newnham College, Cambridge (1871), where they contribute to an atmosphere recalling that of Tennyson's *The Princess*. In the internal decoration fashionable at the time, note must be taken in passing of the Japanese proclivities of Thomas Jeckell (1827-1881) and of E. W. Godwin, two able architects who excelled in the design of ironwork and furniture respectively. Whistler, as is well known, did not think much of Jeckell's work in the famous Peacock room, but he employed Godwin to build him his own *White House* in Chelsea (1877), and the Japanese vogue may well have originated with this influential painter. It informed much of Godwin's furniture; and some of Nesfield's, also, was for a time pronouncedly Anglo-Japanese. A pretty memorial of this fashion is the firegrate made until quite recently by Messrs. Barnard, Bishop and Barnard, in which little medallions of apple blossom and other Japanese elements, in very low relief, float about on a ground of fine diaper or reeding. These grates were designed by Thomas Jeckell and at one time enjoyed great and well-deserved popularity.

Bedford Park (1876), the first, and still the most pleasing, of artistic suburbs, was built entirely in this style, and originally was occupied almost only by artists. Even the church (1878), one of Norman Shaw's most original experiments, is in the style of the surrounding houses, as it is only reasonable that a church that is part of the developement of a building estate should be. On the Chelsea Embankment, in Melbury Road, Kensington, and in Hampstead—artists' quarters all—are many beautiful specimens, and many perhaps less beautiful—of what resulted from the 'Queen Anne' taste when supported by wealth.

In the Albert Hall and the Royal College of Science at South Kensington the use of terra-cotta, and the forms into which it is there cast, have obviously been suggested by buildings of the early Italian Renaissance, as was only to be expected in work with which Alfred Stevens is known to have had a great deal to do. Generally speaking, however, the architects of the time seemed to have been attacked by their craving for terra-cotta after they had made sketching tours in Holland and the Low Countries. Ernest George, for example, early casting off his allegiance to Street, spent a large part of his professional career making very soft and pretty drawings of elaborate Anglo-Dutch architecture and getting them carried out in terra-cotta that is very hard and ugly. A house on the west side of Cadogan Square (No. 52, 1886) is probably the most ambitious thing of the kind that he achieved, and of its sort is extremely well designed. In Collingham and Harrington Gardens, South Kensington (1882), he built what almost amounts to a little Dutch town, although in most of the houses here he gives terra-cotta a rest, and falls back on red brickwork for the principal facing of the walls. This collection of London houses, mostly half-way in size between those of Bedford Park and those on the Chelsea Embankment, expresses very perfectly the reaction in taste among mid-Victorian Londoners from the formal stucco terraces in which hitherto their lives had been spent. Here every man's house was different to that of his neighbour, and in none could you be sure from the outward appearance what you would find inside. Moreover, whereas the early Victorian houses of the West End are apt to appear a little sulky during the intervals of ordinary domestic life between the dinner parties and routs that they seem always to be expecting, in these easy-going gabled homes the front doors call for no red carpet across the pavement, there are no balconies needing awnings, and it would be perfectly possible to come to dinner otherwise than in a carriage and pair. The taste of to-day would send us back into Regency terraces, our necessities drive us into flats of a standardised pattern. Into Regency terraces not many people will be rich enough to go; into standardised flats many will continue to be unwillingly herded. The ideal expressed in such houses as these in Harrington and Collingham Gardens, even if it appealed to us as it did to our fathers, would be no longer within our reach. It should not, however, be allowed to fade without a sigh.

The Anglo-Dutch style of Ernest George and his imitators cannot be confounded with that of Norman Shaw when that master conducts himself most characteristically. Shaw's method of design, almost invariable in essentials, in matters of detail can be classed into four or five varieties. His best known and most easily recognisable work is in the 'Queen Anne' manner, but his most excellent, in the opinion of many, is that in which he developed, rather than abandoned, the Gothic tendencies of his youth. Everything he invented passed gradually into the common practice of the time, but he can hardly be said to have founded a great school, since the difference between his buildings and others resembling them, but not of his designing, is less often the difference between the work of a master and that of his disciples than the difference between valid art and mere skilful imitation. When, for example, he piled up the massive pile of a romantic design like that of Cragside in Northumberland

MAGIC

Grim's Dyke, Harrow Weald, Middlesex (1872)

(1870), he did what only he could do with such certainty in such circumstances. From whatever point, at whatever angle, this dramatic composition is viewed, its silhouette is harmonious and striking; and although such a building may seem an unexpected home for a rich engineer in the nineteenth century, reflection will remind us how characteristic of the sentiments of the time was this flight from the workshop to fairyland. Of his planning in general, it can be said that while not possessing the masterly simplicity and directness of that of Waterhouse, it was invariably ingenious and flexible, and strictly in accord with the external expression of his architecture. If the shapes of his rooms were irregular, they were so as the shapes of mediaeval rooms were irregular—for some definite reason of construction or disposition. The haphazard planning of many of his contemporaries, in which something that you would expect to find in the middle of something else comes all but in the middle but not quite, never found any toleration from Shaw. To special needs arising from special circumstances he was particularly alert, and the architectural strangeness of the block of offices he built in Leadenhall Street, London (New Zealand Chambers), in the year 1872, was difficult for men of commerce to resent, seeing that it provided a much larger window area, where light was all important, than had been provided by any of the so-called 'practical men' whom they were accustomed to employ. This building was not, as it is frequently stated to have been, the first nineteenth-century building to bring red bricks back to the City of London, but their use in the City was still unusual, and with its other accompanying peculiarities created a great deal of excitement when first the façade was uncovered. Much excitement was also caused some years later when at the corner of Pall Mall and St. James's Street, the Alliance Assurance Company built from Shaw's designs (1881) a gabled many-windowed building of gauged brick and stone that seemed to set all the traditions of its neighbourhood at defiance. The appearance of New Scotland Yard (1888) on the Embankment caused a furious outburst of newspaper protest, almost as fierce as that which raged within recent memory over Mr. Epstein's 'Rima,' and there are still people about who are very much annoyed by it. Very few buildings can please everybody, and the attitude of those who contend that the almost fortified appearance of this turreted building, with its pierced lower storeys of Dartmoor granite worked by the convicts, its barrack-like upper storeys, and its somewhat alarming silhouette, are an expression too literary and fanciful for official architecture is one that can be understood. Most critics, however, will prefer to be ranged on the side of those admirers of its talented author who chose it to bear on its front wall the memorial plaque of his features with which they commemorated his fame and their admiration.

Few of Norman Shaw's imitators came to any good, although at one time they must have had nearly three-quarters of the domestic architecture of our country in their hands. Occasionally his particular style was successfully approached, generally it was but caricatured. Of architects who shared his aims but preserved their individuality the number is great; indeed, the more serious among the British architects born in the '30's of the last century constituted a school as artistically capable and effectually cooperative as any these islands have seen. Their agreed style was a renaissance of the Renaissance, a Gothic game played with neo-Classical counters, not very different from the game that had been played all over Europe three centuries before. The nineteenth-century players were more conscious than the sixteenth-century players had been of their audience, more often tempted into picturesque poses, into displays of unnecessary virtuosity. On the other hand, they were much less gross than their Elizabethan ancestors, coached by clumsy Germans High and Low.

In common with all uninhibited artists they had no distaste for elaboration, and their chosen style, the wealth of their age, and the ductility of the materials nearest to their hand, brick and terra-cotta, made elaboration easily obtainable. Looking toward France and Italy rather than toward Germany and Holland, they produced it sometimes in fine stonework, unsparingly and at great expense. The Imperial Institute at South Kensington (1888) is the most conspicuous example of this magnificence, and has not so much a French or Italian as a Spanish flavour at first peculiar to its architect, but afterwards, proving very much to the public taste, continued by a large number of his imitators. In the Imperial Institute red-gauged brickwork is used as though it were a purely decorative material and more precious than the Portland stone of which the greater part of the walls is built. Set in the recesses of deep arches its strong colour intensifies their shadow, while narrow lines of it run horizontally across the many planes and facets of the elaborately modelled elevation, defining and emphasising their perspective. Nowhere else has gauged brickwork been used in exactly this way, a way as effective as it is original. Indeed, the whole building is a *tour de force*, combining as it does extreme delicacy of detail with breadth and grandeur in its general effect. The principal tower is extremely elegant in silhouette, admirably proportioned in itself, entirely useless for any known purpose, and disagreeably oppressive towards the remainder of the elevation.

Our national mania for towers in season and out of season has always been perplexing to foreigners, and this example in particular was criticised at the time of its building in a

HAPPY AND GLORIOUS

The Imperial Institute, S. Kensington (1888)

173

most hostile fashion abroad and even was nervously defended at home. It was rumoured, whether truly or not,
that Thomas Collcutt (1840-1924), the architect of this one,
had sacrificed for its sake the knighthood that is customarily
bestowed upon the architect of so important a public work
by insisting upon building this tower in defiance of the
disapproval of the personage who laid the foundation stone.
In London the Houses of Parliament have three towers, the
Law Courts two, the Natural History Museum has four, the
Foreign Office one, two others being prepared for but never
built, the Local Government Board offices two complete,
four in embryo, the War Office four, the new Admiralty
two, but why go on with a list that would be endless?
Plainly these useless things satisfied some national hunger,
since towers sprouted from houses almost as commonly as
from public buildings. Possibly Englishmen felt, with
Hilda Wangel in *The Master Builder*, that homes for human
beings are not inspiring enough without high towers and
pinnacles above them. Whatever its significance, the fact
remains that in the Bric-à-brac period a tower would have
been added as the finishing touch to any important building
whatever, if the architect's employer had consented to pay
for it. Nor can we be sure that it is anything but economy
that makes us so sparing with our towers to-day.

Beside the Imperial Institute, Collcutt built a great deal
of pleasant enough bric-à-brac, and was chosen as architect
for the façades and internal decoration of the English
National Opera House (1891) that so soon was to fail and
be converted into the Palace Theatre. Here his neo-
Spanish detail is executed in the terra-cotta to which its
form so readily lends itself. That the internal decoration
of this building, as it left Collcutt's hands, was such as to
remind us of old-fashioned liners, is not surprising, because Collcutt was much employed both on sea and land

by the P. & O. Steamship Company. Lloyd's Registry of Shipping in London (1900) was his work and so were innumerable first- and second-class saloons afloat.

If Lower Chelsea is the spiritual home of Norman Shaw and Edward Godwin with their style called Queen Anne, in Upper Chelsea is displayed with profusion the allied style of Bric-à-brac Renaissance. In Pont Street it accumulates at its worst, rivalling in severity the almost contemporary outbreak in Mount Street, Mayfair. Indeed, the Westminster Estate is almost as full of it as is the Cadogan, although for the style in its fullest developement the regions around Sloane Street still afford the best hunting grounds. If it tempt us to impatience, we must nevertheless avoid any unduly critical disparagement of its merits. In unskilful or in callously commercial hands it could fall to the depths in which it wallows in Harrod's Stores (1901), and in that architecturally unhappy thoroughfare, Knightsbridge. In the hands of a conscientious architect it could do great things. It is much to be wished that there were nowadays a body of men building in the streets of London possessed of the artistic ability that Ernest George, and the better among his confrères, never failed to display. To our tired eyes the brilliance and scintillation of this always exciting manner of design has become wearisome, sometimes even painful, and until our sight grows stronger we are likely to turn with relief from every specimen of bric-à-brac to the less exacting spectacles of our own day. It is remarkable, however, and chastening, to observe what a mess the present-day architect makes of it when he attempts, in adding to buildings of the Bric-à-brac period, to adapt their style to his own more prudent tastes and lowered vitality. No doubt many of the less exuberant qualities of which we now are proud are qualities well worth having; nevertheless, when London architecture left Hampstead and Bedford

Park behind it, it left behind there also something of youth and gaiety that we should be blessed indeed if we could recall.

In the Sheffield Town Hall (1890), built a few years later than the Imperial Institute, the style of that building was weakened and adulterated by an inferior architect, and in most of the municipal buildings then rising all over the country the weakening and adulteration were carried further still. In the Birmingham Law Courts (1886), a very good plan is embodied in architecture that shews how great had been the fall in a few years from the standard set by Waterhouse at Manchester. Many inhabitants of Oxford nowadays are very ungrateful to the civic authorities for the new town-hall they were given in 1892; it is difficult to see why. The building is very sensibly planned and the façade in St. Aldate's Street is well-proportioned, and catches cleverly enough the scintillating brilliance of the Italianate variety of English Renaissance, which Oxford, led by Sir Thomas Jackson, has chosen so often to reproduce. The indigestion that style now causes proves the unwisdom of ever attempting to hot it up and serve it again. The tower of the old Schools, the Jacobean tower at Merton and the strange frontispieces in the quadrangle of Wadham, had the value of rarity, until that value was debased by Jackson's and Champneys' broadcasting of their architectural idiom; now they might well strike the uninformed visitor as mere clumsy anticipations of later Victorian glory. Obviously, however, the style was one that no lover of bric-à-brac could be expected to resist, and it is hard to see what it is that makes critics who tolerate the interior of Hertford College Chapel (1875) become so very scornful when they enter the town-hall. Jackson's largest building in Oxford is the Examination Schools (1876) which exhibit in a high degree the elegance of his ornament and the ineptitude of his planning. He was a competent decorator, having a great deal of what people call 'good taste,' and considerable sensitiveness to subtleties of form and proportion. In planning, however, he never seemed able to pack more than two rooms together without crushing something and leaving something else sticking out. It is this unhappy defect of his that makes almost all his work essentially inferior to the perhaps rather slickly competent designs of the architect who built the town-hall. As a man of taste that architect may have been Jackson's inferior, but he was what Jackson was not, a man who understood his job.

In Gothic built during the Bric-à-brac period, some architects employed by Oxford and Cambridge Universities acquitted themselves well. Mansfield College at Oxford (1888) seems delicate and pretty, not only in comparison with the vulgarity of the almost contemporary Manchester College next door, but also in its own right. The Divinity Schools at Cambridge (1876) and the Rylands Library at Manchester (1890) are good examples further afield of the style we see in Mansfield College, and are by the same architect.

The front block of Brasenose College (1886), by Sir Thomas Jackson, is probably the best thing that he did in Oxford. There is nothing to tell us whether its neo-Gothic style or the neo-Renaissance style in which he designed more frequently would be his choice when he was perfectly free to do as he pleased, but it is certainly by his neo-Gothic buildings that he will be longest and most pleasantly remembered. Designed neither by Champneys nor by Jackson, however, are the two Oxford buildings in which the merits of the late-Victorian version of secular Gothic are best of all exemplified. These are the north range of buildings at St. John's College facing on to St. Giles's (1881), and the St. Swithun's quadrangle at Magdalen College

(1880). The first was designed by George Gilbert Scott (1839-1897), son of Sir Gilbert—the second by Thomas Garner (1839-1906) of Messrs. Bodley and Garner. Each in its way has extraordinary merit.

To represent secular Gothic architecture of this date chiefly by buildings at Oxford and Cambridge is not as partial as might appear—seeing that, in the general rout of the style after the onslaught of Queen Anne, it was the older universities and schools that gave it almost its last sanctuary. The brave good sense of Waterhouse and his sympathisers made a stand here and there, Gothic town-halls displaying originality of character giving place only gradually to the pretty pastiches of the prevailing fashion. The town-hall at Congleton in Cheshire (1864), being by Edward Godwin, one of Bric-à-brac's apostles, may be taken as an example of the pre-Bric-à-brac Gothic that continued to be occasionally practised and approved. In 1871 the style burst grandly into flower in the Guildhall and Assize Courts at Plymouth of which Godwin made the designs for a local firm of architects, who carried them into effect. The character of this admirable group of buildings is uncompromisingly mediaeval and rigidly logical within its assumptions. Only in the Universities did the less logical Gothic of sensibility, the Gothic of those who preferred to mingle some pleasant nonsense with their sense, linger in lay architecture, although in ecclesiastical architecture rational and sentimental currents of design flowed with equal strength.

Yet, in spite of the relaxation of Gothic rigour, it is difficult to define any group of Victorian churches that belong indisputably to our Bric-à-brac period in any respect save that of date. Holy Trinity, Sloane Street, London (1890), is a Bric-à-brac church in the sense that the fittings designed for it by its architect are in miscellaneous and entirely unrelated styles, but the general character of its design is the late mediaeval English that we shall find pervading the churches that will be referred to in the next chapter. The strange mixing in the furniture of rococo ironwork, of Italian Renaissance marble work, of semi-naturalistic carving, however, was a peculiarity not shared by many of its architect's contemporary brethren, and never became the characteristic of a school.

The churches built by Norman Shaw are few compared with the large number of buildings built by him for secular uses, but all are stamped with his idiosyncrasy. Mention has already been made of the English church at Lyons, and the church at Bingley in Yorkshire in which as a young man he did homage to Street. A worthy specimen of his later practice is the church at Richard's Castle (1891) that stands, lonely, on the Herefordshire and Shropshire borders, amidst surroundings of great beauty. No design could be devised to adorn its position better than that of this sturdy building, its masses so cleverly accommodated to the sloping ground, its outline so broad and simple. It is not very much like any building older than itself, but it is remarkably like many buildings newer—and less successful.

In the Congleton town-hall can be seen the survival of the primitive details of foreign Gothic that Street and others had popularised during the period of Victorianism in flood. In church-building these forms long lingered and were nowhere used to better effect than in the town churches, most of them what are apt to be called slum churches, designed by James Brooks (1825-1901). Bric-à-brac could hardly be expected in the slums, and all through the period during which it was flourishing elsewhere, Brooks was building simply and well churches of a character that owed something to Butterfield, something to Street, but more to his own invention. In these, of which the churches of St.

Columba (1871) and of St. Chad (1869), Haggerston, are typical specimens, all the mouldings, the tracery, the carving, that seemed to Pugin so necessary an expression of his architectural reform, are discarded by one of the latest, but not least worthy, of his disciples. This asceticism was fortunate, since when Brooks in other works attempted Gothic ornament the results were curiously jejune and amateurish, and his attempts at Bric-à-brac in the South-Eastern Hotel at Deal (1893) and in the huge stables he built in Mayfair for the Marquis of Londonderry (1882) shew him to have been utterly insensitive to values in any style but that which he had made for himself. His gaunt slum churches, and others of the same kind that are not in slums, have considerable nobility, and in their day had many imitators.

The discussion of other developements of English church architecture, contemporary with the activities of Sedding, of Shaw, of Brooks, may allowably be postponed until the next chapter, which will deal with *The Morning After*. That title is meant to connote the morning after the feast of Bric-à-brac, and, since ecclesiastical architects avoided that indulgence, in the story of their work there is no division between the time of excess and that of repentance.

THE frivolous title of this chapter would be misleading if it suggested that English architects, having tried to sleep off their orgy of Bric-à-brac, awoke in any very rueful or disconsolate mood. That their digestions were upset may be inferred from the appearance of their subsequent work, but if they had acknowledged the effect they would probably have denied the cause. Certainly for some time very few of them seemed able to contemplate with comfort any rich architectural fare, and all of them became rather suspiciously occupied with methods of design that were quiet and in 'good taste.' People as determinedly occupied as they were with good taste are very likely not to have too good a taste in their mouths at the moment. Anyway, we are now come to the time when architects began to hope that if not always artists they were always gentlemen—the age when art was praised for being refined —the age when artists fled in outraged panic from the slightest suspicion of vulgarity. Our church department under Mr. Bodley made a speciality of quiet devotional interiors in the true English tradition, our line in Quality-

Street Georgian houses went extraordinarily well, our new cottages could hardly be distinguished from the old ones drawn so prettily by the water-colourists of the day, and our educational buildings (into which class we were gradually bringing our inns and public-houses) were free from any possible offence even to the most fastidious. Of course town-halls would be town-halls, and Carnegie libraries Carnegie libraries, often most regrettably, but even public authorities and the architects serving them might be made gentlemen in the end.

When an architect of the Bric-à-brac school had designed —shall we say?—a picturesque home for a successful merchant, in a suburb or some tidier part of the country, he had been expected to go it a bit with gables and half-timber, and the result of his labours would, of course, have been described by any properly qualified house-agent as a 'replica of a Tudor manor-house.' Neither the architect nor his patron supposed for a moment that the house was anything but a new Victorian thing to suit a new Victorian man, whose personal interests were probably centred in the billiard-room, but whose daughters liked to have things pretty. The Bric-à-brac architects accordingly made things pretty—as pretty as the houses seen in the background of drawings by Randolph Caldecott or by Kate Greenaway, and a great deal prettier than the old farm-houses in the neighbourhood. All the sentimental values of old architecture were skilfully transcribed and heightened; the small panes of the leaded windows were made smaller, the cosy inglenooks cosier, the sheltering eaves more sheltering, the quaint tall chimneys quainter and taller, the broad hospitable front door broader (and probably more hospitable), than in the Doric home of the real countryman. Everything, too, would be extremely tidy, with ventilation and sanitation proudly up to date, and would be most healthily pink and white in its colouring. In short, what nonsense there was about it (and it cannot be denied that any old Englishry in a new England really is nonsense) would be delightful exaggerated nonsense with more than a touch of fantasy to keep it sweet.

Compare such a house with its counterpart in the Morning After, with the 'replica of a Tudor manor-house' as understood then, as still understood to-day! Gone is the piquant, exciting, silhouette, long level roof-lines now serving not to relieve but to echo the monotony of the land-scape. Fled are the healthy hues of youth, the orange-red bricks and the white paint, the glazed Spanish tiles lining the loggia: everything now is toned and mottled in simula-tion of age. The merchant's wife now has no pretty drawing-room; she sits in a yeoman's parlour, her smart clothes strangely discordant with her background of decay-ing tints and textures. She sits there and listens to the sounds of a dance band decanted through the linen-fold panels of her weathered oak wireless set. Really one feels that to harmonise with her surroundings she ought to have had her face not lifted but dropped.

Of course not every house of the Morning After was faked up into any show of antiquity. Of course not every Norman-Shavian house was no worse than gay. Many of the little red and white houses of our Bric-à-brac period were pert and showy, without the power of ageing into anything but shabbiness, and many of the later houses are not soft and sentimental enough to cloy. At the very beginning of his career Sir Edwin Lutyens (1869-1944) used the smart bright architectural technique of Sir Ernest George, in whose office he had worked, but soon he dis-covered that his highly individual manner of design de-manded for its proper expression the capture of sensuous charm in surface and in tint. While pursuing his charm he contrived to design better and better, and if the same had been true of his contemporaries there would be less to complain of in the general sentimentalisation of house-building that marks the Morning After. Unhappily, however, with most of them, the popularity and attractiveness of silver-grey oak and multi-coloured brick, of cottagey casements divided up with thick leads, of rough, soft, roofing tiles warped in the burning, were greedily seized, not as an enrichment of, but as a substitute for, architecture. The Norman-Shavian variations upon old themes were regarded not as developements but as mistakes, and the merchant's house lost aesthetically all of its contemporaneity, and became a not very edifying monument of a not very wholesome nostalgia for the past. Oakwork was no longer wax-polished, but was savagely attacked with wire brushes and eroded with acid. Old cottages and barns were pulled down to provide materials already stained by time; and crumbling stones that the builders ought to have rejected everywhere became headstones of corners. In short, a great many Edwardian architects became terrified of the age they lived in, and ran to ground in the burrows of antiquity.

Even when they had no conscious intention of making their houses look older than they were, they accepted without question the popular opinion that the softly blended hues and bloomy textures that years of weather bestow upon the materials of building were the only hues and textures in which beauty could be found. When putting a building into a landscape their aim was to conciliate rather than to conquer nature. The mood of the eighteenth century, dominating hill and plain with gleaming walls of imported stone, taming the meadow into the park, and spreading the park like a carpet before the portico, was theirs no longer. Nor did they ever share that other ambition of their grandfathers which had led to the heightened picturesque, to the rusticity exaggerated and artificially displayed by the *cottage orné*. All they seem to have desired was that their convenient homes with Company's water, telephone, gas, and electricity, should resemble as closely as possible the uncomfortable homes, possessing none of these conveniences, that everybody knew and loved in the clever water-colours of Mrs. Allingham.

Architecture, however, unlike dressmaking, has no very deep concern with hues and textures, desirable though it may be that the architect, besides practising his proper art, should be skilful in presenting it in a way that is agreeable in these minor respects. The church in Shropshire designed by Norman Shaw that was praised in the last chapter looks in a photograph to be faultlessly adapted to its surroundings. In reality it disturbs the soft colours of the natural landscape by walls of very yellow stone, and roofs covered with tiles that have remained shrimp-pink since the time of its building, and apparently always intend to do so. It is obviously pleasanter not to have to look at buildings through smoked glasses, and the connoisseurship in pretty materials that has developed so greatly since Shaw's day would be a matter for satisfaction if the growth of such sensibility had not been accompanied by a serious loss of enterprise in actual design.

Shaw himself, when, in the last of the houses that he built in Queen's Gate, South Kensington (No. 170, 1888), he deserted the style then called Queen Anne for the style actually used in Queen Anne's day, can little have thought that he was inaugurating an epoch in which all his past work would be, for a time, discredited; and that this house only among the many he had designed would be used as a pattern by the younger generation. It is an excellent house of its kind, possibly a little better in proportions than are most of the old houses it so strongly recalls. A more marked superiority may be found in Bryanston (1890), the great mansion, replacing a less ambitious one by Wyatt, that Shaw built for Lord Portman in Dorset. The comfort and pleasantness of this kind of house-building cause it still to be in current use to-day, and, if it seldom rise to being great architecture, it has the merit of being, in a measure, foolproof. In it unskilful proportion and clumsy detail have but a limited range of possible harm, and if a house so built is not very often worth looking at, it is almost always easy to overlook. Ardenrun Place in Sussex (1906), designed by a pupil of Shaw's, is a pleasant specimen of a country house far more modest than Bryanston, more obviously inspired by Wren than that, but of the same general character. It makes no pretence of being older than it is: it looks well already, and, given proper upkeep, should look better and better as years go on.

With such houses when they were built by Sir Edwin Lutyens the case is different, since in them he seemed often to rob the future of its peculiar charms for our present delight. No one has ever been so artful as he in the choice of attractive materials, building into the walls and roofs of his houses not only bricks and tiles but an imaginary past, an imaginary past much more amusing than any real past could have been, a whimsical, self-conscious past as entertaining as that in a drawing by Rex Whistler. The Salutation at Sandwich (1912), with its staid exterior and its elaborately scenic plan, shews his particular cleverness very well. Its design appears to be simplicity itself, as, in conception, indeed it is. The delicate adjustment of its proportions, however, would be far from simple to any artist less gifted than Lutyens himself. It is exquisitely done. The plan would bring too much drama and too little convenience into daily life to satisfy most people, but probably gave

ESTABLISHED ORDER

Bryanston, Dorset (1890)

what they wanted in the way they wanted it to those for whom it was made.

It may reasonably be held that in spite of the great merits of Lutyens' more formal designs, his special skill was never so happily displayed as in the more irregular houses with which he first made his name, and which to the end of his life he still continued on occasion to produce. Munstead Wood (1896), Little Thakeham (1902), and Grey Walls at Gullane in Scotland (1901) are perhaps the three most admired, but everybody can have his favourite where almost all are agreeable. In general disposition and in grouping, these houses are as original as those of Norman Shaw, and in ornament, also, Lutyens' invention never failed him. In the simple elements of which they are compounded, however, they are much more literally imitative of traditional English building than are the generality of houses of the Bric-à-brac period. Now these smaller elements are all that smaller-minded architects can see and mimic, and it is hard to escape the conclusion that Lutyens' domination of domestic architecture in the years before the 1914-1918 war was largely responsible for the change in ideals deplored at the beginning of this chapter. Other influences certainly tended in the same direction, but none was so powerful or so impelling. To examine one of the more potent of these influences, it will be necessary to go back a little in history and glance at the slender but significant output of Philip Webb.

Philip Webb, mentioned already as having been at one time Street's chief draughtsman, was the architect most closely associated with William Morris, the friend who most nearly realised Morris's ideals in architecture. Like Butterfield he was little affected during his long working life by the moods and fashions of his contemporaries. To think of architecture as being anything other than the sum of independent handicrafts working together in harmony would have been heresy to him, and he therefore never consented to design a house unless he himself could spend the greater part of his time on the work, shaping it as it grew. In the house he built for Morris in 1859, Street's influence was obviously powerful, and in his subsequent work that influence never entirely evaporated, despite the widening divergence between the older and the younger man's philosophies. Nevertheless, the most conspicuous characteristic of Webb's work is always its originality, and its strong personal flavour. His style owes nothing to the Renaissance, and to call it Gothic, although liable to mislead literal-minded people, is no more than a statement of fact. It displays almost always the many-paned sash windows of the conventional Queen Anne, and little of its detail may be recognisably mediaeval, though even less will be recognisably anything else. The disposition of its masses is seldom romantically picturesque. Yet always with Webb the elevation exactly expresses the plan, the architectural features exactly indicate the construction, the nature of materials dictate the forms they are made to assume, any irregular necessity is emphasised and as it were dramatised; and if all that is not to be Gothic, what is?

In nearly everything Webb did can be traced his preference for compact and bulky masses, for long ranges of similar gables, for tall, almost ungainly, windows, and for simple massive chimneys contrasting strangely with the elaborate stacks in which Norman-Shavians delighted. His constancy in the manner of his design throughout a long working life is comparable with that of Butterfield, and it is not only in that respect that an affinity between the two men can be found. If Keble College were translated into plain brickwork with all its Gothic details removed, if Webb's great house Clouds (1880) were streaked and zig-zagged with colour, the two buildings would shew a family likeness truly remarkable.

Philip Webb may be regarded as an architect only of houses, since of commercial and public buildings he designed none and he only built one church. Of his houses

THE MORRIS AFFLATUS

Standen, East Grinstead, Sussex (1892)

Clouds is the largest, most of the rest being of dimensions so moderate as to afford little opportunity for any architectural composition except the simplest. There is indeed no evidence that any complex composition was within either his ambition or his capacity. An attempt therefore to represent him as an architect of powers equal with those of Butterfield would be imprudent, and the comparison between the two men made above was in respect only of certain characteristic preferences in form that both seem to have shared. These preferences in Webb were so marked and so narrow as to give not only a strong tang of personal flavour but a valuable unity in expression to his often rather naïvely composed elevations. Any sensitive architect must feel the awkward charm and the singularity of his work, but his ultimate importance in history is likely to derive less from what he built himself than from the example that he set to others in his care for minute detail both in design and in processes of workmanship.

Eastlake, writing in 1872, comments upon such care for minute detail as a new and remarkable thing. 'The wooden architraves, door panels, staircase railings, etc.,' he says, 'which were once allowed to take their chance at the contractor's hands, or were only selected from patterns submitted for approval, have of late years become to architects the object of as much attention as the plan of a room, or the proportions of a fireplace.' This change in practice, a change which Eastlake exaggerates but which nevertheless was a real one, was probably as much due to Webb as to anybody else. That it was great can be realised now when almost every architect designs or pretends to design everything in a house down to the handrail of the back staircase; and when authorities on seventeenth-century architecture profess to see the hand of Wren himself in every drawing for woodwork submitted by a joiner for his approval. There is no real evidence that Wyatt, Salvin, Burn, or any but a very few of their predecessors or contemporaries, ever themselves drew a bedroom chimney-piece or the back stair banisters in their lives. All matters of process, too, of the pointing of brickwork, or the tooling of stone, had customarily been controlled only by a clerk of the works interpreting a conventional specification, until Webb, and, of course, William Morris, awoke their age to full consciousness of craftsmanship.

Pugin, with his inseparable builder, Myers, had got rid, though not very completely, of some of the un-Gothic glueings and sand-paperings to which woodworkers had been trained in the seventeenth and eighteenth centuries, and of some, but not much, of the mechanical exactness in tracery and carving that workers in stone had been taught by Chambers and by Adam. The tenet, however, that the mark of the worker's tool can add positive value to the finished work, a tenet that is probably based less upon aesthetics than upon sociological sentimentality, was left for Webb to propagate, and was the foundation of the whole movement known as Arts and Crafts. From this preoccupation with craftsmanship there resulted much neglect of architecture at the hands of those sympathisers with Webb who did not share his instinct for good proportion and artistic integration. The desperately earnest building for the Eagle Insurance Company at Birmingham (1900) is an embarrassing example of failure in these respects.

To the purely aesthetic pleasures in broken tints and textures that Edwardians found in the early works of Lutyens must be added the contributory satisfaction that faithful disciples of Morris found in all visual evidence of the nobility of labour. By such attraction a whole generation of architects has been enthralled, and the public has been relieved from the difficult problem of finding out what is good and what is bad design by the assurance of their instructors that if they look after the handicrafts the design will look after itself.

Naturally this came as a great relief to everybody. It is so much easier to say, 'I *do* like that brickwork' than to say,

'Those windows are badly proportioned.' It is so easy to believe that the picturesque values of old and accidental architecture are all that need be looked for in new. Very few people are unmoved by the sentimental charm of ancient buildings, whatever their architectural quality; and now, instead of saying, 'I know nothing about architecture but I do know what I like,' it became possible to say, 'I do know what I like and therefore I know about architecture. If I cannot have a lovely old house, my architect will build me a lovelier, and what looks like an older, one.'

Of course, not everybody felt in this way. Many, indeed, felt very differently, and either persisted in methods of reasonable design that they had established for themselves, or thought the time propitious for novel experiment. No mention has been made hitherto in these chapters of the constant clamour for novelty in architecture that was kept up by people not very wise throughout the whole of the nineteenth century. In High Victorian days it had been neither very important nor very influential, but in the Morning After the orgy of Bric-à-brac, it found a ready audience. As might be expected at such a time, it expressed itself in a demand for the cup that might cheer but could not inebriate—in other words, for an invigorating but essentially negative simplicity.

The extremists among Philip Webb's disciples had indeed attained simplicity of a sort. They had built cottages most primitively planned, with rooms reached only one out of the other, and with ladders instead of staircases. Such resumption, however, of the discomforts endured by the rude forefathers of the hamlet was not at all to the taste of the art suburbs, from which, as always, the cry for novelty proceeded. The class whence artists are chiefly drawn had been suffocated in the parlours of Victorian respectability, and many members of it were ready for almost any reasonable revolt from the characteristic surroundings of their youth. They did not, however, wish to go native. Bedford Park had made a nice change for them, but Bedford Park was not quite enough. Outside and in, its economical little houses still preserved an aroma of gentility, and required a certain amount of conventional living up to. People embracing the simple life, discarding boots for sandals, browsing on health foods at odd hours, and indulging in unlimited freedom of thought—and freedom of conduct as little limited as the neighbours would allow, found that even at its simplest the architecture of Norman Shaw and of Godwin cramped their style. What, on the other hand, could possibly suit them better than the unconventional little white-washed houses, bashfully virgin in their simplicity, that were beginning to be illustrated in the pages of *The Studio*, and which a growing school of earnest young architects was anxious to provide?

The leader of these architects had put his theory into a nutshell when he said that he wrote specifications chiefly in order to tell builders what to leave out; and his meticulous elimination of unnecessaries produced quite agreeable results as often as not. For the brick or tile facing then most usual in small houses, he substituted rough-cast plaster, propping up extremely thin walls, which he thus could weather-proof, by long sloping buttresses—sometimes necessary and sometimes perhaps less so. Walls and rooms alike he made as low as bye-laws would allow, and the usual complication of small roofs he replaced by large simple roofs springing almost from the ground. Windows he made of long ranges of very small leaded casements, varied by small round apertures in unexpected places. His chimneys would be high and large, surmounted by tall, thin chimney-pots. At the eaves, gutters would be projected on prominent iron brackets, the water from them being conducted often into prominent wooden water-butts. At the front door the function of a porch was likely to be served by a large flat projecting shelter, something like the tester

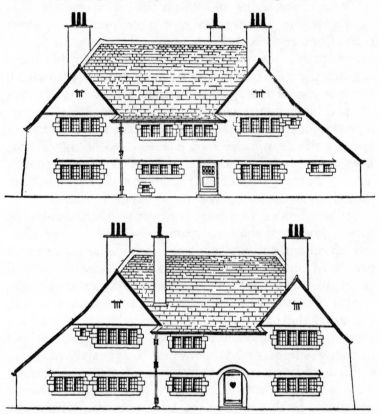

'THE SIMPLE LIFE'

'The Orchard,' Chorley Wood, Hertfordshire (1898)

of an old-fashioned bed, hung out by iron stays from the wall above. If there were any ornamental detail inside or out, it would present combinations of hearts, of straight-stemmed flowers rather like toasting forks, and of birds either perched or in flight. All external woodwork, including the water-butt, would be painted a vivid green.

There is something to be said for many of these little houses, whose disarming lack of pretension must protect them from any pedantic architectural censure. Up to a certain point, they were easy enough to design, but those that actually were the work of C. F. A. Voysey (1857-1941), the inventor of the type, sometimes possess a value that escaped his imitators. To the eyes of those who now are wearying of the recondite tints and textures of the Lutyens fashion, the clean, unaffected newness and brightness that many of them still retain will recommend them strongly. Their architectural value is chiefly negative, but the charm of their innocent unsophistication cannot be denied.

In these houses, however, furniture transferred from the former homes of their occupants would often appear extremely discordant, and even the farm-house antiques, or pretended antiques, then much sought after by tasteful suburbans, were apt to look rather guiltily experienced in surroundings so childishly artless. To furniture design, therefore, the believers in the new architecture turned a great deal of attention, and there arose in Glasgow a school of young designers who, by putting novelty above all other virtues, achieved results that surprised many and greatly pleased a few. Morris's doctrine that objects of domestic use should be shaped to fit their purposes was impetuously discarded, and a great semblance of 'originality' was procured by choosing for everything forms hitherto considered too inconvenient to be eligible. Chairs grew enormously high backs endangering their balance, legs of tables multiplied and were made of almost impossible slenderness. Legs of other pieces of furniture, such as sideboards and piano-cases, were continued up above the objects they supported

and crowned with sharp-cornered tiles of wood not unlike
mortar-board caps. Little panels of ornamental leaded
glazing were inserted in the strangest positions, even in the
heads of beds and the backs of arm-chairs. Generally, the
outlines of this decoration and furniture were rectilinear,
but occasionally the curious humps and wriggles of the
stylisation florale that characterised the textile designs of the
school invaded even the architecture. In a mitigated form
these can be found adhering even to the commercial buildings of the city in which they originated, and their flavour,
faint though it be and disguised, can be detected in two
amusing façades put up about this time in Sloane Street,
London (Nos. 63 and 64, 1897).

The sources of this remarkable Glasgow fashion, though
not directly traceable, arose probably in the workshops of
Morris's art-craftsmen, in the textile and fictile designs of
Gallé and Grosset, in such escapades of Gothic rogues as the
Free Library in Ladbroke Grove (1890), and in the drawings of Aubrey Beardsley. Certainly the architectural
drawings by Charles Mackintosh (1868-1928), the typical
man of the movement, contain much rather childish imitation
of the superficial elements in Beardsley's style. The work
of the Glasgow School was greatly appreciated in Germany,
where it joined forces with the remarkable architectural
salmagundi known and execrated in France as '*le style
munichois.*' Concurrent with it in England was a thin stream
of imitation of the experimental French work that was to
blossom into the '*Art Nouveau*' of the Paris Exposition of
1900. Of this the Horniman Museum at Forest Hill (1901)
may serve as an example. With these eccentricities must
not be confused the rational novelty of such rare designs
as that of the pair of houses built in Palace Court (1890)
by J. M. Maclaren (1843-1890), an architect of very high
ability who died young. That this remarkable work should

be so little known is a sad proof that novelty, when it is rational rather than sensational, obtains scanty recognition.

In the next chapter dealing with the architecture of the

ESCAPADE

Free Library, Ladbroke Grove, London (as first designed) (1890)

years since the end of the 1914-1918 war we shall find among other curious things erupted by that upheaval from the lower strata of our recent history, some Germanised versions of the Glasgow products that are now being eagerly gathered up by collectors of the curious. At the moment our view is bounded by the year 1914, when the fads and fancies of the *Simple Life* school and of the Beardsleian decorators still lay buried beneath many layers of subsequent fashions. English domestic architecture in 1914 was sharply and almost exclusively divided between the formal neo-Georgian derived originally from Nesfield's Kinmel and from the later practice of Norman Shaw, and the discreetly picturesque, conforming more or less to the Bric-à-brac ideal as seen in the cold light of the Morning After. What Shaw's architectural descendants were doing in England was being done, with a difference, in Scotland by a small band of architects whose Shaw had been Sir Rowand Anderson (1834-1921) and whose Lutyens Sir Robert Lorimer (1864-1929). Both in England and in Scotland formal 'Georgian' character had percolated downwards from the large houses in which it originated to even the smallest suburban home of the business man, often capturing by this minification the demure charm of the doll's house. Houses whose character was intentionally picturesque aspired to that quality by means rather of style and of surface texture than of any romantic or irregular composition. Almost all, of either type, were very well and conveniently planned, and were more apt to be symmetrical than not. If at this date domestic architecture was neither very exciting nor very progressive, its general reasonableness and convenience went far toward justifying the boast frequently made—that in this department of design England led the world.

Chapter VIII

THE EDWARDIAN RECOVERY

IF England, at the opening of the present century, boasted, with some justice, that she led the world in the design of dwelling-houses, such a claim on behalf of her more elaborate architecture was never made and certainly could not have been supported. Frequent competitions for the designing of municipal offices had served to improve the general standard of planning such buildings, but the example of Waterhouse had still not yet completely prevailed over the haphazard and artless methods surviving from the age of Bric-à-brac. The municipal offices built in that age at Leicester (1875) followed very closely the sober architectural style Nesfield had displayed at Kinmel, but in this respect were not generally imitated until later. The municipal buildings (1891) surrounding and embodying the old town-hall at Bath, and the Chelsea vestry-hall (1885), shew a retrogression that at their time was considered an advance; they turn their back upon the modernism of the Nesfield developement and mimic the foibles of the eighteenth century as exactly as their author, John McKean Brydon (1840-1901), knew how. It is obvious that had he

been as competent as Sir William Chambers he would have
built as Chambers built, without any variation. His largest
work was the Local Government Board Offices in Whitehall
(1898), executed more or less in accordance with his drawings after his death. It can leave no doubt in our minds that
he thought much more highly of Chambers than Chambers
would have thought of him.

Not many of his contemporaries, however, played for
safety as he did. Most of them boasted openly that the
style in which they cast their works was 'freely treated,' as
indeed it was. The London Sessions House (1907), or the
New Bailey, as it has come to be called, is truly characteristic of the period, of its wealth, its insufficient scholarship,
its professional competence, its fundamental insensitiveness.
The Lambeth Municipal Buildings (1905), (locally in Brixton), are the result of an architectural competition unusually
large and hotly contested, and combine considerable merits
in planning with elements in design that we may not yet be
far enough away from to be able to judge fairly. In truth
the juiciness (there is no other word for it) of this prosperous
period of English architecture is not very much to our taste
to-day, and the many ambitious works in which it is displayed should be brought up for judgement fifty years hence
rather than now.

In the designs of one architect only does this Edwardian
Municipal style always seem to justify itself. It seems
improbable that admirers of Edwin Rickards (1872-1920),
that draughtsman and designer of exuberant fancy, need
fear that any change of fashion will degrade his works from
their supremacy over others of their time. Of the many
proud and handsome buildings arrayed magnificently round
the public park in the city of Cardiff, none surpasses
the first to be built there, the City Hall and Law Courts
(1897), with the designs of which Rickards had won a public

competition. The assessor in this competition was Water-house, who, no doubt, may have found the rich large-featured 'all-out' character of Rickards's drawings rather hard to swallow. He recognised, however, what we can recognise still—the admirable planning, the masterly grouping, and the brilliant detail in these remarkable conceptions, and English architecture owes to his wise award two of the most entirely satisfactory specimens of monumental architecture that municipal enterprise has yet called into being.

The most sumptuous of Rickards's executed designs is that of the Wesleyan Central Hall at Westminster (1905), the first and best form of which had to be modified owing to special requirements of light and air in the hospital which stood opposite to it. In the competition for its designing only two of the competitors had the good sense to make the great hall visibly dominate those subordinate parts of the building that were intended to be let out for commercial purposes. Rickards not only had the sense to do this, but to do it very impressively and well. Everything indeed that he built has extraordinary merits of one kind or another. The Deptford town-hall (1902), with its clear and simple plan, its admirably proportioned architectural treatment, and the charming nautical flavour of its ornament, stands high among cognate buildings of all ages.

Contemporary with the Local Government Board Offices in Whitehall was the new War Office, a building also carried out by the Office of Works from plans made by an architect who had lately died. Little can be said in its praise; indeed, in comparison with it the Local Government Board Offices can claim some honourable distinction. The two taken together are historically significant in marking the return of English civil architecture to the European neo-Classical convention, but not, alas! to that convention as refined by

Cockerell and by Pennethorne. In them English architects can merely be seen rethumbing the primers that architects elsewhere had long outgrown.

When we lament the great inferiority of all the buildings we have just been examining to contemporary work of similar character in France, we must remember that in that country the Roman lamp of Vitruvian architecture lit at the Renaissance had since been carefully tended and never extinguished. At the École des Beaux Arts the accumulated experience of generations concerning such technical difficulties in design as how to combine columns with undiminished pilasters; how to get the Doric entablature round a corner; what may be the appropriate height for an attic storey; how far balustrades and rustications should be kept to a human scale and how far they should be proportioned to the main order of the façade; all this experience was handed down from teacher to pupil, so that, if the pupil chose to experiment, he experimented with his feet on solid ground. Even more important in the curriculum of the École des Beaux Arts, always has been, and still is, the study of order, rhythm, and logic, in planning, and the cultivation of sound sense and reasoning skill in construction. To say that all this in England had been lost at the time we are considering would not be true, because something of it survived Victorian emotionalism, and much of the rest of it we have never had. Cockerell was an architect whose work in its intellectual quality was on a par with that of his great French contemporaries, but Cockerell stood alone, Pennethorne coming far enough after him for no great interest to be expected outside England in his work. It may be that little in the elaborate mental equipment possessed by Cockerell is indispensable for the production of good architecture, but much of it is indispensable for the production of good neo-Classical architecture; and this is what English architects of forty years ago could hardly be expected to understand. Training in the less severe schools of Gothic and of Bric-à-brac had accustomed them to look at architectural form rather with the eye of the scene-painter than with that of the scholar.

When the architect of the Local Government Board Offices drew his design, it is obvious that his aim was rather to produce a building that might have appeared in an agreeable painting by Samuel Scott than to join up with the living European tradition of monumental design. Architecture to him and to his contemporaries was as much a sketch-book affair as it had been in the Gothic Revival, only that now the sketch-books were full not of Chartres and of Amiens, of Winchester and of Beverley; but of Hampton Court, of Somerset House, of Greenwich Hospital, and of the City of Bath. In moving on from the thirteenth century, viâ the seventeenth century of the Bric-à-brac merchants, to the eighteenth century of Gibbs and of Chambers, English architects remained as far from their own nineteenth century as ever before.

When, therefore, the proprietors of *The Morning Post*, having lost their old offices in the clearance necessitated by the formation of Aldwych and Kingsway, built new ones (1903) from the design of a Parisian architect, the accomplishment displayed in that design naturally seemed to shew up cruelly the defect in much native work that had contented us before. Soon the same architect taught us another lesson in the Ritz Hotel (1904) and another again in the Royal Automobile Club (1909). Not that in any of these three buildings there was any pronounced novelty: in fact, they were, by the Parisian standard, unusually, and undesirably, stylistic, the ornamental forms in all of them being closely reproduced from those of the period of *Louis Seize*. Yet here was work of one born to a manner we were painfully acquiring, of one whose *savoir faire* made his English friends look distressingly awkward and inexpert. Designing like this could only be learnt at school, where most English architects at that time had been—shall we call it privately educated?—by the uncertain method of pupilage.

During the years of the *Entente Cordiale* English architects had learnt to admire French proficiency as displayed in France, but had never foreseen, or perhaps desired, its invasion of their own country. The Gothic Revival had produced work that of its kind no other country could equal. Architects and public alike had tired of that, and had now come, by stages, to another kind of work in which it seemed that they could equal nobody else. Presumably what French architects could learn to do with such certainty English architects might eventually learn to do as well; but where were they to be taught and who was to teach them? Schools of a kind existed; but not of a kind to meet the situation, being but evening schools staffed by professors trained in the old ways and incapable of teaching the new.

The change of method in architectural education in this country, begun with the reconstitution of the Architectural Association School in London and the foundation of that in the University of Liverpool, and resulting in the almost universal school-training of to-day, has produced results good and bad, expected and unexpected. Much has been said, and much remains to be said, of what has been gained and what lost by the revolution. The only relevance of the subject here, however, lies in the reminder it affords that all the would-be neo-Classical architecture of the late-Victorian and Edwardian period was designed by individual architects having no collective knowledge of the difficult style coming back into fashion. Remarkable buildings such as the Cardiff Hall and Courts, the additions to the British Museum (1905), and the Institute of Chartered Accountants (1890), were indeed

EXPERTISE RECOVERED

North Front of the British Museum, London (1905)

produced, but produced sporadically by lonely artists working under disadvantages that only a restored tradition and systematic education could remove. The Institute of Chartered Accountants may be regarded as a key building of the period, seeing that it was received with great acclamation, and that its conspicuous peculiarities were very widely imitated. Peculiarities, indeed, of all sorts were welcomed by those who, galled by the yoke of neo-Georgianism newly imposed upon them, wished, with the romantic egotism of their age, that every man should make his designs notably different from those of every other man.

To find the designs most influential in the shaping of distinctively Edwardian monumental design we must, however, turn from municipal architecture to that which it is customary to class as commercial, and observe what it was that kept Norman Shaw so busy in his old age. The formation of Aldwych, to which was due the rebuilding of *The Morning Post* offices, had also involved the destruction of the old Gaiety Theatre, and a new Gaiety was to rise at the corner of the new street. For the general design of that street a competition had been held, but was so badly mismanaged as to come to naught. Meanwhile, the naturally impatient proprietors of the theatre submitted a rather disagreeable design of what they intended to build if nothing happened to stop them. Thus confronted, the London County Council, although abandoning any detailed control of buildings upon the new sites, shewed that it was not prepared to relax all discipline, and accordingly refused to allow this important corner to be occupied by the theatre as it was proposed. After a good deal of negotiation, the Council eventually agreed itself to contribute an important sum of money toward the building of the theatre, provided its exterior were designed by the veteran Norman Shaw, then retired from the ordinary practice of his profession.

George L. Raine, Ph.D., Ph.D.

Shaw's design (1902), when it was made, did not fit the building very well, the elevated colonnade which was its chief feature coming mostly above the roof of the actual building; but the design, for all this, was carried into execution by the architects whose own design Shaw's had replaced, and as a piece of street scenery has ever since been generally admired.

A little later in point of time, the part of the quadrant of Regent Street that adjoined the site of the old St. James's Hall was destroyed together with that building, in order that a large hotel fronting both into Regent Street and Piccadilly might be erected upon the whole site. Here again it was made a condition of consent to the rebuilding that Norman Shaw should design the façades, it being further stipulated that what faced Regent Street should be part of a general design with which the whole of the quadrant could eventually be brought into conformity. The general design made by Shaw (1905) was magnificent, and the fragment of it that consisted of the façade of the hotel was carried out immediately. That fragment, however, proved so costly and unpractical that, as everybody knows, it was never continued; the quadrant being afterwards completed to a more convenient but relatively ineffective design by an inferior architect.

Considered purely scenically, these two products of Shaw's vigorous old age have a robust splendour that no man could capture who was not a great architect. When he conceived them it was already fourteen years since he had encased a country house near the Roman Wall in Northumberland with grandiose architecture of very much the same kind, so that his latest manner of design must be regarded as considered, and as no result of passing impulse. Nevertheless, not even his gusto and bravura can obscure the fact that he was playing a new game of which he was

VICE NASH

The New Quadrant, Regent Street, London (1905)

too old to learn the rules, and playing it in a boisterous and extremely dangerous way. That many other architects joined in the same game has been a great misfortune for London, and for some provincial cities as well; since the rusticated pillars, the enormous carved swags of fruit, the screen colonnades, the violent projections and recessions of surfaces, if tolerable when conducted by Shaw, when imitated by other people have proved to be perhaps of all architectural vulgarities the most distressing. For example, the architects upon whom his collaboration was forced in the Gaiety Theatre produced afterwards, on their own account, two of the worst caricatures that exist of Shaw's latest style, an office building in Storey's Gate (1910), and an Assurance building at the north-east corner of St. James's Street (1907). Hardly a provincial town is without caricatures little less offensive. What in Shaw was insouciance in his apes was usually crass ignorance, and although it is possible that future critics may find in this clumsy misuse of classical material some of the alleviations we now allow to Elizabethanism, it is hardly imaginable that tolerance of them will ever verge upon admiration.

In former chapters it has been convenient to make a special class for educational buildings, but here no class of the kind will be necessary, seeing that when the large-featured neo-Classic of the Morning After was applied to such buildings it was seldom recognisably different from the same style in its civic or in its commercial variety. Even at Oxford the School of Chemistry built in 1913 has a façade differing little from what in its day might have served for the municipal offices of a small provincial town. In the residential buildings of Oxford colleges, the orgies of Jackson and of Champneys seem to have been followed by no morning after, but rather by a deep coma. At Cambridge, the customary neo-Tudor was subjected to some

curious and pleasing modifications in new buildings at
Caius College (1903), and at Emmanuel College (1912).
The great group of buildings for Christ's Hospital School
(1894), near Horsham in Sussex, are agreeably designed in
the same modified convention, beside being very well
planned and laid out. In London, board-schools changed,
as might have been expected, from pure Bric-à-brac to
pure neo-Georgian, and this is true also of most educational
buildings throughout the country.

In short, taking secular architecture as a whole, it may
be said that in the years immediately preceding the 1914
war the general aspect of English architecture had become
remarkably uniform, broken only by isolated experiments,
of which some proved sterile and others bore no important
fruit until later. Before, however, this chapter can be
brought to a close, there is much ground to be made up in
the story of ecclesiastical architecture, since, although in
that the developement cannot be synchronised with the
actions and reactions to be noted in the secular field, yet
in one as in the other, during the period of the Morning
After, there was calm after stress and a greater degree of
unanimity than in earlier more troubled years. Church-
building, however, was no longer the guiding architectural
activity of the country. This it really had been while
Victorianism was in flood.

It may seem strange to have deferred until now any consideration of the work of John Loughborough Pearson
(1817-1897), an architect of great attainments and reputation
who was only Pugin's junior by five years. The reason for
the anachronism is that it was only at the end of his life
that Pearson became a leader, excellent as was much of the
work that he had already done, first under the influence of
Pugin and later under that of Street. In the slender proportions of his Puginistic church built at Weybridge in

1849, in the sumptuous elegance of his Street-like church at Dalton Holme in Yorkshire, built in the early '60's, the strong flavour of the man is equally apparent, but it still was a personal flavour, and not the flavour of a school. In his last phase, however, beginning with the church of St. Augustine, Kilburn (1871), and ending with the church of St. Patrick, Birmingham (1896), his designs are so representative of what was most congenial to all neo-Gothicists before their style was deposed that it is allowable to place them here. George Frederick Bodley himself, although a younger man, must appear here by a similar anachronism. Both Pearson and he had done excellent work all through the long reign of Street, but it was not until that master was in his grave that they attained their full influence and importance. Both had been early in turning from foreign models to those of our own country, and, from the works of theirs that are the most characteristic, it would be impossible to guess that they had ever been abroad in their lives. In this particular, Pearson's cathedral at Truro (1878) stands in strong contrast with the cathedral built by Burges at Cork, of which mention has been made in a former chapter.

In matters of style Pearson's preference appears to have been for Gothic of the thirteenth century, although on occasions he adapted to his use the forms known as 'Perpendicular.' Among his contemporaries he stood alone in his almost invariable practice of covering his churches with some form of fire-resisting vaulting whenever money could be found to pay for it. In the design of such vaulting he had no equal, a statement that even a superficial study of his churches will corroborate.

Bodley, on the other hand, worked most frequently and most naturally in a style very near to that which had been recommended as a *point de départ* by the Puginists, and seems often not to have desired for his buildings any covering

ENGLISH HISTORICAL

Truro Cathedral, Cornwall (1878)

more permanent than a wooden roof suspending an arched ceiling finely carved and painted. The church of St. John at Cowley, by Oxford (1894), that of St. Augustine at Pendlebury near Manchester (1877), and those at Clumber in Nottinghamshire (1886), at Hoar Cross in Staffordshire (1871), and at Eccleston in Cheshire (1899), are representative examples of his sensitive and fastidious manner of design.

In the design of ornament Bodley shewed greater accomplishment than Pearson, and gained by it as many admirers as by his architecture. As a colourist, also, he had a great reputation, although one difficult now to account for. He delighted in brownish tones, and if compelled to retain existing stained glass by Pugin or Wailes would coat it with umber glaze. His decoration as a whole is hardly as inventive as had been Pugin's, but surpasses it in what Victorians called 'refinement'; and what is thought of it will depend upon what is thought of that quality. It certainly has another quality, that of harmony, which it would be wrong to belittle.

Pearson had few close imitators, except in matters of unimportant detail. The particular style of Bodley, on the other hand, was very faithfully mimicked, both by his many pupils and by others with whom he had had no personal encounter. It satisfied completely the aspirations of those who believed that the road to national sanctity lay through the older public schools and universities, guarded by Anglican scholarship from the intruding errors of Geneva or of Rome. It was not exactly what the Ecclesiologists had hoped would emerge from their campaign; they had intended something a little more popular, a little more at home in the slums, a little less aloof from the 'progressive' temper of the day. But it was they who were responsible for it, it was they who had long-drawn the aisles, had storied

REFINEMENT

St. Mary's Church, Eccleston, Cheshire (1899)

the windows, had segregated the surpliced clergy and choir in screened enclosure, had converted the draped table into the vested altar, and had turned the eyes of architects back to a style that had proved harder to develope than to imitate. Things might not have turned out quite as they expected, but in the result there was much more to rejoice over than there was to deplore.

Whatever be our verdict upon Bodley's ornamentation and colouring, there can be no doubt that in both he was immeasurably surpassed by John Francis Bentley (1839-1902), whose rare and delicate talent in neo-mediaeval design, although plentifully exerted in the furniture and decoration of churches, found regrettably few opportunities in their architecture. In the exquisite and wonderfully original altars and other furniture that he designed for the church of St. James, Spanish Place, London; in the no less beautiful chapels he added to the Redentorist church[1] at Clapham (1883), in the marblework, woodwork, metalwork, and stained glass he was constantly devising, to be placed too often in buildings unworthy to contain them, the fourteenth and nineteenth centuries meet in a peculiar perfection of its kind unprecedented. Of the few complete churches for which he was responsible all are very good, that of the Holy Rood at Watford (1887) having strong claims to be considered the most lovely church the nineteenth century gave to England. Nothing in it is quite like anything seen before, but nothing in it could have been made what it is without an affectionate understanding on the part of its creator of the achievements and experience of his forerunners. Bentley's great cathedral at Westminster (1895) is well known as a work of extraordinary beauty and grandeur, and as a model of permanent construction; of construction, that is to say, without the assistance of metallic reinforcement. Its architectural character was

[1] Our Lady of Victories.

PERFECTION

Church and Presbytery of the Holy Rood, Watford, Hertfordshire (1887)

intended to be generally Catholic rather than particularly western or eastern, mediaeval, or modern. Its plan was to be congregational, its fabric massive and lasting. Its whole internal surface was to be veiled by an unbroken sheet of coloured and glittering mosaic.

In its external ornamentation an interesting experiment has been made. A mosaic-lined church vaulted domically, as this one is, inevitably awakens associations with Byzantine art, but in that art there is no convention for external architecture that could be appropriately applicable in the atmosphere and surroundings of a London residential quarter. A new convention, a nonce-style, has therefore been created by Bentley in which the neo-Renaissance procedure of his time has been, as it were, infused with Byzantine suggestion. Sometimes it seems that he is expressing Byzantine notions in Renaissance language, sometimes Renaissance notions in Byzantine; the balance is delicate and delicately maintained. Earlier in the century, French eclectics such as Ballu had made of neo-Gothic and neo-Classical elements a mixture very different in strength and consistency from the mixture made of them at the Renaissance; in the Bric-à-brac period the architect of Holy Trinity Church, Sloane Street, had thrown them together without any attempt at mixture or even conciliation. None had done as Bentley did, none other than he had succeeded in fusing distinct architectural metals into a smooth indissoluble alloy. Opinions may differ concerning the necessity or the wisdom of the experiment, but there can be nothing but agreement as to the skill with which it has been conducted.

The unhappy severance in England during the nineteenth century of the professions of architect and engineer was either a cause or a symptom of the misfortune that neo-Gothic architecture and adventurous engineering ran in parallel courses and never joined their streams. Side by

CONSTRUCTION PARAMOUNT

Cathedral Church of the Most Precious Blood, Westminster (1895)

side in the St. Pancras railway station the architect painfully roofed the booking-hall with cautious stylistic timberwork and the engineer lightly threw across the railway shed the broadest roof of glass and iron that then existed in the world. The proposition that the language of Gothic architecture was nothing more than engineering formally emphasised, although acknowledged in principle by every disciple of Pugin, was never in England developed into a practical philosophy as it was in France by Viollet-le-Duc. English neo-Gothic architecture, therefore, although wonderfully strong and logical in the hands of men of strong and logical intellect, in the hands of intellectual weaklings was disastrously subject to whims. Of these there was a serious epidemic early in the present century, betrayed in such symptoms as battered walls, arches with dropped centres, windows trisected by buttresses, hugely haunched gables, seaweed tracery, unexpected mouldings and still more unexpected absences of mouldings, unlikely materials put to unlikely purposes. The rankest forms of these proliferated in nonconformist chapels outside the law, others less gross insinuated themselves (with the connivance of the then architect to the Ecclesiastical Commissioners) into the joints of Pearson and Bodley's stronghold and reduced its security. Neo-Gothic began to play to the gallery.

A staunch and able defender of the style's honour was Temple Lushington Moore (1856-1920), skilful and responsible as a constructor, poetical and imaginative as a designer. His preferences were as English as those of Bodley, whom he equalled in resource and in vigour surpassed. His work, although what would now be described, and by silly men decried, as 'traditional,' has the true novelty of unprecedented excellence in its kind, a kind admittedly circumstricted by his sympathies and his descent. Wherever a church of his may stand, it is impossible to forget that its designer was a Yorkshireman. It is impossible to forget this when inspecting his noble church of All Saints in the London suburb, Upper Tooting (1909). It would be impossible not to remember it with reverence when admiring his magnificent addition to the architectural glories of his own countryside, the church of St. Wilfrid at Harrogate (1905).

All the later churches of Pearson, and of Bodley, all the churches of Moore, accord very much better with what at the moment is considered to be good taste than any designs by the equally competent architects of the generation preceding theirs. This, of course, is only natural, seeing that they have not had so much time as the others have had in which to get out of date. That the sort of building these men delighted to produce, with its masonry finely designed and sympathetically executed, with its sober colouring, its graceful proportions, and its careful avoidance of all vulgarity and violence, is an excellent sort cannot be denied, and that Moore's designs in particular shew great force and freedom in the new handling of old forms is obvious. Nevertheless, the material they handled always is old, correctly mediaeval, and unadventurous, and we cannot look back from it with anything but regret to the days when Butterfield and Street, their heads full of adventurous fancies, eagerly took toward novelty and developement steps their successors made a point of re-tracing. All that these successors could teach to their disciples was good taste, and the history of art has shewn, here as always, that in the not very long run, the wages of good taste is death.

For, in its old form, the Gothic Revival is now as dead as Queen Anne, and any hope for its future must be based upon its possible reappearance in a form changed to suit changed methods of construction. In so far as the limited kind of utilitarianism which is called 'functionalism' is art at all it is Gothic art, and although at the present time there are signs that 'functionalism' will soon be forgotten, much of its instruction may prove to have been a useful preparation for a newer and a truer faith.

Chapter IX

THE END OF AN
EPOCH?

IN a published criticism of an exhibition of architectural
designs held in 1923, two drawings by Charles Rennie
Mackintosh, appearing rather unexpectedly at that date,
were described as 'curiously old-fashioned.' So they were
regarded then, because those young enough to discover
Mackintosh as a novelty were still too young to go to
architectural exhibitions. To students of architecture the
name of Mackintosh was certainly not unfamiliar, but that
his work should be represented in an exhibition of contemporary architecture was disconcerting, as disconcerting
as would have been the announcement of a new comedy
by Oscar Wilde, or a new drawing by Aubrey Beardsley.
What is called 'period value' had not in those days been
acquired by productions of the 'nineties, and it was even
difficult to obtain recognition for the merits they possessed.
They seemed 'curiously old-fashioned' to most people,
and to many people little else.

We need not be concerned at this moment with the
worth or the triviality of Mackintosh's designs; what
concerns us lies rather in their peculiarity. Now, in peculiar

architecture, whether it be good or bad, the peculiarity is all that the unphilosophical critic will see; and, if it be unfamiliar to him, it will stimulate or depress him according to his idiosyncrasy. If it stimulate him, he will often seek to justify his interest in it by claiming as its cause some value not aesthetic, such as that of courage, of originality, or of truth. Of what to him is a pleasant invigorant he makes a medicine for the age. The age takes it, feels perhaps a little better; and then loses faith in it. In a later age the same medicine, forgotten and rediscovered, may have a second vogue.

Immediately after the armistice of 1918 English architecture certainly seemed to need a dose of something. Many nostrums were tried and none given a fair chance. Most of them were stale, having lain packed up and forgotten during the years of war. Some were fresh but not very wholesome. It would probably be wrong to see in this sick striving after health the result of the four dreadful years that preceded it. Both the sickness and the striving can be detected in most of what Englishmen had built since the opening of the century. They were symptoms not specifically post-war but specifically post-Victorian. And even in Victorian days their incipience can be plainly traced.

There is now an easy belief proclaimed that Mackintosh, George Walton (1867-1933), and the others of the Glasgow group were disregarded clairvoyants; that during a long period of neglect over here their visionary germs were cultured abroad in a gelatinous 'ismus,' that the European war stirred the minds of our architects to discontent with their former productions; until a new courage, a new originality, and a new truth, popped conveniently out of the laboratory bottles. On such a thesis the resumption of our survey at the year 1918 after four years' interruption by war, might have been a turning of the hopeless dawn of a Morning After into the dawn of hope in a New Age. There is no evidence, however, that the Glasgow group had any prevision of the new methods of construction that afterwards retrospectively gave meaning to some of their meaningless innovations, and it is rash to claim that the laboratory culture of Glasgow peculiarities abroad resulted in anything more important than amusement. No doubt the war stirred the minds of English architects; but their minds had not generally had enough to do with their architectural productions for those to be visibly affected. When the war ended, English architecture began again very much where it had left off.

It has been contended in these pages that the experiment and vitality of the late-Victorian orgy of Bric-à-brac were ill exchanged for the prudence of a *fin-de-siècle* Morning After that, accordingly, the architecture of the Imperial Institute is much less negligible critically than that of the new War Office, and that the style of Norman Shaw's Chelsea and Hampstead is much more vital than that of the later revivals of pure Georgianism in old Westminster. From this point of view a whole villageful of modern Cotswoldry could be bartered with advantage for a stylish little house by Shaw, Nesfield, or Godwin; and the 'quiet good taste' of the tired Edwardian smells badly of decay. Decay not necessarily of architecture as a whole, but of one aspect of it, of that aspect toward which Victorian eyes were almost exclusively turned, and from which nowadays the eyes of many are deliberately averted.

The conception of architecture as a game played with pieces of construction, a game in which the movements of those pieces are governed only by their aesthetic significance, is as old as Roman engineering with its veneer of pilaster and entablature. In the Roman game and its Renaissance replay the pieces of construction were obviously conventionalised and unreal; pilasters being representations—sculptural representations—of columns, and not real columns walled in; applied pediments and entablatures representing, but never simulating, the gables and eaves of non-existent roofs.

The Victorian game differed essentially from the Roman in that the pieces were not tokens but realities. Whereas the Roman had manœuvred his pilasters, his pediments, his entablatures into pleasing combinations on the surface of a postulated construction, the Victorian compromised with his construction to produce combinations of gables, of chimneys, of wall surfaces that, if not postulated, were certainly at the back of his mind from the first moment he occupied himself with his design. He thought always of his building, not as a thing whose proper shape he should emphasise and adorn, but as a thing upon which he must impose a shape conformable at the same time with convenience and with his preferences in picturesque arrangement.

In his excellent book, entitled *The Picturesque*, Mr. Christopher Hussey, with admirable acuteness of analysis, has found in the direction toward this quality one of those changes of helm by means of which the course of all arts has been diverted, and the latitude of human creativeness permanently increased. In picturesque architecture and gardening the laws governing bi-dimensional design within a frame are extended into the boundless world of tri-dimensional reality; solid objects are marshalled and composed so as to present to the eye patterns similar to those the painter would make with his representational symbols. Now, this is a thing that no Chinese, no Egyptian, no Etruscan, no Greek, no Roman, no Byzantine, no man of the Middle Ages, ever dreamt of doing. To all of these a building was a building, as incapable of consciously aesthetic pose as was an animal. The symmetry and grace of an animal it might emulate; often, too, it might be jewelled and clothed, but it never would sit for its portrait. In it the painter must find his picture where he could, nowhere would there be offered to him a picture already conceived and artfully arranged. In it the picturesque where it occurred would be purely accidental.

The architects of the Early Renaissance in Italy went to the other extreme, and attempted to build the architecture that the painters of the time had imagined. Architects of the generation succeeding theirs put an end to the experiment, and returned to the realities of building, under Sanmicheli and Peruzzi. Of Baroque architecture, when it arrived, the character was sculpturesque rather than picturesque—a distinction of great importance, but one not needing elaboration here; since in Palladianism, in neo-Romanism, in neo-Grecianism, and even in the earliest neo-Mediaevalism, both the picturesque and the sculpturesque ceased to be objective points in architectural operations. In the architecture produced by these movements no contrivance was made of any such effects as those that the painter or the sculptor extracts from the chances of Nature.

For the genesis and growth of picturesque architecture and gardening reference must be made to Mr. Hussey's account: here we are concerned with their dominion and their decay. The title of this chapter, *The End of an Epoch?*, finishes with a question-mark, since it may be that the end is further off than now seems probable. If, however, any essential change is really taking place in English architecture to-day, that change is almost certainly due to the decay of the Picturesque; and if any governing character has unified the English architecture we have reviewed already, that character was due, unquestionably, to the Picturesque's former dominion.

Architects who learnt their trade early in the twentieth century will remember being told that they ought while designing a house to test their work at short intervals by outlining it accurately in perspective. 'Only so,' they were warned, 'can you be sure that your chimneys will *tell*— that your roofs will compose into a good mass.' If your chimneys refused to tell, and your roofs remained uncomposed, you were to dodge your plan about until they saw their way to becoming more amenable. 'Keep it low' was another common counsel to the house-designer, 'and get all your windows as far as you can from the corners.' It was also desirable to prolong the main roof downward over a porch or what not, to 'get a good sweep.' Most of this advice still is good enough, if houses are to be regarded primarily as subjects for conventionally pretty pictures. Many people will see no strong reason why houses should not be so regarded, if the comfort of their inhabitants be nowhere compromised. A large number of young people, however, does see very strong reasons indeed why such a standpoint should be ridiculed and made untenable, and this conviction of theirs suggests that we may very well be coming to the End of an Epoch.

In the twenty years between the two last wars, Picturesque house-building certainly strengthened the case of its opponents. Whatever the little houses that lined our new roads may not have been, they were undeniably picturesque in intention, composing their features in studied grimaces toward the passer-by, and expressing their real feelings only at the back. Special characteristics in Art can often be apprehended most easily in caricature, and the architectural perversions in modern speculative building can be exceedingly illuminating to the student of their origins. What Lutyens did yesterday, Jerry will do to-day; with a difference wide enough to separate success from failure, but too narrow to establish a distinction in kind. Since the decay of neo-Grecianism at the end of the Regency, almost all our domestic architecture has been in the same boat, steering with an unwavering though often faulty course toward pictorial effectiveness.

One of the earliest actions of Picturesque doctrine was to discard bilateral symmetry, which thenceforward, during eighty years or so, became a quality rare in domestic design. If Palladian elements occurred in a Victorian house they would, no doubt, be symmetrically disposed, since with conventional pieces it is hard not to play a conventional game. The idea, however, of making a symmetrical arrangement with humble things like cottage gables and outhouses, of balancing water-butt with water-butt, is a defiance of Picturesque principles which—although differing essentially from the unforced regularity of Regency farm-houses and inns—betrays, nevertheless, a tendency away from pictorial toward purely architectural design. However pictorialised by the method of its portrayal, bilateral symmetry, in itself, is essentially unpictorial. Such symmetrically designed houses, therefore, as that with which Mr. Curtis Green won a *Country Life* competition immediately before the first war, as Lutyens' house, earlier in date, at Knebworth (1901), as the prize-winning design in the much publicised competition for small houses at Gidea Park (1910), marked a highly significant retreat from Picturesque practice.

High Picturesque, however, is not concerned only with design and composition, but also with qualities of colour and of texture. Broken colour and varied texture have proved so especially suitable for representation by the painter that they have come quite naturally to be seen by our painter-suckled generation as especially 'artistic.' Those to whom 'artistic' means beautiful are certainly wise in indulging while they can their pleasure in spottiness and shimmer, until a popular acceptance of the standards of Cézanne or of Van Gogh shall have made the 'artistic' the definite and the crude. Where public taste is allowed its influence in matters of texture and colour, Picturesque preferences are likely to die harder and more slowly than in matters of form and composition, since in matters of colour and texture very few people have any taste robust enough to be independent of fashion. At the present time it is not unusual to see the jazz architecture of the cinema façade carried out in bricks 'multi-coloured' and mellow enough to be worthy of the old-time golf club at its richest and best. There is sentimental inconsistency in this, but not necessarily any aesthetic fault. At Oxford, the tender colouring of walls and roof in the new buildings of Lady Margaret Hall is probably as much admired now as was the untender colouring of the walls and roof of the New Museum seventy years ago; every age is entitled to its fancies. But, whereas that of the New Museum would certainly never have been imitated by utilitarians opposed to Ruskinism, that of the building at Lady Margaret Hall would cause no surprise if it reappeared in a severely 'functionalist' motor garage.

These two characteristics, then,—the importation of bilateral symmetry into simple rustic constructions and the intensification of the search for soft, pretty, tints and surfaces,—are the only novelties prominent in most English house-building between the two last wars. Planning changed in its details, but not in its general character; the small new houses of our country still remained what for some time they had been—the most comfortable of their kind in the world. Often, too, they were highly agreeable to look at, and it is very seldom that they were offensive in any marked degree. Large houses in great number were pulled down; the number of large houses built was very small.

In the last chapter but one a house by Lutyens at Sandwich, and a Sussex house closely modelled upon the so-called 'Wren' house at Chichester, were mentioned as examples of the houses of moderate size that it has become customary to cast in the style of the eighteenth century. The plan of Lutyens' house was romantically theatrical, the plan of the other house was prosaic and convenient. Externally both houses were fashionably anachronistic, the Sussex house designed with sense, Lutyens' house with great sensibility. The output of architecture of this kind was large, much of it—and that not the worst—being provided by firms of decorators without any external assistance. If it was not completely Picturesque in character, it certainly had not enough logical aesthetic in it to qualify as neo-Classical. Although it suggested another age than its own, and gave little scope, normally, for Fancy, it fulfilled the material needs of the life for which it was designed, and made for that life an agreeable background. In a form emaciated by the last war, it is with us yet.

The adjective *neo-Classical* is one that may be interpreted variously, but hardly so as to include this souvenir style of semi-Picturesque Georgianism. In France, where the aesthetic science of architecture has been pursued continuously since the Renaissance, and Picturesque irrationality continuously eschewed, its intended meaning could be conveyed by the simple word *architectural*. *Architectural* means to a Frenchman all that the Wesleyan Central Hall at Westminster is and that Church House is not, all that the Radcliffe Camera at Oxford is and that the old Schools quadrangle is not, all that Buckingham Palace is and that St. James's Palace, through successive alterations, has ceased to be. It means, in two words, logically organised.

Neither Church House, nor the old Schools quadrangle, nor again St. James's Palace, is a building strictly *architectural*, which is not to deny that Time in its mercy has given charm to the last two of them and in due course may give it to the first. All possess, in different degrees, the power of giving pleasure by pictorial suggestion, having agreeable parts whose most serious short-coming is their lack of inter-relation. Inconsistence has never been objected to by followers of the Picturesque, content as they are if an archi-tectural design can be pictorially integrated in the vision of the beholder, whether or not it be integral in itself. On the other hand, inconsistence, to believers in the *architectural* —or 'neo-Classical'—faith, is fatal to serious art.

In the ten years preceding the last war, architecturalism—organised architecture, that is to say—was much reviled by young and enthusiastic utilitarians. In this it is now clear that they were barking up the wrong tree, having mistaken their enemy. Architecturalism as it was embodied in the teaching of the École des Beaux Arts was absolutely prac-tical and rational in method, although based, no doubt, upon aesthetic and moral hypotheses that material utilitarians would reject. Agreeing to differ upon these, the neo-Classicist and the utilitarian should have been able to work harmoniously along parallel lines, each accepting as axio-matic that all architectural ends, whether aesthetic or physical, must be attained by means that are logical and direct. What every logical utilitarian should violently abhor is not the neo-Classical but the Picturesque. The Picturesque that flouts reason, that entertains caprice, that hastily and half-heartedly makes terms with necessity and then abandons itself to unregulated fancy. The Picturesque that when it charms and delights us does so in a way the utilitarian must regard as monstrously unfair.

If, as many young people believed twenty years ago, and as many middle-aged people believe now, both architec-turalism and the Picturesque were about to be completely vanquished by utilitarianism, it would be little worth while to analyse the contrariety of moribund philosophies. Upon the better grounded supposition that architecturalism, in some form or another, must survive as long as civilisation, that the Picturesque has no guarantee of long-continued approval, and that utilitarianism is an aesthetic negative which will die out of art when its work of destruction is accomplished, it is necessary to lay stress upon that contrariety which in domestic architecture may not always be very easy to descry. In the more spacious field, however, of the architecture commonly called monumental it seldom can escape us.

Consider for a moment such a building as Somerset House. Here is architecture in which the painter may delight, but not that in which the architect's pre-occupation has been pictorial. The plan is nobly and appropriately disposed, and the elevations follow naturally from it. All the Palladian details that contribute to its design are obedient to their nature, and arranged in accordance with the conventions they were invented to serve. So natural, so inevitable does everything in it appear that Sir William Chambers's function almost seems to have been that merely of an accoucheur, assisting at the happy delivery of a child of Architecture.

Contrast with Somerset House the picturesque new London headquarters of the Midland Bank in the City of London (1926). What is that temple up in the sky? Why is it up there? What is its dome for? Ah! The painter could tell you, but not the architect. Lutyens had to set back the upper storeys; the Building Act required it. This necessity suggested a picture to his mind, a very romantic picture most sensitively conceived. So he built the picture in solid stone, and built it with real rooms and real staircases and real lifts and real lavatories all packed away somehow inside it. He did just what Norman Shaw had done in the Piccadilly Hotel and the Gaiety Theatre, just what Decimus Burton had done in the Arch at Constitution Hill (for there are rooms packed away inside that, also), just what most English architects of the nineteenth century who were outside the Gothic camp had done, amid general applause that only now is abating.

The pictorial value of Lutyens' buildings is outstanding, no other architect of his time having equalled him in poetic imagination or happy ingenuity. His productions are, perhaps, less truly architecture than they are scene-painting; or, rather, scene-construction, he having had a sculptor's skill in the management of masses 'in the round.' Less exuberant and whimsical than those of the Baroque period, his buildings have a vitality and inconsequence that are Baroque in essence. The offices of the Anglo-Persian Oil Company in Finsbury Circus (1920) shew him at his most entertaining, with their (entirely false) suggestion of palatially rich upper apartments supported by a grim substructure of store-rooms and apartments for slaves.

The gulf separating Lutyens from his imitators can be measured by a comparison of his Midland Bank with the huge blocks built by the Imperial Chemical Industries in Westminster (1927). These shew, as most of Lutyens' larger buildings also shew, a close if miscellaneous derivation from the style of Wren, but the pastiche is not happy. They may be noted, however, for a peculiarity that steel constuction has lately made frequent in urban architecture. When the maximum height that is allowed for walls abutting upon streets has been reached, the addition of further storeys is allowed, if they be set back from the frontage line. Formerly these storeys were customarily contrived within sloping roofs, but nowadays it has become more usual to face them with vertical walls supported by girders inside the building.

PIRANESI IN FINSBURY

Britannic House (Anglo-Persian Oil Company), Finsbury Circus, London (1920)

Architects are therefore now able to produce the surprising appearance of a small building standing upon the roof of a big one, an ability that is exploited at the Midland Bank with aesthetic success. In its occurrence in the buildings for the Imperial Chemical Industries no aesthetic success can be claimed for it, and the excuse of necessity may be doubted, because the frontage faces the Thames, where restrictions upon height ought not to have been unsurmountable.

For tall or tallish buildings, whether set back at the top or not, the Americans have evolved a sort of neo-Roman style that has become to them an accepted symbol of high finance. This architecture or near-architecture, whichever we may decide that it is, has been brought to a pitch of rare perfection by the multiple firms of architects that supply the needs of American commerce, and has generally proved beyond the scope of architects having only English experience. That an Englishman should have produced single-handed a specimen equal to America's best is undoubtedly gratifying, although the flawless magnificence of Martin's Bank at Liverpool (1926) may evoke in us admiration unmingled with affection. This building is a remarkable one, displaying great technical accomplishment on the part of its designer, and, now that it seems certain to be the last of its sort, can be praised without anxiety. Whatever may be true of its class, this particular specimen is no near-architecture, but architecture itself, excellently planned and consistently worked out in all its elaborate and variously derivative details.

Nevertheless, in these exploitations for commercial purposes of ancient Roman magnificence, the ridiculous stalks closely behind the sublime, especially when to architectural richness is added any elaboration of figure-sculpture. 'Take,' says Mr. Massingham in his book *London Scene*, 'the National Provincial Bank in Prince's Street. It

is crowded with allegorical heads and figures. Lady-
mermaids grasp cornucopiae. They appear to be land-
mermaids because they have tails of leaves and fruit emerg-
ing from their night-dresses, and they appear to be women
because they also have feet which stand on tasselled
cushions. Night-gowned gents in buskins and Phrygian
caps grasp keys.' Mr. Massingham is perfectly right in
thus describing classically allusive sculpture dumped in a
London street, in describing it, that is to say, as the man
in the street must see it. He has missed the best joke of all,
which—can it be believed?—is a figure of Britannia placed
between two other ladies personifying the higher and the
lower mathematics! Nobody is going to bother about
what any of these tiresome pomposities signify, nor will
anybody but the least sophisticated be favourably impressed
by the large amount of money that must have been wasted
upon them. If the purpose of external walls in a city building were to display figure-sculpture and to keep out the
light, those of the National Provincial Bank would be hard
to better.

The designers of Early Victorian banking houses, and of
those few earlier banking houses still that have come down
to us, avoided display, and emphasised the appearances of
security and of solidity. Hoare's Bank in Fleet Street
(1830) remains to remind us of an admirable class of buildings most of which have passed away. The old Westminster
Bank (1837) was a particularly good specimen, its simple but
dignified façade being the work of no less an architect than
Charles Robert Cockerell. It has unfortunately now given
place to a successor grander in size and pretension, but
wearing a second-hand style of which the best that can
be said is that it is still quite serviceable.

To the deliberate architectural restraint that marked the
old private bank, a quaint provincial flavour had been

added by Norman Shaw, when in his building for Messrs. Baring (1881) he had brought red brick up to the City of London. In this he had several belated followers, some straggling as late as the eve of the last war. The material can hardly be said to be more suitable to the place than tweed breeches and cap would be as a City man's attire, and it is certain that these buildings, pleasantly coloured when new, will get dark and ogreish with smoke, as Shaw's early block of offices in Leadenhall Street has done already.

If the new upper storeys of the Bank of England (1925) had been built in red brick they could hardly have appeared more discordant with Soane's classical work below than they are made already by their incongruous and ignorant design. To the outrage done to what of Soane's masterpiece has been allowed to remain it would be pleasanter to make no reference, but the undertaking, in virtue of its size, requires this minimum record.

The elegant and appropriate branch house of the Westminster Bank in Piccadilly (1927) may be taken to represent the best among the many buildings of the kind that have arisen during the twenty years before the last war in the streets of all our large towns. Few were as good as this, although English bankers appeared generally to be paying a more consistent attention to architectural elegance and propriety than had been their wont. In this design, the top storeys are typically picturesque, providing a loggia the first object of which is obviously appearance rather than use. This we know with our minds, but to our eyes the loggia appears so disarmingly usable that we can fancy it not to be an 'architectural feature' but a necessary cunningly architecturalised. May we not therefore sharpen our distinction between the architectural and the picturesque by deciding that, whereas in the architectural the aesthetic result must spring ultimately from a normal necessity, in the Picturesque an abnormal necessity may be feigned in order to justify an aesthetic result? *Normal* and *abnormal* may seem question-begging words, and the distinction in which they are here implicated cannot, no doubt, be exact or indisputable. Nevertheless, even without any exactitude of application, it can be truly said that the formulas of Palladio and Vignola, upon which all neo-Classical architecture is based, admit of only those inutilities that are natural extensions of normal utilities, whereas, in architecture primarily pictorial, a pretended necessity can be aesthetically justificative of any inutility whatever.

Looking, for example, at the house of the Auctioneers' and Estate Agents' Institute in Lincoln's Inn Fields (1922), the votary of the Picturesque might satisfy any scruple of reason remaining in him by making believe that the top floor was occupied by people unusually sensitive to the glare of the sun, and therefore that on that floor, and on that floor only, the persienne shutters that appear so surprisingly upon the elevation were needed for utility. The architecturalist would be less imaginative and less easily satisfied. To him an exceptional need of shade in one part of a building ought to be a root factor in the whole design, and not merely the occasion for a happy makeshift with wooden shutters. To tack on a few wooden shutters without any need would, of course, never occur to him. This unobjectionable little building was one of the first to be awarded the Royal Institute of British Architects' medal for the best London building of the year, and therefore shews the kind of thing that a reasonably representative jury considered, in the year 1924, to be especially worthy of encouragement and honour. Obviously in that year the official architectural outlook was still pictorial.

The competition for the design of the London County Hall was decided before the first war, but the building, partly redesigned after the architect's appointment, was finished only a few years before the second. It can, therefore, allowably be instanced here as an example of the monumental Picturesque on a really large scale. The excessively scenic recessing of the middle of the river front in a concave semicircle had no rational genesis beyond that of the occurrence, in the original design, of a similar recessing on the opposite side of the building. This recessing had there been necessary in order to embrace a circular council-chamber. When it was decided to put the council-chamber elsewhere, the semicircle seemed too good to lose, and so it was trotted round to the front. Thus is the Picturesque begotten. The truth should also be told about the enormous chimneys that break through the roof so dramatically, in a way that might cause anxiety as to the adequacy of that central heating system upon which the comfort of the L.C.C. staff normally depends. The anxiety would be needless because the chimneys contain very few flues, the major part of the interiors of most of them being occupied by convenient stairs giving access to the top for purposes of repair.

While unnecessary chimneys, apparently, were things to be simulated at Lambeth, at Buckingham Palace the dissimulation of necessary chimneys that existed is said to have been one of the principal preoccupations of the architect responsible for its refronting (1913). The Palace in its old form was certainly very disorderly at the top, and to conceal its irregularities by means of a lofty mask was certainly an effectual way of making it tidy. Another pretext, no doubt, for falsely heightening the façade was the height of the memorial that had been placed in front of it, by which the old building had become dwarfed. Furthermore, the front that Blore had designed on the Prince Consort's instructions was built of perishable stone, which alternate coats of paint and London dirt had made unsightly. It was of very respectable architecture, however, with the proportions and placing of the windows well adjusted to the surrounding wall-surface. That these window-openings could ever be reconciled with an entirely different ordonnance must have seemed improbable to any architect, yet the unpromising task was attempted by one well known for his experience and common sense. The whole thing had to be done in a hurry, and the result, to those who pass it in a hurry, may seem tolerable. Such deformities, nevertheless, as the false centering of some of the windows between the columns, the crushing of the central arch by the balcony above it and the disagreeable proportions of the middle and flanking features, are distressing consequences of a cavalier treatment of neo-Classical obligations, such as never could have occurred in the first house of any land in which neo-Classicism was generally valued and understood.

For, let there be no mistake about it, neo-Classical architecture never has been generally valued and understood in England. Our Wren and our Lutyens, our Hawksmoor and our Rickards, our Vanbrugh and our Norman Shaw have had great powers of poetic imagination, and have achieved results that have more than compensated us for the havoc wrought by their imitators. But the steady accumulation of aesthetic experience at the disposal of all, the systematisation of architectural good sense, the communicable skill of a continued tradition, which were Italy's and France's gift to civilisation in the century after the Renaissance, which still persist in France,—these have never come among us to stay. Chambers and Adam we have had, men of skill and learning; Soane and Cockerell, men of invention and masterly resource. Each has won a success almost entirely personal; none has succeeded in raising a stock company of trained artists or in securing a critically intelligent body of patrons. The eighteenth century gave us many tasteful carpenters dancing to the pipes of a Burlington or a Dean Aldrich; the nineteenth, many skilled purveyors of Grecianism à la Smirke or Italianism à la Barry. But in giving us these it gave us no more. In our Gothic Revival our native genius shone brightly, although Time has quenched it now to a murky flicker.

At that movement's close we rushed into the neo-Classical, in rabble formation, flying the banner of the Picturesque. Gradually since then we have been organising ourselves; slowly since then we have learnt that, of two alternatives equally eligible by Taste, Reason may shew one to be right and the other wrong. All the would-be monumental architecture described in this chapter has been less aimless and undisciplined than our productions of the same kind forty years ago. If all such monumental architecture is coming to an end, ours will perish less ingloriously than it would have done had it perished earlier. If any of it is to survive, ours may yet attain equality with that of countries continuing the main European tradition.

From that tradition such public buildings as the town-hall built at Beckenham in 1927 are already not at all remote. Indeed, the planning of this Beckenham town-hall is as good from every aspect, practical or aesthetic, as any country could produce at the present time. Its exterior, with the exception of the useless but customary tower, is rational and appropriate. That it should be extremely unrhetorical is not unfitting in what is merely a block of offices, albeit municipal ones, with a council-chamber unavoidably buried in its midst and therefore not architecturally expressible. The St. Marylebone town-hall (1914), begun before the first war and finished after it, piles on the Corinthian agony very competently; but in a way that the present

242

generation feels, probably rightly, to be incongruous. English *mairies* contain no magnificent *salles de mariage*, English mayors have but few ceremonial duties. The chief civic building of a town or suburb should, no doubt, be something better than workmanlike, but gorgeousness is out of place in a Rates Office, grandeur ridiculous in the department of a Borough Surveyor.

A curious symptom of the utilitarianism becoming fashionable in the nineteen-twenties may be detected in the extravagant praise accorded to the offices of the Ministry of Pensions [1] at Acton at the time of their building. In the design of these offices it is difficult now to see any particular merit other than that of discretion, of keeping out of trouble. The proportions of the windows are not noticeably well adjusted, the design of the doorways pretends but fails to be expressive, there is nothing remarkably good about the cornice, and nothing else that can be remarked at all. Yet the negative virtues of this unassuming piece of architecture evoked a chorus of praise as loud as it would have deserved had they been positive: criticism, in rejoicing that so much had not been attempted, failing to perceive how very little had been attained.

In Commercial Architecture, recent neo-Classical designing has a record far less stainless than in Municipal. Regent Street is fortunately a horror by itself, having been perpetrated, under the authority of a body now happily reconstituted, in a style thirty years behind its own time, and bad at that. Kingsway (1905—), though earlier in date, contains architecture more advanced and of much better quality. Africa House (1920) is a fair to good specimen of an unadventurous street façade that could not hurt a fly. Further south there are other buildings that within their convention are both original and stimulating. It seems so certain, how-

[1] Now called 'Government Building.'

ever, that in commercial architecture the end of the neo-Classical epoch is approaching, that no time need be wasted in gloating over the moribund. No commercial offices can have too much natural light, and now that steel frames have made light-obstructing walls unnecessary, an architecture depending upon wall surface for the display of its characteristics cannot long survive.

For many-storeyed shops and showrooms it is now becoming increasingly recognised that internal wall space is more valuable than apertures admitting natural light, which is seldom strong enough to make artificial light unnecessary. The ultimately logical architecture for them would therefore be not all-window but no-window, as in the latest building of the Galeries Lafayette in Paris (1936). This theory, however, has not yet been put into practice in England, where it still is frequently assumed that a building resembling a conservatory will be convenient for mercantile use. Selfridge's (1908) was partly built before the first war, but its design must be remembered here as a temporary compromise that once looked as though it might prolong the existence of Commercial Grandeur, Old Style. By this compromise steel stanchions, cased as columns, were allowed to appear unencumbered for exactly the height customary in stone columns of the same diameter, but for no more. If that height were three storeys, then three storeys of the building were adequately lighted. Above that, however, the stanchions had to disappear and burrow through a horizontal band of stonework made to resemble the architrave, frieze, and cornice, that masonry columns would have supported. In the storey behind this band, lighting became precarious; such windows being engineered in the frieze as architectural conventions would allow, and the deficit of necessary light made up by skylights.

Disingenuous and partly ineffectual as this compromise

was, it was extremely popular for a time, and has furnished most of our English towns with chaste and classical temples for the supply of dry goods. It certainly fitted the necessities of its programme better than such uneasy adjustments of traditional Georgianism as the first of the new shops built in Kensington High Street by Messrs. John Barker (1924) (on the north side), or the Bond Street scent-shop (1922) built in American collegiate Gothic, and crowned by a flèche containing a tubular carillon. Upon Messrs. Liberty's Tudor indiscretion (1922) it is kinder not to dilate.

In London streets, nowadays, most of the buildings that are not shops and offices are hotels and blocks of flats. If the new Cumberland Hotel (1932) by the Marble Arch did nothing else, it shewed us how grateful we ought to have been for the new Devonshire House (1924); just as the new Devonshire House seemed, when it was built, greatly to enhance our appreciation of the Ritz. The Ritz most elegantly suggested American taste in Paris, Devonshire House American taste on the loose. The new Cumberland suggested something on the loose that was neither American nor tasteful. The designs of the two older buildings were purely architectural, that of the Cumberland impurely architectural.

That of the new Grosvenor House (1926) on the other hand was purely Picturesque. Seen from Hyde Park, in twilight or a fog, the outline of its box-like towers is as romantic as it was intended to be; indeed, like many unbeautiful people it has its moments. No doubt the stone architecture that creeps round its base has its moments too, if infrequent. The tall little windows of Georgian pattern that puncture the building's surface are not convenient for buildings of this class, in whose small rooms one such window will often prove insufficient, and two excessive.

Even where two windows together do not give too much light, the piece of wall between them casts an undesirable shadow in the middle of a room. This disadvantage had been recognised as early as the end of the eighteenth century, and had been counteracted by the invention of the 'Wyatt window,' the broad opening containing a large pair of sashes flanked on either side by a small one; and it is curious that most neo-Georgian flat-builders should have rejected this improvement. The new flats that line one side and a half of Portman Square (1928) have these same narrow windows, as indeed has the majority of the flats built in recent years. Otherwise, the Portman Square flats are very fairly representative of the better buildings of their sort, having no positive vices and many negative virtues. The virtues of Stratton House in Piccadilly (1927) are positive and exceptional, and, if many of our new street buildings were as good as this, London would soon become a handsome city indeed. Here the windows are of a sensible shape.

Collegiate architecture moved slowly, and the account of its progress given in former chapters needs little supplement in this. Bristol acquired a large new university (1915) in the conventional Gothic that might have been expected at any time during the fifty years preceding its erection; the building is remarkably sumptuous, and presents the curiosity in planning of a square tower poised over part but not all of an oblong hall of entrance. The Cambridge School of Agriculture (1919) was housed in buildings of agreeable appearance, by the architect who had lately behaved himself equally well in additions made to Somerville College in Oxford (1933). These buildings, together with the important university this architect had built at Nottingham (1922), were in a more or less picturesque version of the neo-Classical manner that for so long had been banished

POLISHED URBANITY

Stratton House, Piccadilly, London (1927)

from architecture of the kind. The same is true of the new buildings at Clare College, Cambridge (1924), and at Lady Margaret Hall, Oxford (1931), the former of which was very much to the taste of its time and received loud applause. The new University Library at Cambridge (1934) was arising in a curious form which was watched with mingled hope and anxiety.

In Church architecture surprising developements had begun, but the normal practice shewed little change of character. Bodleyan Gothic struggled manfully on in the Church of the Annunciation, near the Marble Arch (1912), and then seemed to disappear. Only its window tracery remained, like the grin of the Cheshire cat, in some clever simplifications of its type, such as the interesting church of St. Saviour, Acton (1930); and soon even that faded from sight and memory.

In the main, however, the churches that were not professedly original harked back to a round-arched style strongly recalling the Romanesque. The church of St. Alphege at Bath (1929) is an example of this kind that is unusually stylistic, but also unusually agreeable. In the new Western Avenue leading from London there stood for some years an excellent church, St. Catherine's, Hammersmith (1923), in a similar style but of much greater simplicity. Its shape on plan was an aisle-less, unbroken rectangle, large enough to contain the whole congregation in sight of the high altar.

This elementary shape, discarded indignantly as Hanoverian by the early Ecclesiologists, was actually less far from the mediaeval ideal than they thought. Long experience of ancient churches whose aisles had been closely pewed after the Reformation led later Protestants to suppose that worshippers in the Middle Ages were expected to hear Mass without necessarily seeing the priest; to kneel contentedly behind pillars and screens listening to a distant murmur from an unseen altar. The supposition is almost certainly untrue. The naves of mediaeval churches were commonly large enough to contain all the congregation present at any one Mass, aisles and transepts being used only occasionally, and then for other purposes. The body of such a church as St. Catherine's, Hammersmith, is therefore a logical descendant of the mediaeval nave, shorn of its subordinate accretions. Nevertheless, a nave upon such a scale, with its proportionately high walls and its roof of wide span, costs more money than an aisled building of the same area with narrower roof and lower walls. Economy, therefore, has often dictated a return to the Victorian subdivided plan, the inconveniences of which have by competent architects been skilfully minimised.

St. Matthew's Church at Clubmoor near Liverpool (1928), built with the same neo-Romanesque impetus, has merit exceptional enough to claim mention. It is the work of a young architect who has later distinguished himself in designs of a less stylistic character. The exterior of St. Matthew's is very good of its kind, and the interior something better even than that. Few modern churches can shew any furniture in the same class with the original and delightful baldacchino over the high altar, a baldacchino whose design is traditional enough only to throw into strong relief the originality of its treatment in detail.

Neo-Romanesque has not proved to be a fashion in church-building likely to last any longer than has the picturesque neo-anything in secular architecture or indeed the ecclesiastical neo-Gothic, already a thing of the past. It may be bold to date the death of the Gothic Revival within the years in which the central tower of the Cathedral Church of Christ at Liverpool (1925) was beginning to rise, and yet that date appears certain. Of that Liverpool

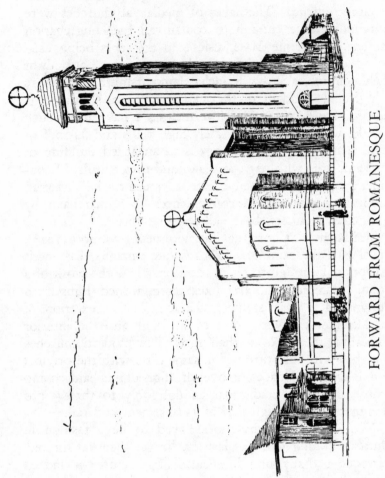

FORWARD FROM ROMANESQUE

St. Matthew's Church, Clubmoor, Liverpool (1928)

GOTHIC DRAMA

Cathedral Church of Christ, Liverpool; Central Tower (1925)

cathedral passing mention has been made already. It is a scenic prodigy, displaying the great imaginative power of its designer, and producing upon many spectators an emotional effect of extraordinary intensity. It stands aloof from architectural reality, having neither the functional nor the constructional inevitability of the ancient buildings whence its forms are ultimately derived—it is either a great engine of emotion or nothing. Those susceptible to its spell need not, indeed should not, disenchant themselves by any attempted exercise of criticism. It has not the guarantee of permanent enjoyability that more rational architecture may hope to possess; for much in it that gives pleasure no justification would remain should that pleasure ever be wanting. Nevertheless, it has permanence as the memorial of long and arduous labour on the part of an architect exceptionally sensitive to the tastes and aspirations of his contemporaries, and permanence also as a memorial of the lofty aims of countless able artists who, in three generations, spent their efforts in the service of Romance. Perhaps the tremendous tower that now crowns this great building may become of romantic architecture the venerated last resting-place.

THIS book has hitherto been concerned with the architectural 'all that' to which many young people wish
to say an impatient good-bye. It has hinted that by
doing so incautiously they may find that they have said
good-bye to architecture. Discriminating between the
architectural and the *picturesque*, it has suggested that it is
against the *picturesque* that youth's real grievance lies. The
mood of the malcontents has been referred to as 'utilitarian.'
Now, between the architectural and the utilitarian there
is no enmity—merely order of precedence. In buildings
made for the service of man, architecture begins where
utilitarianism leaves off, endowing practical contrivance
with aesthetic significance. This does not mean putting
ornament on to plain engineering, a mischievous proceed-
ing against which the new Lambeth Bridge (1928) should
prove a sufficient warning. It does not even mean coaxing
plain engineering into agreeable combinations of form,
cleverly as this has been done in the new Battersea Power
Station (1928). It means rather that the processes of con-
triving and of making significant should be interwoven,

one with the other, in the performance of one man, and should be simultaneous and inseparable.

The concocter of the picturesque contrives for use, and prettifies his contrivance whether successively or simultaneously; he conceives his task to be that of reconciling use and elegance rather than that of being useful elegantly. Sometimes his attempts at reconciliation are efficacious enough; but, more often, what he produces would obviously be more useful if it were less elegant, or more elegant if less useful. These unsatisfying results of his method are so common as to warrant that method's condemnation despite its occasional efficacy. If those who feel the need to hit something would hit the prettifiers no one need wish to restrain them. Unfortunately, with misdirected aim they are apt to hit not the prettifier but the architect on the head, and might, if they had their way, exterminate all whose senses are quickened to an art that ministers to perceptions finer than the mere recognition of the serviceable.

The irresponsible assailants of architecture have here been spoken of in the present, seeing that much that still is said and written about buildings is tainted by a doctrine that to architecture spells death. That doctrine, called 'functionalism,' belongs to the past, although to a past so recent as to be chiefly included in the period with which this chapter is concerned. Functionalism may be regarded as a close architectural analogue of Puritanism, with its insistence upon moral values, its distaste for aesthetic values, its righteous slow-wittedness, and its abhorrence of gaiety. Like Puritanism it offered the consolations of assured virtue to those whom a naughty world might otherwise abash. It was built upon three major assumptions —that every requirement of structure or of use could be perfectly met in one certainly best way; that that way, being perceived as appropriate, was bound to please; and that a building thus pleasing came necessarily into the category of architecture. With the second assumption, the assumption that what works well looks well, a conditional agreement can be given, but the others are contrary to experience and good sense. Hardly any two purely utilitarian engineers have ever constructed even the simplest thing in the very same way. If building that is merely suitable is to be called architecture, what word is left for building which is intentionally expressive of emotion?

Functionalism was first preached in England by Professor W. R. Lethaby (1857-1931) many years ago, but enjoyed no vogue until it was restated more recently by M. le Corbusier, and by him put into practice. M. le Corbusier himself has never definitely said that he wishes his buildings to be regarded as architecture; indeed, the title of his well-known book, *Vers une Architecture*, suggests that he modestly regards himself and his disciples rather as indicators than as performers. The agreeable appearance of some of his constructions may be a reminder, salutary to many, that architecture is no more necessary in everything that is built than melodious structure in every sentence that is spoken. A house need be no more aesthetically significant than a motor-car; mere utility can fully justify the one as well as the other. The mistake of the Functionalists lay not in limiting their ambition to utilitarian building but in calling utilitarian building Architecture.

Although the theory of Functionalism was Lethaby's and therefore English, it nevertheless seemed for many years as though the country of its origin was the only part of Europe in which it never was to be put into practice. If in Lethaby's own strange buildings all was done for convenience and nothing for looks, the convenience must have been that of the builder rather than that of the occupier. In estimating the worth of such theories as his, it is important not to lose sight of the distinction between functionalism concerned with the means and functionalism concerned with the end. The first requires that a thing should be made in the simplest and most effectual way, the second that the thing itself should be the simplest and most effectual satisfaction of the need it is to serve. The first regards the functions of tools and materials, the second regards the functions of what the tools and materials are used to make. The first was practised by Lethaby and his followers, although without any acceptance of the new tools and materials peculiar to their own age. The second they seldom faced squarely, being content for the most part to build conventional but seldom convenient buildings in a convenient but unconventional way.

Most of the architecture described in the last chapter was not even Lethabitic, being neither simply made nor satisfactory for use. Confronted with office-buildings so under-windowed and over-sculptured, with houses so disingenuous and artfully pictorial, with churches so vaguely and timorously traditional, it was natural for would-be reformers to dream of a brave new world full of up-to-date architectural machinery perfectly adapted to every need of daily life. Not until they tried to translate their dream into reality was it borne in upon them that the needs of daily life are exceedingly difficult to define. If you wish to take from the artisan his prim parlour, from the city clerk his Tudorish grill-room, from the ageing siren the becoming half-light of her pretty boudoir, from the cinema haunter his splendour of incongruous marble and gilding,—if you wish to sweep these away and plunge their possessors into a clinical bareness, flooded with ultra-violet rays, you must be a reformer not of architecture but of humanity. The young architect will often try to be that, neglecting his proper job for one in which he is unlikely to have any special competence.

The architect's proper job is to find an aesthetically satisfying way of supplying wants not ideal but actual, and
although he may modify those wants by persuasion he
seldom can safely force the pace. The more docile supporters of Functionalism have been successively induced by
their prophets to count among their daily needs a large
number of strange things supposed to be for their good—
they have needed slippery ramps instead of staircases, they
have learnt to thrive only in houses lifted airily on stilts,
they have realised the turpitude of sitting on chairs that have
any back legs. Never do they seem to have been obstinate,
to have still required ramps after staircases had been dis-
covered to be better for them after all, or to have suffered
when floors were lowered to the ground again and deprived
of aeration. These docile supporters, however, have not
been very many in number, and the world at large has done
what the world at large always will do when assailed by
-isms and movements and reforms. It has adopted what
amuses it in the results of a theory to which, as to all
reforming theories, it has paid no attention at all.

Of the functionalism concerned with fitness for purpose
the results that amuse the world at large are those that
eliminate conventions with which the world at large is
already beginning to be a little bored. The new starkness
made a nice change from our too prettily upholstered past,
and novelty is always entertaining. At the Ideal Home
Exhibition the specimen houses began all to go modern,
and the public fancy was greatly tickled. The theoretical
designer might storm at the public and accuse it of missing
the point of his work. The public would reply sweetly
that it preferred to miss the point of his work, but rather
liked it all the same. Should the theorist, however, try
to push this little advantage, and recommend his mass-
production, his standardised dwellings, his communal

amenities, his efforts would be quite otherwise received. The public would then obstinately persist that whatever anyone might say, it did like its house to be 'different.'

In fact, the disgusting truth from the young reformer's point of view was that in the best of English domestic architecture there was little in the way of convenience that needed reform. The discomforts tolerated in new houses abroad have with us long been banished, and the step from the comfort of Welwyn Garden City to that of a suburb designed by le Corbusier would to most unreformed people be a step backward. On the other hand, many of the forms popularised by the Functionalist are a genuine enrichment of the architectural vocabulary, and although few of our designers yet have employed them with the skill of a Lurçat or a Mallet-Stevens it would not be fair to judge their capacities by many utterly undesigned buildings to which 'modernism' gives countenance. The new hotel (1932) built by a railway company at Morecambe, although a romantic rather than a functionalistic design, shewed good aesthetic use made of forms in origin utilitarian. The house called 'High and Over' at Amersham (1931) went further still with its approved glass staircase functionally preserving the goings-up and the comings-down of its inhabitants from any shameful secrecy. In general outline and proportions this house, if novel in England only, would anywhere be rather stimulating and agreeable.

In commercial buildings there is much more scope for the reformer than in domestic, and in them it may be hoped that the gospel of adaptation to use will soon bring order into the somewhat inconsistent practices of its evangelists. The new building of the *Daily Express* newspaper (1931) must certainly be a lighter and airier place to work in than any of the older offices around it, and in Fleet Street lightness and airiness are of great importance. It has long been urged that buildings in smoky towns should be faced with materials that are washable and non-absorbent, and buildings so faced have often succeeded in everything, except attracting imitation. The black glass chosen for the wall surfaces of the *Daily Express* building possesses no obvious advantages over the more ordinary polished granite or glazed terra-cotta, and has not proved any more persuasive than they in tempting conservative architects away from brick and stone. Nevertheless, if glass is no better than granite or fireclay, it is not necessarily any worse—and it is perfectly allowable to prefer its appearance. In this instance of its use the design of the façades is scarcely developed enough to qualify them as works of architecture, so that the aesthetic potentialities of their material are not seriously tested.

The title of this chapter, *The Preferment of Engineering*, might be misunderstood as implying that the Engineer and the Architect should be separate persons, which would be utterly contrary to its intentions. They are so at present, but their separation is recent, regrettable, and—it may be hoped—impermanent. The separation that is essential and irreconcileable is not between engineer and architect, but between engineering and architecture; not between men but between functions; functions wholly disparate, each of which, nevertheless, can often be best performed by the man also performing the other. Engineering is construction uninfluenced by the exercise of aesthetic choice. Architecture is aesthetic choice exerted not only upon construction but upon the arrangement of what is to be constructed. If to the words Engineering and Architecture we give wider meanings than these, we blur our thought by blurring our vocabulary. The two arts when combined are interactive, but they need not be combined always; there are occasions upon which one only need be employed. There are some things built whose design involves no aesthetic choice at all, the appearance of stability being sufficient. There are other things designed whose building is so rudimentary that stability can never be in question with the spectator. It would be wrong to say that the first should be the exclusive concern of the engineer, the second of the architect, because, ideally, if these men are not united in one they ought to be in constant collaboration. But it would be more wrong to say that the first is not exclusively the concern of engineering, that the second is not exclusively the concern of architecture—that would be the blurring of thought against which we must guard. The versatility of man is one thing, the immutable disparity of functions is another.

The preferment of engineering—its heightened status, its enlarged scope—in architecture has two aspects to-day. The first, in which the pleasure-giving appearances of usefulness have competed for public favour with qualities that are aesthetic need not engage our attention. The public has been offered an alternative to architecture, which it has received, for the most part, with indifference. The second aspect, that in which the evidence of constructive method is made prominent, in which the spectator is asked to share the maker's knowledge of how a thing is made, and thus vicariously to share his pleasure in making it,—to this aspect too much attention can hardly be called. In the last chapter it was pointed out how in the Selfridge building the stanchions of a steel-framed structure, although cased in make-believe columns of stone, were allowed a little more say in the design of the façade than those that the Ritz Hotel demurely but flatly refuses to acknowledge. Partial and unsatisfactory as this concession obviously was, several years passed before it was extended to its logical conclusion in the admirable façade of Heal's shop in the Tottenham Court Road (1914), where the stanchions are frankly made the basis of the whole design.

Heal's shop was finished before the armistice of 1918, but remained for many years afterwards a lonely example of good sense and discretion. Its peculiarity lay in its homogeneity. In many buildings coeval with it the presence of stanchions might be avowed in part of the design, but always the architect would have taken fright before their complete revelation, and have draped their upper or their lower portions with a thick screen of architectural pretence. At this point it may be explained that the casing of stone, brick, or concrete, by means of which a steel stanchion is converted into such a pier as is to be seen in Heal's building, is no mere concession to any fancied claims of appearance. In London, where our architectural currency is chiefly minted, it has for some time been against the law for steel stanchions to stand naked, the object for this restriction being their protection from heat and water in case of fire. In the provinces apparently steel must be robuster, or its destruction must matter less, since the protective casing has not always been insisted upon. English architects, however, have rarely shewn much enterprise in visibly metallic construction, and everywhere have accepted with relief any excuse for covering it up. The casing required by the London Building Act is therefore usual throughout the whole of England.

Tall, thin, piers proportioned to the stanchions they contained were certainly not amenable to the accepted conventions of masonry design, and it must have been for that reason that at first they were so charily used. Suddenly, however, taste changed. Verticality in design became the rage, and these tall thin piers became things of which it seemed to be thought impossible to have too many. Those

COMMON SENSE

Messrs. Heal's Premises, Tottenham Court Road,
London (1914)

containing stanchions were supplemented by others not containing stanchions, and performing no function except the undesirable one of blocking out useful light. Adelaide House (1920) is a typical specimen of this malpractice; only in the top storey is the spectator allowed to see how few uprights would really have been needed to carry the frame. Many other buildings of the period outdid even Adelaide House in the close spacing and dominance of its vertical piers. The better among them attained pictorial impressiveness that shewed how even the starkest implements of construction can be made playthings in the romantic nursery.

If we look at the steelwork of any modern building before the outside walls are hung upon the frame, what we shall see is a skeleton that the architect may treat as he chooses. He may allow it to shew through its covering, as a painter will often delight to do; or, if he will, he may flesh it so fully that only an architectural anatomist could guess its structure. Thus, the London building of the National Radiator Company (1928), with its plating of black granite slabs, exemplifies an entirely reasonable manner of design. If the handsome face of this building answers no questions, it also tells no lies. Older steel-frame buildings like the Ritz Hotel had told lies in plenty, and told them so plausibly and agreeably that even against their tellers our objection cannot be aesthetic. Against them we must merely say that to copy without practical significance what was practically significant to its first maker, to refuse to extract from new ways of building forms practically significant to ourselves, is to embrace impotence, to accept aesthetic emasculation. There is no sign of impotence or of emasculation in the design of the Radiator Building, and if all commercial architecture needed no more window-space than is here provided, there would be little to regret

POWER

Broadway House, Westminster (1927)

had there been any general imitation of its character. This character reappears in the head offices of the Underground Railway in Westminster (1927), where the happy adoption of the X-shaped plan, used many years before by Waterhouse in the University College Hospital (1896), has secured for the building much more sunlight than would have been possible in buildings toeing the frontage line of a narrow street. In this admirable design the steel skeleton is very comfortably fleshed over, and the windows are sufficient in their favoured situation. It happens, however, that most of our commercial architecture, being less advantageously placed, requires a great deal more window-space than this, requires indeed that the openings by which daylight enters should be as wide and unbroken as possible, should stretch from stanchion to stanchion without interruption.

In these circumstances there is no permissible escape from the conspicuous revelation of cased stanchions where they pass through a band of window, seeing that in that band everything that is not cased stanchion ought to be glass. This necessity, for reasonably viewed it is no less, seems to have led some architects to remove supporting stanchions from the outside walls altogether, placing them within the building (just where normally they will be most in the way). By this method the horizontal bands of window can be made absolutely unbroken and continuous, they and the bands of walling between them being supported on cantilevers projecting from within. The occasions upon which such an arrangement will be convenient must be extremely rare, and it is impossible not to suspect that its frequent adoption by some foreign architects has been due to whim rather than to conviction. The appearance, so contrived, of bands of walling, entirely without visible means of subsistence, floating in air above bands of transparent glass, proved entertaining enough to tempt for

a time even former Functionalists from the paths of recti-
tude, but its amusement value has not survived its novelty.

In the steel frame we have been attempting to visualise,—
the skeleton that now is a constant character in our street
scenes,—it will be remembered that the girders supporting
the floors are fully as prominent as the upright stanchions.
Like the stanchions they must be cased, but unlike the
stanchions they will force themselves into no inevitable
prominence in the finished building. If the architect wish
to make them apparent he may do so, but between them
there is no necessity for continuous glass, in fact for a distance of two to three feet above their upper surfaces glass
would be rather a nuisance than an advantage. To the solid
bands that convenience requires below sill-level has been
given the name of *leg-screens*, which defines the nature of
that convenience. Legs of men and of furniture need neither
illumination nor especial aeration, and the low wall that
obscures them will also give to men the feeling of security
they naturally look for when lifted high above the ground.

Reduced to its simplest terms, then, the façade of a modern
commercial building should consist of narrow vertical
stripes—cased stanchions—and broader horizontal bands—
leg-screens—the interstices of this trellis being filled with
glass. Whether the stripes shall interrupt the bands or the
bands the stripes, or again, whether both shall present one
continuous surface, are matters the architect will decide
according to his fancy. In designs of emphasised verticality
the face of the leg-screens may be behind that of the
stanchions and thus only appear between them. Alterna-
tively the stanchions may be behind the leg-screens
and thus be cut by them into the semblance of piers no
higher than the bands of windows they interrupt. This
last method of design can be well seen in Messrs. Crawford's building in Holborn (1930), the low piers simulated

here being differentiated further from the rest of the wall by their casings of stainless steel. In this building can be seen a horizontality almost as emphatic as the verticality of the earlier specimens—indeed, in the course of a few years fashion moved from one extreme to the other. Fashion apart, it would seem more reasonable to project leg-screens than to recess them, seeing that the shallow embrasures their projection will cause internally between the stanchions cannot but add useful space to the areas of the floors. If the facts of construction are to suggest its architectural expression, the casings of stanchions when recessed behind leg-screens, should be so shaped in each of their reappearances as to indicate their underlying continuity. In the head offices of Hay's Wharf (1930) the enclosed storeys had to be raised over an open car-park, and an attempt has been made to reconcile this necessity with an architectural expression of stability by shaping the stanchion casings so as to suggest that they are threaded through the structure like posts through a scaffold. In ordinary buildings, enclosed down to the ground, no necessity demands this expedient, which in such cases becomes merely one of many eligible methods of design.

In certain recent architecture abroad horizontality has been exaggerated, so as to produce buildings that can be described according to taste either as noble streamline compositions or as imitation railway accidents made of piled-up Pullman cars. In the fully developed form of such façades, the window-bands are kept free of any interruption by the pushing back of the stanchions into the building in the way already described. Such exaggeration has worn too solemn a face to offer much amusement, and does not seem serious enough to offer much else. On its first importation into this country it was highly valued, but has now descended into the bargain basement of novelties become flyblown. Horizontality of a kind less exaggerated and more rational is the ruling characteristic of the block of flats called 'Mount Royal' which in the year 1934 made a rather surprising arrival in Oxford Street. The façades of this building consist of alternate bands of red and dun-coloured brickwork, windows occurring in the red bands only intermittently, instead of stretching from stanchion to stanchion. In a block of flats this moderate allowance of window-space is perfectly proper: people do not want to *live* in glasshouses although convenience may suggest that they should *work* in them. The striping of this building is just the architect's fun; it is purely decorative and arises from no necessity. Fun more riotous still can be seen in Westminster (1928), where Lutyens has clothed the Duke of Westminster's tenants in a loudly checked livery of brick and plaster. In these experiments, also, it may be doubted whether the power to amuse will long survive their novelty. Both, however, have weight behind the shock tactics of their oddity, and should not be unnamed in any record of recent architectural adventure.

No true architect can become the slave of stanchions and girders, and nothing said above must be taken to imply that any design revealing construction is intrinsically better than any other in which construction has to be guessed at. It is indeed probable that an architect, by neglecting the aesthetic suggestions of new engineering possibilities, condemns himself to death; but his death may often be a lingering and a beautiful one. The thread with which our designers of the picturesque weave nets for our senses will soon be paid out, and when it ends, their power is gone. Nevertheless, they will often snare us yet. But the architect who is alert to the hints thrown out by engineering progress, who sees in new fulfilments of function the raw material for new aesthetic expression,—he is the man we must encourage if we wish future ages to have any architecture at all. His designs, however, we must judge by their architectural value only; in looking at his buildings we must put out of our minds all thoughts of whether or not its designer is working on what we consider to be the right lines. However we may approve or deplore his aims, we must as architectural critics base our judgement exclusively upon his achievements.

The results of efforts to get on architectural terms with the steel frame have obviously not yet any finality, and there is some excuse for thinking that these efforts have not for the most part been very energetic. On the other hand, efforts to get on architectural terms with ferro-concrete construction have in some other countries been almost frenzied. For a little while after its first systematisation the French, to whom that systematisation was due, regarded it without emotion: to them it was a substitute for masonry, strong and light, that had its appropriate but not very extensive uses. No doubt it could do all sorts of surprising things, but their architects did not particularly want any surprising things done. Surprising things, however, were very much in the line of the brilliant French engineering; and the Hennebique system, slighted by architects and by them hidden, as often as not, behind conventional masks of stone or of faience, by engineers was largely and worthily exploited. Bridges and water-towers, strong but of unprecedented slenderness, were produced by the system, while architects were continuing on their complacent and unimaginative way. Gradually, however, ferro-concrete made itself so indispensable to them, by its neat performance of the small tasks allotted to it, that they were mostly willing to collaborate in its glorification when the moment for that suddenly arrived.

What brought that moment is hard to discover. At one

minute the imagination of architects seemed bounded by the possibilities of masonry construction, at the next nothing would content it but forms that in masonry would have been actually and visibly unstable. Flat roofs were projected far over porches and loggias without any supporting columns; balconies were thrust out as unconcernedly as though they were drawers pulled out in a piece of furniture. Everything seemed to stick by its edge to something else that was doubtfully secure in itself. Doubtfully secure, that is to say, to eyes accustomed to the forms that betoken security in masonry, and it was as a substitute for masonry that ferro-concrete at first was regarded.

If it be regarded, however, as a material having affinities with cardboard or sheet metal no such doubts occur. Now, a wall of ferro-concrete is not altogether unlike a sheet of metal in many of its capabilities, and, once this has been accepted, those capabilities seem no more surprising in one than in the other. After all, conjuring tricks lose most of their effect when their audience has learnt how they are done. In so far, then, as the ferro-concrete fanatics set up as conjurors, their vogue was soon over, they soon had had their day. The specific gravity and degree of tenacity of ferro-concrete entered public consciousness, so that the stability of a cement-faced column of exaggerated height and slenderness soon came to excite no more emotion than would the rigidity of a knitting needle. The peculiar capabilities of this method of construction had thereafter to be valued for their usefulness and aesthetic potency, and could no longer be valued for their wonder. Their usefulness was very little tested in everyday English building, various circumstances combining to make the system unduly expensive and inconvenient. Their aesthetic potency, however, resulted rather curiously in a perceptible modification of our current architectural idiom. For example, the stone façade of the large addition made in 1929 to the exhibition building at Olympia had many ferro-concrete-begotten characteristics, although ferro-concrete was nowhere employed in it; and this façade was typical of much work in which the same influence can be traced.

Early in this book it was stated, and supported by examples, that architecture has always tended to use mimic construction as a means of dramatising the real construction that is its prime motive. Reminder of this tendency may be useful in enabling us to contemplate without bewilderment the non-utilitarian use of new utilitarian forms that gradually reflavoured modern English architecture between the last two wars, without effecting any general change in its constructive method. There was a strong smell of ferro-concrete about much of what we built at that time, and yet the very few buildings in which the material really was present were as likely as not to appear innocent of it. Olympia would be suspected of its harbourage—although wrongly—whereas the Dorchester Hotel (1930), in spite of its tiled skin, would seem to assure us by its pleasingly conventional architecture that no novelties had been attempted in its construction. Yet the Dorchester Hotel is built of ferro-concrete, and so, it is said, are not a few of the demure neo-Georgian buildings produced by the Office of Works. Plainly we can learn little by appearances, except about appearances, and since architectural expression is a management of appearances it is usually impertinent for the critic to pry into what they have been made to conceal. There are very few things feasible in ferro-concrete that are not feasible also with steel construction, and most things that both can do have no special appropriateness to either. Many, however, would never have been thought of for steel construction, had not ferro-concrete pointed the way. Even where no difficult construction is involved—where

simple brick-building fulfils all utilitarian needs, the forms
of that brick-building tend, inevitably and not necessarily
wrongly, to be influenced by our experience of other
methods. When house-building started again after the
1914-18 war people having what used to be called 'advanced
views' and no great sympathy with popular taste, built in
several parts of England houses that closely resembled what
the illustrated papers shewed them were being built by
people with advanced views abroad. Most of these houses
had flat roofs, glass-walled staircases, heavy balconies, and
enormous windows; and, though generally inferior to
their foreign models, often displayed some of the virtues
of their rigid but romantic style. Few of them looked as
though they were built of brick, but almost all of them were.
Indeed, in brickwork their forms proved easily realisable,
although they were not forms which that material is likely
ever to have originally suggested. If it comes to that, no
more could the triglyphs and mutules of the Doric temple
ever have been originally suggested by blocks of marble;
yet we do not condemn those for not being of wood.

Houses of the kind described above can give to the well-
to-do a delightful sense of emancipation, and, when designed by an architect who is an artist, can greatly please
the eye; but they are expensive to live in. Flat roofs are
more apt than any others to need constant attention, large,
plain, wall-surfaces get shabby in no time and have to be
recoloured, large areas of windows make heating bills
enormous. On the Continent houses containing these
elements became the height of fashion, but in England
those who could afford to pay for them were usually not
those who wanted them. Good specimens in this country
are therefore few, although their more easily reproducible
characteristics have been travestied over and over again in
little mongrels of houses, half-conventional and half what

their designers, ignorant of the meanings of words, have generally been pleased to describe as 'contemporary.' Of these it is kinder to say no more. Of the good specimens, the house 'High and Over' has already been mentioned, and another clever entertainment by the same architects may here be bracketed with it—the house called 'Pollard' at Grayswood (1932) on the Surrey heights.

If a design containing the utilitarian causes for its own effects could be declared superior in itself to any design whose effects are borrowed ready-made from those that have sprung from useful causes elsewhere, the estimation of architecture might prove easier than it actually is. If it could be established as unjustifiable to bury steel canti-levers out of sight in order to gain the pleasing effect caused by their absence in ferro-concrete—if it could be established that this was as foolish as it is for the automobile manu-facturer to disguise an engine as a luggage trunk when the engine occurs at the back of the chassis, most of the English building following the continental vogue could be condemned. Obviously, however, it cannot. The automobile manufacturer does not regard the form of a luggage trunk as indispensable to his aesthetic conception; he merely tells a lie to save the face of the man that buys a motor-car with the engine at what his friends may think the wrong end. The architect, suppressing his cantilevers or walling his rooms with glass, acts with a different intention; he has seen and admired the simple shadows that unbrack-eted projections can cast, he has enjoyed the holiday flavour of hot-weather houses in countries where weather is often hot, and he is anxious to secure similar shadows and a similar flavour in his own design. Purists may fume if they find out that all is not ferro-concrete that looks like it, that the glass walls, during most of the year, let in what it would be desirable to exclude, but very likely they never *will* find

273

FOR A NEW WAY OF LIVING

'Pollard,' Grayswood, Surrey (1932)

out. Their grievance, anyhow, must be moral rather than aesthetic.

Whatever may be thought of the continental new style, there can be no doubt of its suitability to factories and warehouses. In buildings of this nature it ought to be merely the new style natural to what really is new, because the most recent developements in construction are all such as may be advantageously used. Often, however, for one reason or another, they may not be, and yet if a new commercial building is really old-fashioned, it would be bad advertising for it to look so. In advertisement the picturesque principle, fatal though it be to developement in the long run, is inescapable; the necessity of catching the eye surpasses from a commercial point of view all other considerations. Indeed, this is the art of the hoarding rather than architecture, and the danger of its invasion into other spheres must not scare us from acknowledging its success in its own. Factories and warehouses have come to share the obligation of the shop-front, they must attract, and must declare the prosperity of their owners.

The factories built in prominent roadside positions between the two wars made a veritable *Journal des Modes*, beginning with the neo-Classical, passing through the colossal Wagnerian, coquetting with the style of the Cambridge University Library, and eventually settling down into the modernistic undenominational. Most of them followed the art of the hoarding only too literally in having façades entirely unrelated to what stood behind. Many had towers.

Little has been said in these pages of theatres or of cinemas because in an account as brief as this they have little claim to a place. Among London theatres no recent ones and very few less recent are as good as the play-going public has a right to expect. Their exteriors have, almost without exception, made no pretension to being more than routine products of architects whose forte was a knowledge of the requirements of the stage. Their interiors have been the work of similarly specialising decorators of whom no more has been required than they were experienced, but seldom inspired, in providing. Among the newer ones, the interiors of the Cambridge (1930) and of the Savoy (1929) (the latter a redecoration only) stand out as being distinctly agreeable, which is more than can be said for most of the rest. Like commercial architecture generally, that of theatres reflects passing fashions, not always very favourably, and in its latest developement before the last war had become a trifle stark.

The Shakespeare Theatre at Stratford-on-Avon (1927), however, is a monument of some importance, being most carefully and sensitively designed both without and within. As with most buildings of the last hundred years whose value has proved enduring, its design was the outcome of a hotly contested architectural competition. Its style is perhaps a little too much of its moment to be likely to retain its full relish when that moment is past—the same was true of the theatre that once occupied its site and is now but a memory. Both that theatre and this one have been considered not wholly suitable to their surroundings. But the present building is a notable work of architecture, well befitting its purpose; which is not that of an opera-house to accommodate glittering crowds, nor of an old-world home of Elizabethan drama for the frequentation of pious pilgrims, but of a people's theatre in which the play is the thing. The architectural harmony of all the parts of this complex design, one with the other, is a quality as admirable as it is rare.

The first cinemas built in England were hardly more aspiring architecturally than the floridly ornamented but ephemeral buildings of contemporary exhibitions, being sheds with more or less elaborate frontispieces toward the street. Some, of course, had been grander than this, but it was not until the '20's of this century that magnificence in them became expected. That magnificence was usually of a rather blatant and unsophisticated kind. The New Victoria Cinema (1930) was the first in England to depend largely upon coloured lighting for the decoration of its interior, suggesting how great the advantage would have been, and still would be, if in every cinema the solid decoration could be extinguished, never to reappear, with the first lowering of the lights. The outside of the New Victoria is excellent advertising, and near to being good architecture. The outside of the Kensington Cinema[1] (1925), another early specimen, is good architecture without any qualification, stylistic in detail, no doubt, but in mass and arrangement as adventurous as need be. The enormously long lintel spanning the recess in the façade would certainly never have been tolerated before the preferment of engineering: such a lintel would be impossible without steel support, and here makes no pretence of not having it. Nevertheless, despite the invitation of the recessed doorways, the general character of this façade is edifying rather than entertaining, and for that reason among others must be ranked lower than that of the famous Regent at Brighton (1921), which not very long after the first war set a standard of appropriate and attractive cinema design too exacting for many to have been able to approach.

In the design of buildings coming within the category of public architecture, of town-halls, libraries, museums, and so forth, engineering has found little preferment. The neo-Classical convention has relaxed, but in most examples has remained the hidden hand that has regulated and dis-

[1] Now the Odeon Cinema.

posed mildly unconventional material, neo-Gothic in the town-hall at Lewisham (1928), nondescript in that at Wandsworth (1934), and in other places most often promiscuously Scandinavian. In hardly any have novel methods of construction been dramatised; where such methods have been employed they have almost always been kept out of sight. The new hall of the Royal Horticultural Society in Westminster (1926) is a notable example of architectural sanity; nothing in its admirable façade is derivative for derivation's sake, but nothing, on the other hand, is done to advertise or exaggerate the originality exerted in its conception. The hall behind this façade is a noble feat of novel construction, suggested, perhaps, by the great French hangar for aeroplanes that supplied, shortly after the first war, what still is the best generally applicable model for the design of large-roofed spaces lit from above. The only objection to which the design of this hall is open is with respect to its height, which, however advantageous it may be for ventilation, tends to dwarf the floral exhibitions the hall was built to contain.

Hospitals make a large and special department of architecture in which the functionalism of use for many years seemed at war with architects' preconceptions as to appearance. In the Royal Masonic Hospital at Ravenscourt Park (1929) a truce has perhaps been established rather than the cause of contention removed. This entertaining building manages to satisfy every medical requirement within a most arbitrarily picturesque exterior. In its romantic attire (which fits its board-room very badly, but otherwise seems fairly comfortable) it sits for its portrait to the photographers as self-consciously as any professional beauty of the Norman Shaw Picturesque.

In school architecture, advances in notions of health and convenience have been continuously reflected during the

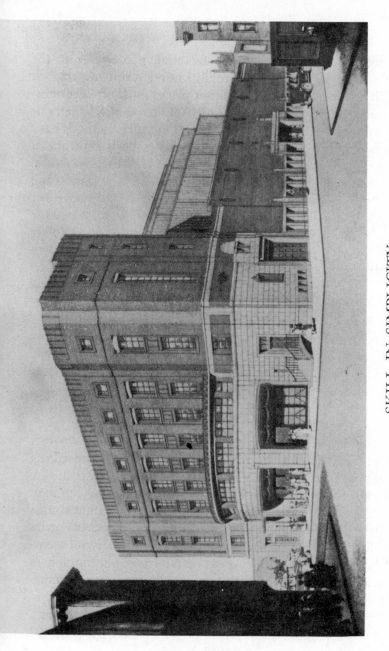

SKILL IN SIMPLICITY

Royal Horticultural Society's New Hall, Westminster (1926)

century in successive changes in methods of planning, which have involved much substitution of new methods of construction for old. Coincident with this, and perhaps related to it, has been a change of sentiment, influenced by which the architectural expression of school-buildings has become more and more that of the workshop and less and less that of the home. The desirability of this change is an appropriate subject for debate by educationalists, but not by architects, who must mind their own business of performing well the tasks required of them. As a rule school architects have proved themselves efficient, but unable, through the needless meticulousness of instructions imposed by authority, to exercise any aesthetic invention.

In residential schools the replacement of the architectural associations of home by those of the workshop has naturally taken place in less degree, although at least one of the lesser public schools has gone 'modern' in a gentlemanlike way. The flirtation of universities with the latest fashions in architecture has been too mild to call for attention: nothing parallel with Butterfield's Victorian rebellion at Keble seems likely to trouble this less zealous age. Among buildings connected with schools, the chapel added in 1928 to Sutton Valence School may be noted as a model of the sensitive asceticism into which such buildings have rebounded from their former Gothic exuberance.

Mention of this chapel can lead this summary to the class of buildings with which it must conclude—to that of churches and other places of worship. Many queer buildings of the kind arose on the Continent after the first war; experimental churches in France, ferocious churches in Germany and Austria, whimsical churches in Italy and Scandinavia. All of these have been copiously illustrated in the architectural press, and have been proposed by some for imitation in this country. The English church architect, however, while not disdaining to borrow from here or anywhere little bits that tickle his fancy, has in the main been unable and perhaps unwilling to embark upon strange adventures. He has, in fact, usually gone on producing the sort of building he has been producing for some time; gentle more or less Romanesque simplicities with a great deal of whitewash inside and a nice touch of pure colour at the high altar.

Against this uninspiring background, one or two churches of valuable originality have stood out in high relief. The church at Clubmoor, mentioned with admiration in the last chapter, was shortly followed by another, that of St. Gabriel, Blackburn (1933), in the design of which the same architect moved farther from traditional conventions. Inside this church is arcuated, whether in brick or not does not appear. Arches are dear to clergy and people, but the architect of these days, using modern constructional methods, may often feel it his duty to do without them. In the well-known church of St. Nicholas at Burnage (1932) they are dispensed with altogether, without any loss of what is called 'ecclesiastical character.'

One of the first obligations of a church-designer to-day would seem to be the provision of a roof that can withstand both fire and beetle. In other words, the era of the timber roof is gone for ever. Not everyone, perhaps, can be brought to tolerate the flat ceilings of the Burnage design, and for those who object to them the alternative of a vault is eligible. Vaults having curved surfaces, however, are natural only to construction in brick, stone, or concrete without reinforcement; once metal is introduced into a fire-resisting ceiling, whether in the form of large members or of small reinforcements, the logical form for that ceiling is extremely unlikely to be curved. Over the roof of a church in the southern counties, built in 1932, a ferro-concrete ceiling has been constructed whose shape consists of five sides of a dodecagon, the form of this ceiling and the requirements for its support having been made the regulating factor in the church's design. The only arches in this building are those that carry brick facing over small spans, for which purpose it was found that the old way of building was actually the cheapest and most convenient.

That old ways of building still often are the cheapest and the most convenient is a moral with which this book well may end. The preferment of engineering has been so sudden and rapid as to tempt that art to false shame at the humble occupations of its youth. It is now a little apt to put on grand manners on occasions when simplicity would become it better. Nothing could restore its social poise so effectively as reunion with the art from which it sprang. May the future bring that reunion, profitable alike to architecture, to engineering, and to the world!

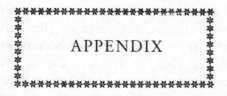

APPENDIX

Goodhart-Rendel's intention to discuss architecture rather than architects led him to omit from his text many of the names of architects. These are indexed with the buildings concerned, presenting the reader with a considerable task of cross- referencing. The present running list supplies page numbers, the names of architects, and other details, such as demolitions of buildings, revised dates, and other variants.

p. 19 Unitatian Chapel, Devonport: Mount Zion Baptist Chapel by John Foulston, 1823–24, dem.

Crockfords Club, St. James's Street, W1, 1827, Benjamin Dean Wyatt and Philip Wyatt, alt.

p. 22 'Government Buildings now rising in Whitehall': designed by E. Vincent Harris, 1935

p. 25–26 Fonthill Abbey, Wilts, 1796–1812 James Wyatt. John Rutter *Delineations of Fonthill and its Abbey* 1823

p. 27 Endsleigh Cottage, nr. Milton Abbot, Devon, 1810, Sir Jeffry Wyattville

p. 29 'Greek' Thomson: Alexander Thomson 1817–75

p. 32 Walton House, Walton-on-Thames, Surrey, reconstructed 1835–39, Sir Charles Barry

Xaverian Seminary, Queen's Park, Brighton E. Sussex, 1829, Sir Charles Barry

p. 33 Trelissick House, nr. Truro, Cornwall, 1824, P. F. Robinson

The Grange, Grange Park, Hants, 1805–09, William Wilkins

p. 35 East Cowes Castle, Isle of Wight, 1798–, John Nash, dem.

Belvoir Castle, Leics, remodelled 1801–13, James Wyatt

Eastnor Castle, Hereford & Worcester, 1812–20, Sir Robert Smirke

Kinfauns Castle, Perthshire, 1820–22, Sir Robert Smirke

p. 35 Gwych Castle, Denbeighshire (Clwyd), 1816, Thomas Rickman

Mitchelstown Castle, Co. Cork, Ireland, J. & G. R. Pain

p. 38 Toddington Park, Glos., 1820–35, Charles Hanbury Tracy, Baron Sudely

p. 39 St. John's College, Cambridge, New Court, 1827–31, Thomas Rickman

Peterhouse, Cambridge, Gisborne Court, 1825–26, William McIntosh Brookes

Balliol College, Oxford, W. side of Garden Quadrangle, 1826–27, George Basevi

Hertford College, Oxford, N. & S. blocks of street front, 1820–22, William Garbett

Pembroke College, Oxford, refacing of master's Lodgings etc., 1830, Daniel Evans

Sidney Sussex College, Cambridge, remodelled 1821–22, Sir Jeffry Wyattville

p. 40 Rugby School, Warwicks., 1809–15, Henry Hakewill

St. David's College, Lampeter, Cardiganshire (Dyfed) 1822–27, C. R. Cockerell

p. 41 King's College, Cambridge, screen 1824–28, William Wilkins

General Post Office, St. Martin's le Grand, EC1, 1824–29, Sir Robert Smirke, dem.

Appendix

The British Museum, Great Russell Street WC1, 1823– 46, Sir Robert Smirke

Royal Institution of Fine Arts, Manchester (now City Art Gallery) 1824, Sir Charles Barry

The Royal High School, Regent Road, Edinburgh, 1825–29, Thomas Hamilton

University College, Gower Street, WC1, 1827–28, William Wilkins

Board of Trade and Privy Council Offices, Whitehall, W1, 1924–26, Sir John Soane

St. George's Hospital, Hyde Park Corner, SW1, 1828– 29, William Wilkins

p. 44n Rex Whistler, painter and illustrator, 1905–1944

p. 48 Covent Garden Market, WC2, 1828–30, and Hungerford Market, WC2, 1831–33 dem., John Fowler

Winchester Corn Exchange, Hants., 1836–38, Owen Browne Carter

p. 49 National Gallery, Trafalgar Square, WC2, 1834–38, William Wilkins

p. 50 St. Marylebone New Church, Marylebone Road W1, 1813–17, Thomas Hardwick

St. James's Church, Thurland Road, SE16, 1827–29, James Savage, assisted by George Allen

p. 52 St. Pancras New Church, Euston Road, NW1, 1819–22, William and Henry William Inwood

p. 53 St. Peter's Church (Parish Church), Brighton, 1824–28, Sir Charles Barry

St. Luke's Church, Sydney Street, SW3, 1820–24, James Savage

St. John's (Episcopal) Chapel, Princes Street, Edinburgh, 1816–18, William Burn

Holy Trinity Church, Theale, Berks, nave 1820–22, Edward William Garbett, tower 1827–28, John Buckler

Holy Trinity Church, Wolverton, Bucks, 1810–15, Henry Hakewill

p. 55 St. Dunstan's-in-the-West, Fleet Street, London EC4, 1825–29, John Shaw Sr.

p. 58 St. Katherine's Hospital, Regent's Park, London NW1, 1826–28, Ambrose Poynter

Christ's Hospital (old), Newgate Street, EC1, 1825–29, John Shaw Sr. dem.

p. 59 The illustration, whose origin has not been traced, shows the design as evolved much later than 1835

p. 60 E. W. Pugin *Who was the art-architect of the Houses of Parliament?* 1867

p. 62 Longleat, Wilts, remodelling and stables, 1806–13; Wollaton Hall, Notts, alterations and additions, c. 1801 and 1823; Sir Jeffry Wyattville

Babraham Hall, Cambs. 1829–32, Philip Hardwick

p. 64 Law Life Assurance Office, No. 187 Fleet Street EC4, 1834, John Shaw Jr. dem.

Peckforton Castle, Cheshire, 1844–50; Scotney Castle, Kent, 1835–43; Anthony Salvin

p. 65 Aldermaston Manor, Berks, 1848–51, Philip Charles Hardwick

p. 66 Facades of houses in Princes Gate, London SW7, 1843–46, Harvey Lonsdale Elmes

p. 68 'Two club-houses newly built in Waterloo Place': The United Services Club (now Institute of Directors), Pall Mall W1, 1826–28, John Nash; The Athenaeum Club, Waterloo Place W1, 1827–30, Decimus Burton

p. 70 George Smith *A Collection of Designs for Furniture* 1808 and *Cabinet-Makers and Upholsterers' Guide* 1828

p. 74 The Sun Fire Assurance Office, Threadneedle Street, EC2, 1841–42, C. R. Cockerell dem.

p. 75 Fitzwilliam Museum, Cambridge, 1836–45, George Basevi; 'another hand': E. M. Barry

284

llu, architect (with Franz Christian Gau) of Ste. Clotilde, Paris,

g design at Gidea Park, 1910, by Geoffrey Lucas
ge and Chapel, Lady Margaret Hall, Oxford, 1931, Sir Giles

use, Westminster, SW1, 1937–40, Sir Herbert Baker
k, SW1, 1927, Sir Frank Baines
nk (now Barclay's), Water Street, Liverpool, 1926, H. J. Rowse
ial Bank (now National Westminster Bank), Prince's Street, EC2,
Cooper
leet Street, EC4, 1830, R. Parker
nk, Bishopsgate, EC2, 1881, R. Norman Shaw dem.
e Bank of England, Threadneedle Street, EC2, 1925–37, Sir Herbert

minster Bank, Piccadilly W1, 1927, W. Curtis Green
ncoln's Inn Fields, WC2, 1922, Greenaway and Newbury
y Hall, SE1, 1908–22, Ralph Knott
am Palace, SW1, E. front 1913, Sir Aston Webb
m Town Hall, Kent, 1927, Lanchester and Lodge dem.
e Town Hall, Marylebone Road, W1, 1910, Sir Edwin Cooper
of Pensions Building, Bromyard Avenue, W6, 1922, Sir James G.

, Kingsway, WC2, 1920, Trehearne and Norman
s, Oxford Street, W1, 1908–19, Daniel Burnham of Chicago with R.
son, completed by Burnet and Tait
, 26–64 Kensington High Street (N side) W8, 1924, Sir Reginald

ow Ferragamo) 24 Old Bond Street, 1926, E. Vincent Harris
reat Marlborough Street, W1, 1922, E. Stanley Hall
Hotel, Marble Arch, W1, 1932, F. J. Wills
House, Piccadilly, W1, 1924, Thomas Hastings of New York and C.

House, Park Lane, W1, 1926, Sir Edwin Lutyens, with Wimperis and

rd Court, Portman Square, W1, 1928, Messrs. Joseph
ing, University of Bristol, 1925, Sir George Oatley
nstitute of Agricultural Botany, Huntingdon Road, Cambridge, 1919–
ley Horder
orial Court, Clare College, Cambridge, 1923–34; Cambridge University
934; Lady Margaret Hall see p. [230]; Sir Giles Gilbert Scott
ch of the Annunciation, Old Quebec Street, Marble Arch, W1, 1912, Sir
pper
r's Church, Old Oak Road, W3, 1930, A. W. Kenyon
ge's Church, Oldfield Lane, Bath, 1929, Sir Giles Gilbert Scott
rine's Church, Westway, Hammersmith, W12, 1923, Robert Atkinson

Matthew, Queen's Drive, Clubmoor, Liverpool, 1928, F. X. Velarde
l Church of Christ the King, Liverpool, 1903–80, Sir Giles Gilbert Scott
beth Bridge, London, 1928, Sir Reginald Blomfield

p. 77 Blackwall Station, 1840, Sir William Tite dem.
London Bridge Station, 1841–44, Henry Roberts dem.
Brighton Station, 1840, David Mocatta dem.
Nine Elms Station, 1838, Sir William Tite dem.
Southampton Station, 1839, Sir William Tite
Cambridge Station, 1845, Sancton Wood
Newcastle Station, 1846–50, John Dobson
King's Cross Station, 1852, Lewis Cubitt

p. 78 All Saints Church, Hassop, Derbys. (RC), 1818, Joseph Ireland
St. Leonard's Church, Woore, Staffs, 1830, George Ernest Hamilton
St. Mary's Church, Grantham, Lincs (RC), 1832, Edward James Wilson

p. 78 Holy Trinity, Southside Street, Plymouth, Devon, 1840–42, George Wightwick, dem.
The Spanish Chapel, Manchester Square, W1, 1793–96, Joseph Bonomi, dem.

p. 79 SS. Mary and Nicholas, Wilton, Wilts, 1841–45, T. H. Wyatt and David Brandon
Christ Church, Watney Street, E1, 1841, John Shaw Jnr. dem.
St. Jude's Church, Old Bethnal Green Road, E2, 1842, Henry Clutton dem.
Christ Church, Christchurch Road, Streatham, SW2, 1841–42, James Wild
St. John the Evangelist's Church, Duncan Terrace, N1 (RC), 1839, J. J. Scoles

p. 82 A. W. N. Pugin *True Principles of Pointed or Christian Architecture* 1841

p. 83 Sir Gilbert Scott *Personal and Professional Recollections* 1879, p. 88

p. 84 Scarisbrick Hall: Pugin's involvement dates from 1836, and his work continued at least until 1845

p. 87 St. Marie's Church, Norfolk Row, Sheffield, 1846, Hadfield and Weightman
St. Mary's Church, Yorkshire Street, Burnley, Lancs (RC), 1846, Hadfield and Weightman
St. John the Baptist's church, The Triangle, E8, 1847, W. W. Wardell
Our Lady of Victories, Park Road, SW4 (RC), 1850; Our Lady Star of the Sea, Croom's Hill, SE10, 1851, W. W. Wardell

p. 88 SS. Mary and Nicholas, Littlemore, Oxon, 1835, H. J. Underwood
Chapel of the Convent of the Sacred Heart, Roehampton, Surrey, 1853, W. W. Wardell part dem.

p. 92 St. Saviour's Church, Cavalier Hill, Leeds, 1842, J. McD. Derick
St. Peter (Parish Church), Leeds, 1838, R. D. Chantrell

p. 95 St. Martin's Church, Osmaston, Derbyshire, 1845, I. H. Stevens
St. John the Evangelist, Ladbroke Grove, W11, 1844, J. H. Stevens and G. Alexander

p. 96 St. James's Church, Weybridge, Surrey, 1846, J. L. Pearson
SS. Thomas and Clement Church, Southgate Street, Winchester, 1845, E. W. Elmslie

p. 97 St. James the Less, Nutley, East Sussex, 1844, R. C. Carpenter
St. James the Great, Morpeth, Northumberland, 1844, Benjamin Ferrey

p. 98 The caption appears to be in error. Kemerton is in Worcestershire and the church is dedicated to St. Nicholas. It was designed by R. C. Carpenter, 1847, and resembles in outline but not in detail the print used here, which cannot be traced to source. I am grateful to the Rev. F. Wright for his assistance.
James Fergusson *History of the Modern Styles of Architecture* 2nd ed. 1873 pp. 556, 558

Appendix

Charles Lock Eastlake *A History of the Gothic Revival in England* 1872, p. 282
New University Museum, Oxford, 1854, Thomas Deane and Benjamin Woodward. Quote from Eastlake op. cit. p. 285

p. 104 Paddington Station, 1850–54, I. K. Brunel, with M. D. Wyatt
Sir Joseph Paxton designed Mentmore in collaboration with his son-in-law G. H. Stokes
Great Western Hotel, Paddington, London W2, 1852, P. C. Hardwick
Alexandra Hotel, Knightsbridge, SW1, 1857, F. R. Beeston dem.
Westminster Palace Hotel, Victoria Street, SW1, 1858, Messrs. Mosely
Charing Cross Station Hotel, Strand WC2, 1863, E. M. Barry
Cannon Street Station Hotel, EC4, 1863, E. M. Barry dem.
Hydropathic Hotel, Ilkley, W. Yorks, 1854, Cuthbert Brodrick

p. 107 Dorchester House, Park Lane, W1, 1849, Lewis Vulliamy dem.
Harrington House, Kensington Palace Gardens, W8, 1852, Decimus Burton and C. J. Richardson

p. 113 National Schools, Bisley and Ripley, Surrey, 1846, H. Woodyer
Leeds Town Hall, W. Yorks, 1853, Cuthbert Brodrick
Bolton Town Hall, Lancs, 1866–74, William Hill
Portsmouth Town Hall, Hants, 1886, William Hill
Wolverhampton Market, Staffs, and Bolton Market, Lancs, 1851, G. T. Robinson
Bank of Scotland, St. Vincent Place and George Street, Glasgow, 1865, J. T. Rochead

p. 115 Burlington House, Piccadilly, W1, 1872, additions by Charles Barry Jnr.

p. 116–117 Quotations from Scott op. cit. pp. 180, 195–98 passim.

p. 118 Stationery Office, Princes Street, SW1, 1847, Sir James Pennethorne dem.

p. 119 Pembroke College, Oxford, N. range of Chapel Quad 1844–46, Hall 1848, John Hayward

p. 120 Lincoln's Inn Hall, WC1, 1843, P. C. Hardwick
St. Michael's College, Tenbury, Worcs, 1855, H. Woodyer

p. 136 Churches by E. B. Lamb: St. Mary Magdalen, Canning Road, Addiscombe, Surrey; Christ Church, Church Square, W. Hartlepool, Durham; St. Martin's, Vicars Road, NW3.

p. 148 Burges's house in Kensington: Tower House, Melbury Road, W8, 1875–81. For 'the fate of the remaining treasures' see J. M. Crook *William Burges* 1981. Dates from Crook for works listed: St. Finbar's Cathedral, Cork, Ireland, 1863–1904; Church of Christ the Consoler, Skelton-on-Ure, W. Yorks, 1870–76; Church of St. Mary, Aldford-cum-Studley, W. Yorks, 1870–78; Castell Coch, Glamorgan, 1872–91; Cardiff Castle, Glamorgan, 1866–1928; Worcester College Chapel, Oxford, 1864–69

p. 150 Church of Our Lady of the Assumption and St. Mary Magdalen, (RC), Tavistock, Devon; St. Mary's Church, Woburn, Beds.

p. 153 J. T. Micklethwaite *Modern Parish Churches* 1874 p. 258n.

p. 154 Holy Trinity, Bingley, W. Yorks, 1866, R. Norman Shaw dem.
St. Luke's Church, Oseney Crescent, NW5, 1869, Basil Champneys

p. 156 Town Hall, Preston, Lancs, 1862, Sir Gilbert Scott dem.
Eastlake op. cit. pp. 361–62

p. 166 Newnham College, Cambridge, 1871–1910, Basil Champneys
White House, Tite Street, SW3, 1877, E. W. Godwin dem.

p. 170 Cragside, Rothbury, Northumberland, 1869–1885, R. Norman Shaw

Appendix

Battersea Power Station, SW8, 1929–35, Sir Giles Gilbert Scott and J. T. Halliday

p. 258 Midland Hotel, Morecambe, Lancs, 1932, Oliver Hill
High and Over, Amersham, Bucks, 1931, A. D. Connell

p. 258 Daily Express, Fleet Street, EC4, 1930–32, Ellis and Clarke with Sir Owen Williams

p. 261 Heal's, Tottenham Court Road, W1, 1914–16, A. D. Smith and Cecil Brewer (extended 1938 by Sir Edward Maufe)

p. 263 Adelaide House, London Bridge, EC3, 1924–25, Sir John Burnet and Tait
National Radiator Company, Great Marlborough Street, W1, 1928, S. Gordon Jeeves with Raymond Hood of New York

p. 265 55 Broadway, W1 (London Transport), 1927, Charles Holden (Adams, Holden and Pearson)

p. 266 Crawford's, No. 233 High Holborn, WC1, 1930, Frederick Etchells and Herbert Welch

p. 267 Hay's Wharf, Tooley Street, SE1, 1929–31, H. S. Goodhart-Rendel

p. 268 Mount Royal, Oxford Street, W1, 1932–33, Sir John Burnet, Tait and Lorne
Flats in Page Street, SW1, 1929, Sir Edwin Lutyens

p. 271 Olympia, W14, remodelling 1929, Joseph Emberton
Dorchester Hotel, Park Lane, W1, 1930, W. Curtis Green (concrete design by Sir Owen Williams)
'Pollard' (New Farm), Grayswood, Surrey, 1932, Connell, Ward and Lucas

p. 276 Cambridge Theatre, Earlham Street, WC2, 1930, Wimperis Simpson and Guthrie with S. Chermayeff
Savoy Theatre, Carting Lane, Strand, WC2, redecoration 1929, Basil Ionides
Shakespeare Memorial Theatre, Stratford-on-Avon, Warwickshire, 1927, Scott, Chesterton and Shepherd

p. 277 New Victoria Cinema, (now Apollo Victoria Theatre), Wilton Road, SW1, 1930, W. E. Trent and E. Wamsley Lewis
Kensington Cinema (Odeon), Kensington High Street W8, 1925, Leathart and Granger
Regent Cinema, Brighton, 1921, Robert Atkinson dem.

p. 278 Town Hall, Lewisham, SE6, 1928, J. Bradshaw Gass and A. J. Hope
Wandsworth Town Hall, SW18, 1934, E. A. Hunt
Royal Horticultural Society New Hall, Greycoat Street, SW1, 1926, Easton and Robertson
Royal Masonic Hospital, Ravenscourt Park, W6, 1929, Sir John Burnet Tait and Lorne

p. 280 Sutton Valence School Chapel, Kent, 1928, Charles Holden (Adams, Holden and Pearson)

p. 281 St. Gabriel, Blackburn, Lancs, 1933, F. X. Verlarde
St. Nicholas, Burnage, Manchester, 1932, N. F. Cachemaille-Day
'a church in the southern counties': St. Wilfrid's, Brighton, 1932, H. S. Goodhart-Rendel

Appendix

p. 77 Blackwall Station, 1840, Sir William Tite dem.

London Bridge Station, 1841–44, Henry Roberts dem.

Brighton Station, 1840, David Mocatta dem.

Nine Elms Station, 1838, Sir William Tite dem.

Southampton Station, 1839, Sir William Tite

Cambridge Station, 1845, Sancton Wood

Newcastle Station, 1846–50, John Dobson

King's Cross Station, 1852, Lewis Cubitt

p. 78 All Saints Church, Hassop, Derbys. (RC), 1818, Joseph Ireland

St. Leonard's Church, Woore, Staffs, 1830, George Ernest Hamilton

St. Mary's Church, Grantham, Lincs (RC), 1832, Edward James Wilson

p. 78 Holy Trinity, Southside Street, Plymouth, Devon, 1840–42, George Wightwick, dem.

The Spanish Chapel, Manchester Square, W1, 1793–96, Joseph Bonomi, dem.

p. 79 SS. Mary and Nicholas, Wilton, Wilts, 1841–45, T. H. Wyatt and David Brandon

Christ Church, Watney Street, E1, 1841, John Shaw Jnr. dem.

St. Jude's Church, Old Bethnal Green Road, E2, 1842, Henry Clutton dem.

Christ Church, Christchurch Road, Streatham, SW2, 1841–42, James Wild

St. John the Evangelist's Church, Duncan Terrace, N1 (RC), 1839, J. J. Scoles

p. 82 A. W. N. Pugin *True Principles of Pointed or Christian Architecture* 1841

p. 83 Sir Gilbert Scott *Personal and Professional Recollections* 1879, p. 88

p. 84 Scarisbrick Hall: Pugin's involvement dates from 1836, and his work continued at least until 1845

p. 87 St. Marie's Church, Norfolk Row, Sheffield, 1846, Hadfield and Weightman

St. Mary's Church, Yorkshire Street, Burnley, Lancs (RC), 1846, Hadfield and Weightman

St. John the Baptist's church, The Triangle, E8, 1847, W. W. Wardell

Our Lady of Victories, Park Road, SW4 (RC), 1850; Our Lady Star of the Sea, Croom's Hill, SE10, 1851, W. W. Wardell

p. 88 SS. Mary and Nicholas, Littlemore, Oxon, 1835, H. J. Underwood

Chapel of the Convent of the Sacred Heart, Roehampton, Surrey, 1853, W. W. Wardell part dem.

p. 92 St. Saviour's Church, Cavalier Hill, Leeds, 1842, J. McD. Derick

St. Peter (Parish Church), Leeds, 1838, R. D. Chantrell

p. 95 St. Martin's Church, Osmaston, Derbyshire, 1845, I. H. Stevens

St. John the Evangelist, Ladbroke Grove, W11, 1844, J. H. Stevens and G. Alexander

p. 96 St. James's Church, Weybridge, Surrey, 1846, J. L. Pearson

SS. Thomas and Clement Church, Southgate Street, Winchester, 1845, E. W. Elmslie

p. 97 St. James the Less, Nutley, East Sussex, 1844, R. C. Carpenter

St. James the Great, Morpeth, Northumberland, 1844, Benjamin Ferrey

p. 98 The caption appears to be in error. Kemerton is in Worcestershire and the church is dedicated to St. Nicholas. It was designed by R. C. Carpenter, 1847, and resembles in outline but not in detail the print used here, which cannot be traced to source. I am grateful to the Rev. F. Wright for his assistance.

James Fergusson *History of the Modern Styles of Architecture* 2nd ed. 1873 pp. 556, 558

Appendix

Charles Lock Eastlake *A History of the Gothic Revival in England* 1872, p. 282
New University Museum, Oxford, 1854, Thomas Deane and Benjamin Woodward. Quote from Eastlake op. cit. p. 285

p. 104 Paddington Station, 1850–54, I. K. Brunel, with M. D. Wyatt
Sir Joseph Paxton designed Mentmore in collaboration with his son-in-law G. H. Stokes
Great Western Hotel, Paddington, London W2, 1852, P. C. Hardwick
Alexandra Hotel, Knightsbridge, SW1, 1857, F. R. Beeston dem.
Westminster Palace Hotel, Victoria Street, SW1, 1858, Messrs. Mosely
Charing Cross Station Hotel, Strand WC2, 1863, E. M. Barry
Cannon Street Station Hotel, EC4, 1863, E. M. Barry dem.
Hydropathic Hotel, Ilkley, W. Yorks, 1854, Cuthbert Brodrick

p. 107 Dorchester House, Park Lane, W1, 1849, Lewis Vulliamy dem.
Harrington House, Kensington Palace Gardens, W8, 1852, Decimus Burton and C. J. Richardson

p. 113 National Schools, Bisley and Ripley, Surrey, 1846, H. Woodyer
Leeds Town Hall, W. Yorks, 1853, Cuthbert Brodrick
Bolton Town Hall, Lancs, 1866–74, William Hill
Portsmouth Town Hall, Hants, 1886, William Hill
Wolverhampton Market, Staffs, and Bolton Market, Lancs, 1851, G. T. Robinson
Bank of Scotland, St. Vincent Place and George Street, Glasgow, 1865, J. T. Rochead

p. 115 Burlington House, Piccadilly, W1, 1872, additions by Charles Barry Jnr.

p. 116–117 Quotations from Scott op. cit. pp. 180, 195–98 passim.

p. 118 Stationery Office, Princes Street, SW1, 1847, Sir James Pennethorne dem.

p. 119 Pembroke College, Oxford, N. range of Chapel Quad 1844–46, Hall 1848, John Hayward

p. 120 Lincoln's Inn Hall, WC1, 1843, P. C. Hardwick
St. Michael's College, Tenbury, Worcs, 1855, H. Woodyer

p. 136 Churches by E. B. Lamb: St. Mary Magdalen, Canning Road, Addiscombe, Surrey; Christ Church, Church Square, W. Hartlepool, Durham; St. Martin's, Vicars Road, NW3.

p. 148 Burges's house in Kensington: Tower House, Melbury Road, W8, 1875–81. For 'the fate of the remaining treasures' see J. M. Crook *William Burges* 1981. Dates from Crook for works listed: St. Finbar's Cathedral, Cork, Ireland, 1863–1904; Church of Christ the Consoler, Skelton-on-Ure, W. Yorks, 1870–76; Church of St. Mary, Aldford-cum-Studley, W. Yorks, 1870–78; Castell Coch, Glamorgan, 1872–91; Cardiff Castle, Glamorgan, 1866–1928; Worcester College Chapel, Oxford, 1864–69

p. 150 Church of Our Lady of the Assumption and St. Mary Magdalen, (RC), Tavistock, Devon; St. Mary's Church, Woburn, Beds.

p. 153 J. T. Micklethwaite *Modern Parish Churches* 1874 p. 258n.

p. 154 Holy Trinity, Bingley, W. Yorks, 1866, R. Norman Shaw dem.
St. Luke's Church, Oseney Crescent, NW5, 1869, Basil Champneys

p. 156 Town Hall, Preston, Lancs, 1862, Sir Gilbert Scott dem.
Eastlake op. cit. pp. 361–62

p. 166 Newnham College, Cambridge, 1871–1910, Basil Champneys
White House, Tite Street, SW3, 1877, E. W. Godwin dem.

p. 170 Cragside, Rothbury, Northumberland, 1869–1885, R. Norman Shaw

Appendix

p. 172 Imperial Institute, SW7 (later Imperial College), 1887–93, T. E. Colcutt dem. except for tower

p. 176 Sheffield Town Hall, W. Yorks, 1890, E. W. Mountford
Birmingham Victoria Law Courts, Corporation Street, 1886–91, Sir Aston Webb and Ingress Bell
Town Hall, St. Aldate's, Oxford, 1892, H. T. Hare
Hertford College Chapel, Oxford, 1908, T. G. Jackson

p. 177 Mansfield College, Oxford, 1888, Basil Champneys
Manchester College, Oxford, 1891–93, T. Worthington

p. 178 Holy Trinity Church, Sloane Street, SW3, 1888–90, J. D. Sedding and Henry Wilson

p. 186 Ardenrun Place, Crowhurst, Surrey, 1906, Sir Ernest Newton dem.

p. 191 Eastlake op. cit. p. 344

p. 192 Eagle Insurance Co., Colmore Row, Birmingham, 1900, W. R. Lethaby

p. 194 'The leader of these architects': C. F. A. Voysey

p. 195 Nos. 63 and 65 Sloane Street, SW3, 1897, Fairfax B. Wade

p. 197 Free Library, Ladbroke Grove, W10, 1890, Henry Wilson
Horniman Museum, London Road, Forest Hill, SE23, 1901, C. Harrison Townsend
Nos. 10 and 12 Palace Court, Bayswater Rd. W8, 1890, J. M. Maclaren

p. 200 Leicester Town Hall, 1875, F. J. Hames

p. 201 London Sessions House (Central Criminal Court), Old Bailey, EC4, 1907, E. W. Mountford
Lambeth Town Hall, Brixton Hill, SW2, 1905, Septimus Warwick and H. Austen Hall
E. A. Rickards worked in partnership with H. V. Lanchester (1863–1953) and James Stewart

p. 202 War Office, Whitehall, SW1, 1898, W. Young

p. 204 Morning Post (Inveresk House) Aldwych, WC2, 1906–07; Ritz Hotel Piccadilly, W1, 1903–06; Royal Automobile Club, Pall Mall, SW1, 1908–11, Charles Mewes and Arthur J. Davis

p. 205 King Edward VII Galleries, British Museum, Montagu Place, WC1, 1904–14, Sir J. J. Burnet
Institute of Chartered Accountants, Swan Alley, Moorgate, EC2, 1890, Sir John Belcher

p. 207–08 The original design of the Gaiety Theatre was by Ernest Runtz (1859–1913)

p. 208 Apart from the elevation of the Piccadilly Hotel, the facades of the Regent Street quadrant are by Sir Reginald Blomfield, 1916–26
Country house by Norman Shaw in Northumberland: Chesters, Humshaugh, 1890–94
Office building in Storey's Gate, Birdcage Walk, SW1, 1910, Ernest Runtz
Norwich Union Assurance Office, NE corner of St. James's Street, SW1, 1907, Ernest Runtz
School of Chemistry, Oxford, 1913, Paul Waterhouse
St. Michael's Court, Gonville and Caius College, Cambridge, 1903, Sir Aston Webb
North Court, Emmanuel College, Cambridge, 1910, Leonard Stokes
Christ's Hospital, Horsham, Sussex, 1894, Sir Aston Webb

Appendix

p. 218 Theodore Ballu, architect (with Franz Christian Gau) of Ste. Clotilde, Paris, 1846–57

p. 229 Prize-winning design at Gidea Park, 1910, by Geoffrey Lucas

p. 230 Deneke Range and Chapel, Lady Margaret Hall, Oxford, 1931, Sir Giles Gilbert Scott

p. 231 Church House, Westminster, SW1, 1937–40, Sir Herbert Baker

p. 234 ICI, Millbank, SW1, 1927, Sir Frank Baines

p. 236 Martin's Bank (now Barclay's), Water Street, Liverpool, 1926, H. J. Rowse
National Provincial Bank (now National Westminster Bank), Prince's Street, EC2, 1930, Sir Edwin Cooper
Hoare's Bank, Fleet Street, EC4, 1830, R. Parker

p. 238 Baring's Bank, Bishopsgate, EC2, 1881, R. Norman Shaw dem.
Extensions to the Bank of England, Threadneedle Street, EC2, 1925–37, Sir Herbert Baker
National Westminster Bank, Piccadilly W1, 1927, W. Curtis Green

p. 239 No. 29 Lincoln's Inn Fields, WC2, 1922, Greenaway and Newbury
London County Hall, SE1, 1908–22, Ralph Knott

p. 240 Buckingham Palace, SW1, E. front 1913, Sir Aston Webb

p. 242 Beckenham Town Hall, Kent, 1927, Lanchester and Lodge dem.
St. Marylebone Town Hall, Marylebone Road, W1, 1910, Sir Edwin Cooper

p. 243 Ministry of Pensions Building, Bromyard Avenue, W6, 1922, Sir James G. West
Africa House, Kingsway, WC2, 1920, Trehearne and Norman

p. 244 Selfridges, Oxford Street, W1, 1908–19, Daniel Burnham of Chicago with R. Frank Atkinson, completed by Burnet and Tait

p. 245 Barkers, 26–64 Kensington High Street (N side) W8, 1924, Sir Reginald Blomfield
Atkinsons (now Ferragamo) 24 Old Bond Street, 1926, E. Vincent Harris
Liberty's, Great Marlborough Street, W1, 1922, E. Stanley Hall
Cumberland Hotel, Marble Arch, W1, 1932, F. J. Wills
Devonshire House, Piccadilly, W1, 1924, Thomas Hastings of New York and C. H. Reilly
Grosvenor House, Park Lane, W1, 1926, Sir Edwin Lutyens, with Wimperis and Simpson

p. 246 Orchard Court, Portman Square, W1, 1928, Messrs. Joseph
Wills Building, University of Bristol, 1925, Sir George Oatley
National Institute of Agricultural Botany, Huntingdon Road, Cambridge, 1919–21, P. Morley Horder

p. 246 Memorial Court, Clare College, Cambridge, 1923–34; Cambridge University Library, 1934; Lady Margaret Hall see p. [230]; Sir Giles Gilbert Scott

p. 248 Church of the Annunciation, Old Quebec Street, Marble Arch, W1, 1912, Sir Walter Tapper
St. Saviour's Church, Old Oak Road, W3, 1930, A. W. Kenyon
St. Alphege's Church, Oldfield Lane, Bath, 1929, Sir Giles Gilbert Scott
St. Catherine's Church, Westway, Hammersmith, W12, 1923, Robert Atkinson dem.

p. 249 St. Matthew, Queen's Drive, Clubmoor, Liverpool, 1928, F. X. Velarde
Cathedral Church of Christ the King, Liverpool, 1903–80, Sir Giles Gilbert Scott

p. 253 Lambeth Bridge, London, 1928, Sir Reginald Blomfield

Index

Index

293

Index

294

Index

295

Index

Index

LIST OF ARCHITECTS WHOSE WORK IS MENTIONED